Anonymous

Sermons by American Rabbis

Anonymous

Sermons by American Rabbis

ISBN/EAN: 9783744752046

Printed in Europe, USA, Canada, Australia, Japan

Cover: Foto ©Lupo / pixelio.de

More available books at **www.hansebooks.com**

Sermons
by
American Rabbis

Edited and Published under the Auspices of the
Central Conference of American Rabbis,

The Central Conference Publication Committee.

CHICAGO, 1896.

PREFACE.

In accordance with a resolution adopted by the Central Conference of American Rabbis, at Rochester, N. Y., in July 1895, the Publication Committee presents herewith this collection of thirty-seven sermons preached in the American Jewish pulpit by twenty-seven different rabbis. The intention is to publish a similar volume from time to time in the hope that this may prove a medium for the clearer expression and the better understanding of the fundamental doctrines and characteristic aims of modern Judaism and a historical record of the development of the content and expression of Jewish religious thought. It is anticipated that this book will be of interest to preachers and laymen of all denominations, who may desire to learn what Judaism has to say in regard to the vital questions of the day.

The plan of the book has been suggested by its need. The sermons for the festivals occupy a larger space than is given to the other discourses, because they reflect clearly and directly the main ideas of Judaism, and, moreover, because they will be of special benefit to the smaller communities which have no rabbis and wish to conduct divine services on the chief holy days.

THE COMMITTEE.

CONTENTS.

Preface... iii
Introduction. By Isaac M. Wise vii

THE NEW YEAR'S DAY.

I. The Eternal Verities. By David Philipson........ 1
II. The Message of the New Year. By Leon Harrison.. 11
III. Seeing God. By Max Heller...................... 18
IV. Our Refuge. By Gustave Gottheil................ 29
V. Religion's Call. By Samuel Schulman............. 36

THE DAY OF ATONEMENT.

VI. The Glory of Religion. By K. Kohler............ 47
VII. Sin and Forgiveness. By I. S. Moses 55
VIII. Sin and Penitence. By Stephen S. Wise.......... 66
IX. A Definition of Judaism. By I. S. Moses........ 74
X. I Am a Hebrew. By Leon Harrison............... 87

THE FEAST OF TABERNACLES.

XI. The Harvest Festival. By Emil G. Hirsch........ 94
XII. Israel's Religion a Message of Gladness.
By Samuel Sale..................................... 114

'HANUKKAH AND PURIM.

XIII. The Ancient Anti-Semite and his modern successors. By Emil G. Hirsch... 122
XIV. 'Hanukkah. By G. Gottheil..................... 147
XV. Silence Means Ruin. By Max Heller............. 151

PASSOVER.

XVI. Liberty and Light. By Oscar J. Cohen......... 158
XVII. Four Sentiments. By Max Landsberg.......... 163
XVIII. Judaism and Temperance. By G. Gottheil...... 176
XIX. Freedom, Justice and Fidelity. By Isaac M. Wise. 180

THE FEAST OF WEEKS.

XX. The Ten Commandments. By Henry Berkowitz. 189

XXI. Genius in History and the History of Genius; a Lecture. By Isaac M. Wise............... 200
XXII. The Need of a Living Creed. By K. Kohler..... 217
XXIII. Who is the Real Atheist? By Adolph Moses... 223
XXIV. What we Have to be Thankful for. By Adolph Moses........................ 233
XXV. Judaism and the Congress of Liberal Religious Societies. By Joseph Stolz 244
XXVI. Judaism and Liberal Christianity. By Moses J. Gries........................ 250
XXVII. Jewish Theology. By Joseph Silverman........ 259
XXVIII. Judaism and Unitarianism. By Maurice H. Harris 270
XXIX. Dedication Address. By Joseph Stolz.......... 285
XXX. Faith With Reason. By Joseph Krauskopf..... 292
XXXI. The Hope of Immortality. By Rudolph Grossman 306
XXXII. The Law. By Louis Grossman................. 316
XXXIII. Life. By Samuel Greenfield.................... 329
XXXIV. The Weaknesses of Bible Heroes. By Edward N. Calisch.............. 338
XXXV. Manhood. By E. Schreiber.................... 344
XXXVI. The Deluge. By F. De Sola Mendes........... 353
XXXVII. The Jewish House a Sanctuary of the Lord. By B. Felsenthal........................ 360

INTRODUCTION.

I. READING OF SCRIPTURES.

The reading of Holy Writ, in devotional assemblies, (called in Isaiah, i, 13, מקרא קרא,) on the Sabbath, New Moon and Holy Days, followed by prayers (Ibid, verse 15)—is ancient custom in Israel. It is older than the Synagogue; according to Talmudical statements, older than the Temple of Solomon: Moses ordained it and Ezra added that the Thorah should also be read on the afternoon of every Sabbath and on every Monday and Thursday. That this was done conscientiously during Israel's second commonwealth is evident from Nehemiah viii and ix, from the books of the Maccabees, the Mishnah in Taanith and Yoma, also from the Acts of the Apostles, and the homilies of Philo, which frequently close, like the five books of Psalms, with a solemn doxology. The numerous provisions and ordinances in the ancient rabbinical literature concerning the How, When and What to read from Holy Writ in public assemblies, are no mean evidence that this reading was ancient custom, when those provisions had become laws.

II. EXPOUNDING SCRIPTURES.

As long as the Israelites lived in their own land and spoke their own language, the mere reading of Sacred Scriptures may have sufficed to convey the sacred lessons to the popular mind. Still also then and there, as is evident from the oratorical tone of many prophetical sections and didactic psalms, (especially Psalms cxix, II Kings iv, 22-23, and Isaiah lxvi, 23) sermons were preached at stated times, Holy Writ

CONTENTS.

PASSOVER.

XVI. Liberty and Light. By Oscar J. Cohen......... 158
XVII. Four Sentiments. By Max Landsberg.......... 16ᴊ
XVIII. Judaism and Temperance. By G. Gottheil...... 176
XIX. Freedom, Justice and Fidelity. By Isaac M. Wise. 180

THE FEAST OF WEEKS.

XX. The Ten Commandments. By Henry Berkowitz. 189

XXI. Genius in History and the History of Genius; a Lecture. By Isaac M. Wise............... 200
XXII. The Need of a Living Creed. By K. Kohler..... 217
XXIII. Who is the Real Atheist? By Adolph Moses... 223
XXIV. What we Have to be Thankful for. By Adolph Moses........................ 233
XXV. Judaism and the Congress of Liberal Religious Societies. By Joseph Stolz 244
XXVI. Judaism and Liberal Christianity. By Moses J. Gries........................ 250
XXVII. Jewish Theology. By Joseph Silverman........ 259
XXVIII. Judaism and Unitarianism. By Maurice H. Harris 270
XXIX. Dedication Address. By Joseph Stolz.......... 285
XXX. Faith With Reason. By Joseph Krauskopf..... 292
XXXI. The Hope of Immortality. By Rudolph Grossman 306
XXXII. The Law. By Louis Grossman................ 316
XXXIII. Life. By Samuel Greenfield.................... 329
XXXIV. The Weaknesses of Bible Heroes. By Edward N. Calisch..................... 338
XXXV. Manhood. By E. Schreiber................... 344
XXXVI. The Deluge. By F. De Sola Mendes............ 353
XXXVII. The Jewish House a Sanctuary of the Lord. By B. Felsenthal........................ 360

INTRODUCTION.

I. READING OF SCRIPTURES.

The reading of Holy Writ, in devotional assemblies, (called in Isaiah, i, 13, מקרא קרא,) on the Sabbath, New Moon and Holy Days, followed by prayers (Ibid, verse 15)—is ancient custom in Israel. It is older than the Synagogue; according to Talmudical statements, older than the Temple of Solomon: Moses ordained it and Ezra added that the Thorah should also be read on the afternoon of every Sabbath and on every Monday and Thursday. That this was done conscientiously during Israel's second commonwealth is evident from Nehemiah viii and ix, from the books of the Maccabees, the Mishnah in Taanith and Yoma, also from the Acts of the Apostles, and the homilies of Philo, which frequently close, like the five books of Psalms, with a solemn doxology. The numerous provisions and ordinances in the ancient rabbinical literature concerning the How, When and What to read from Holy Writ in public assemblies, are no mean evidence that this reading was ancient custom, when those provisions had become laws.

II. EXPOUNDING SCRIPTURES.

As long as the Israelites lived in their own land and spoke their own language, the mere reading of Sacred Scriptures may have sufficed to convey the sacred lessons to the popular mind. Still also then and there, as is evident from the oratorical tone of many prophetical sections and didactic psalms, (especially Psalms cxix, II Kings iv, 22-23, and Isaiah lxvi, 23) sermons were preached at stated times, Holy Writ being expounded by prophetical orators or other men of learning and inspiration. When Hebrew was no longer the people's vernacular and the environs and circumstances had changed, the translator and expounder of the Hebrew texts had to come, and this was the *Meturgam* in the synagogues, academies and courts. These were the first actual and official preachers. We meet with the *Meturgam* among the oldest *Tanaim* in Palestine and the *Amoraim* and *Gaonim* of the east, down to the tenth Christian century. We possess the sketches and fragments of their sermons and exhortations in the Talmudical Hagadah, the *Targumim*, the ancient *Midrashim* and *Pesiktoth* including *Aboth* of Rabbi Nathan, *Tana debei Eliah*, *Sheiltoth* and *Pirkei Rabbi Eliezer*: a homiletic literature, in bulk and richness of thought, in poetical forms and oratorical ornamentation, the largest and most valuable in the world's literature after the Bible. The liturgical poets of the synagogue and the moralists of subsequent ages down to our time derived from those ancient homiletic sources their inspiration, their material always, and the form very frequently; the old preachers did the same; and with but few exceptions from and after the days of Mr. Jacobson it is still done to this day. Most of the preachers based their discourses not merely on Holy Writ but also—and not seldom, chiefly,—on the rabbinical homiletic literature, expounding and interpreting both.

Aside of Talmudical Hagadath, Targumim, Midrashim, Pesiktoth, etc. (as mentioned above), we possess no homiletic literature prior to the sixteenth century, except the *Derashoth* of Rabbenu Nissim, the Derashoth of Rabbi Moses ben Nachman, the exhortations of Jonah Girondi, and the philosophical sermons of Isaac Arama and Aba Mari Antoli.

III. THE MAGGID AND DARSHON.

The *Meturgam* was superceded by the *Maggid*, also called the *Baal Darshon*, the homiletic preacher of the synagogue. Their literary productions are called *Derashoth* in contradistinction to the ancient *Midrash*. Both terms are derived from דרש "to inquire" (Leviticus x, 16), which in New Hebrew also received the meaning of expounding. So those two terms signified both inquiry and expounding, and the whole homiletic literature, ancient and modern, pretends to be no more than inquiries into and expositions of Holy Writ. The preacher is the expounder of the Law, as the modern phrase runs.

This *Derusha-literature* is vast and varied. Several thousands of such sermons were published mostly in rabbinical Hebrew; some were also published in Spanish, Italian and Dutch. Zunz, in his book "Gottesdienstliche Vortraege," furnishes an historical summary of that whole homiletic literature, most of which was adopted by Dr. Graetz in his "History of the Jews."

There exist a number of index books to the *Derashoth*, as for instance, Asaph ham Mazkin, by Zachariah of Porto (Rome, 1675). Most all of these Derashoths expound more of the Rabbinical than of the Biblical literature, are more witty than exegetic, more smart than logical, more ethical than theological, and nearly all without organic systematic construction, with many *bon mots* strung together loosely. All of these stand upon a high moral plane, more or less austere and ascetic according to the happy or unhappy conditions of the preachers and people at any particular time.

IV. THE RETROGRESSION.

From the beginning of the sixteenth to nearly the end of the eighteenth centuries the synagogue, especially in Germany and the Eastern countries steadily declined to the somber and disspirited locality for prayer-meetings and the performance of ceremonial observances. Gradually the prayers and observances became so lengthy and all-important that no time for instruction or exhortation was left, and the rabbis preached only a few times a year. This led to the belief that the sermon was no integral portion of the divine service. If the Maggid or Darshon did preach at all it was in the afternoon of the Sabbath.

This state of affairs prevailed almost all over Europe, and America also, till Moses Mendelssohn, with his compeers and disciples, started the reformatory commotion among the German-speaking Hebrews of Europe. The French revolution and subsequent invasions on the continent roused the benumbed energies of the inert masses of the nations, which also reacted upon the petrified synagogue; and a new era began in Judaism. Then even a generation had to pass away before the spirit could return to the dead walls of the synagogue, so that the writer of this summary not only knew the first preachers in the synagogue: Mannheimer in Vienna, Zunz and Sachs in Prague, Solomon and Kley in Hamburg, Wolf in Copenhagen, and later on Kreuzenach, Hess, Leopold Stein, Abraham Geiger, Kirchenrath Mayer, Samuel Hirsch, Samuel Adler, Holdheim, Einhorn, Phillipson, Wechsler, Levy and Aub, Prof. Marks in London— but was himself one of the first who, fifty-three years ago, preached in the synagogue in the pure vernacular of the country and made the sermon an integral portion of the divine service. So young is the modern sermon in the synagogue.

V. THE SERMON IN AMERICA.

The Israelites coming to this country from Europe

direct or via Brazil, arrived here with the same conceptions of the synagogue and divine worship, as were entertained by their brethren abroad. They organized congregations, benevolent societies, and schools for religious instruction on that very same pattern, according to the Portuguese, German or Polish rites. The *Parnass*, or president, was the autocrat of the congregation, the vestry was his cabinet. The *Hazan*, *i. e.*, the precentor, was the minister, the reverend, actually the reader of the prayers and Scriptures and the master of ceremonies. In the smaller congregations the *Hazan* was the factotum; he taught the children to read Hebrew, performed the prescribed ceremonial observances, and also took care that the *Kosher* meat and *matzos* should be uncontaminated. The first preaching *Hazanim*, very respectable and profoundly religious pastors, were Rev. S. M. Isaacs of New York, Rev. Isaac Leeser of Philadelphia, Rev. Mr. Nathan and Rev. Mr. Jacobs.

Shortly after them came Rev. Mr. Posnanski in the reform congregation of Charleston, S. C., and Rev. Mr. Braun in the reform congregation of Baltimore. They preached only occasionally; and in Philadelphia, a sermon was preached provided the Parnass gave the Hazan permission. Rev. Isaac Leeser published his sermons (English), and this is the only homiletic literature we possess from those primeval days.

In 1843, Dr. Merzbacher came to New York from Fuerth, Bavaria. He preached in the three German congregations of New York occasionally and voluntarily, till 1845, when the Emanuel reform congregation was established and elected him their permanent rabbipreacher. The same year Dr. Max Lilienthal came to New York from Munich, Bavaria, and was elected chief rabbi and permanent preacher of the three German congregations, to preach alternately in one of the three synagogues. These were the first ordained rabbis that came to this country and also the first permanent preachers in the American synagogue. Lilienthal afterwards published a number of his sermons (English) in the *American Israelite*, his book of German sermons having been published in Europe in 1839. The style of those sermons was the puritanic, profoundly moralistic and edifying, in the very spirit and tone of Dr. Salomon of Hamburg.

July 26, 1846, Isaac M. Wise arrived in New York, and shortly after his arrival he was elected rabbi and permanent preacher of the Beth-El Congregation of Albany, N. Y. He preached regularly every Sabbath and Holy Day during divine service in the morning up to 1866; when in Cincinnati he added to it the Friday evening lecture for every week from October to May. His homiletic productions appeared in the *Occident, Asmonean, American Israelite, Deborah* (German), and in various political and literary organs almost all over the land. This introduced into the American pulpit the philosophical sermon and the historical lecture. Some of his sermons have appeared in *The American Jewish Pulpit*, a volume published by Bloch & Co., Cincinnati; and many of his lectures have also appeared in books, reprints from the *American Israelite*.

About the same time, James K. Gutheim came to America from Germany, a young man, talented and aspiring. In 1847 he was elected *Hazan* of the Bene Yeshurun Congregation in Cincinnati. He was the first preacher in any synagogue west of the Allegheny Mountains, the first also who preached in English in any German congregation. Several of his sermons appeared in the *Occident, American Israelite* and in his book called "The American Pulpit." His style was chiefly the sentimental, more puritanical than rabbinical, inclining to Isaac Leeser's pastoral tone. In and shortly after the year 1848 a number of rabbi-preachers came to America and occupied pulpits permanently and regularly. The most noteworthy of them were Rabbi Kalisch in Cleveland, Rabbi Illowi in New York, and the Rabbis Reiss, Guinzburg and Hochheimer in Baltimore. They preached well, wrote considerably for public organs, especially Mr. Reiss for the orthodox and Mr. Kalisch for the reformatory side, but contributed nothing of importance to our homiletic literature, as they published no sermons with the exception of some German addresses by Rabbi Hochheimer in the *Deborah* and elsewhere.

In the year 1850 Dr. Raphall came over from England. He introduced himself to the public with six lectures on the poetry of the Bible. He was elected rabbi-preacher for the Bene Yeshurun Congregation of New York, and preached there with great success. A number of his sermons were published in various journals, and but one of them preserved in a collection of addresses on the slavery question, published in New York in 1860. Although Dr. Raphall was a very able pulpit orator, he exercised no influence on the American pulpit. Besides the Reverend Hazanim Henry and Rosenfeld, none are known to have adopted Raphall's style and diction. The sermons published in Germany by Mannheimer, Mayer, Ludwig Phillipson, Leopold Stein, Prof. Marks in London and Rev. Mr. Isaacs of Liverpool were the main patterns and literature of the preaching Hazanim of that period, up to 1855.

From and after the year 1855 there came to this country Dr. Samuel Adler, Dr. David Einhorn, Dr. Samuel Hirsch, Dr. Deutsch the grammarian, Dr. Elkan Cohen and Dr. Schlesinger; later on Dr. Jastrow, Dr. Szold; each of them occupied a prominent pulpit in the eastern part of our country. Then came Dr. Adolph Huebsch, Dr. M. Mielziner, Dr. Isaac Schwab. All of these preachers, being learned Talmudists, stood in the middle between the *Derasha* of olden times and the modern sermon, and understood well how to harmonize the two systems. This was a new feature in the homiletic literature, especially in the east, where there were yet men who appreciated the sagacious interpretation of a Midrash or an ingenious application of a rabbinical maxim or story, framed into a rationalistic discourse of a reformatory character or applied philosophically. Excepting Dr. Raphall all these preachers belong to the new school, and all excepting Gutheim and Wise spoke in German only.

Another new element, introduced more specially by Dr. Einhorn, was polemics in the pulpit, which had been entirely unknown here. The American preacher, English or German, reform or orthodox, was always sentimental, philosophical or apologetic. Enlightenment was the object of the sermon on the one side, edification on the other. And yet Dr. Einhorn contributed the largest share to our homiletic literature in his "Sinai" and in the posthumous volume published by Dr. Kohler.

These are the elements with which the sermon in the American synagogue started and became not only an integral part but the main part of the divine service. The living word took the place of the dead letter. Here begins the transition from the German to the English, from the foreign to the American, from the derashic to the modern form of the sermon, a collection of which has been compiled in this volume, showing the progress of the synagogal pulpit in the first half-century of its existence.

I. M. W.

SERMONS.

THE ETERNAL VERITIES.

A NEW YEAR'S SERMON, BY REV. DR. DAVID PHILIPSON.

The uppermost thought in the mind of the serious man on days such as this is the transitoriness of things earthly. The New Year's Day is the mile-stone whereat the traveler o'er life's journey halts, and resting for a brief space he cannot but let his thoughts engage themselves with the significance, if there be any, of the way he has traversed. From out the depths of space a voice seems to inquire of each one of us, as it did of the prophet of old: "Watchman, what of the night?" for truly we, who are living at this latest moment of time, are like watchmen standing on the highest point of vantage, peering, peering into the night of the future, and according to the power of our mental sight, will be the vision that is unrolled to us. There be those who will give back answer to that questioning voice; the night is all dark, life is a blank, vanity of vanities; man were better off had he never been born. For such the firmament of life is all o'ercast with thick clouds; the stars of hope are hid; the bright messenger of coming dawn unnoted. But pessimism is not the true philosophy of life; as night is not real, but only the absence of light, so is pessimism but the absence of the true conception of life and its meaning.

The strongest refutation to these wailings is offered by the past achievements of the race. In the light of the progress, the advancement, the civilization that have gone before, the shadows conjured up by pessimists dissolve like the fancies of a mind diseased. Trace the philosophy of the pessimist to its source and you will, in all likelihood, find that it took its rise in some physical ailment or in some individual disappointment. Then there be other watchmen on the ramparts of life who in response to the voice, "What of the night, what of the future?" give back the careless reply, it matters not to us what the future may have to say; let us eat and drink and be merry, for to-morrow we die; let us live in the present moment. Wherefore be serious? wherefore be thoughtful? Let us quaff the cup of sensual delight. The pleasure-philosophy has its myriads of devotees; multitudes crowd the chariots whose streamers bear its motto. But is this the true philosophy? Is life best lived in the mad chase after the pleasures of the senses? Answer, ye hundreds who have made sensuality your god and pleasure your divinity; answer truly, ye thousands who have given the strength of your young years to the pursuit of sense delights. Dies not the pleasure in the very moment of its satisfaction? Is the game worth the pursuit? Appetites cloyed, senses wearied, existence blasé, the light of life blurred and dimmed by the haze of satiety, are not these the result of your devotion and worship at the shrine of eudæmonism and epicureanism? So, then, we cannot accept this as the true solution to the question of the voice crying unto us, Watchman, what of life? For further answer, let us turn to another of our great prophets unto whom, also, a voice came out of the depths of reflection. "A voice saith, Proclaim; and I said, "What shall I proclaim? All flesh is grass and all its goodliness as the flower of the field; the grass withereth, the flower fadeth, but the word of our God will stand firm forever"—(Isaiah xl, 6.) An answer, the result of experience, observation and faith. No one can close his eyes to the facts of life, and therefore no one, least of all the prophet, would for a moment deny the transitoriness, the change, the passing away of earthly things.

Yes, the grass withers, the flower fades, all flesh is as grass, but—but—there is the permanent, undying, everlasting, eternal element at the ground of things. The phenomenon is transitory, the essence is permanent. The appearance is passing, the principle is eternal. Let us make this thought the burden of our reflections on this New Year's morning.

Unto the majority of men the most palpable significance of a day that marks the passing of the years is the never-ceasing flow of time. There is no present, to speak of. Even as I address you, the present moment passes into the lap of the past and takes its place in the silent shades of the eternity that is behind us. But with the passing, with the never-ceasing flow of the currents in the ocean of time, there is joined the permanency of things real that passes not away, but belongs to the undying order of God's everlasting creation. The grass that now flourishes on your lawn will wither when the biting breath of the frost will nip it, but the principle of growth, God's everlasting law, works eternally; it is permanent; that particular growth of grass will pass away, but there is the permanent element that passes not with it, but will cause the new growth to appear in the coming springtime; the flower fades, the beauteous rose withers and dies, but that which made the flower dies not. God's everlasting law of growth that transfigures the dull brown and black of the clod of earth into the brilliant red, the modest blue, the glowing yellow and the dazzling white of the flowers of the field is the permanent element. The particular flower may fade, this or that growth may wither, but the principle of the flower, that which is in reality the plant, neither fades nor withers; it stands forever; it belongs to the eternal scheme of things. This is the principle that runs through all creation, through all history, through all life. Time and eternity, appearance and reality, phenomenon and principle, permanence and transitoriness; these are the two sides of the coin of existence, and when we bewail the passing of time let us not forget that this is only the now of eternity, and when the appearance of things earthly fades away, let us recall the fact of the reality that persists and lasts.

As the grass and the flower are the appearances that bring to our visual perception the patent proof of the existence of the principle of growth, so in all things is the principle exemplified by the phenomenon—the real by the appearance. Let me illustrate: The sculptor, by power of his genius, conjures up within his own soul a dream of beauty; before the clay that is to be molded is touched, the statue is complete in the sculptor's brain; with mallet and chisel it is to be given appearance, but that statue may not express to the onlooker a tithe of the beauty and grace and loveliness that the artist dreamt; that particular statue may be destroyed, but the eternal laws of form and beauty that gave it birth exist forever, and now and then in other brains will take concrete shape and produce new appearances. The harmonies that the great composers hear and shape into palpable musical compositions are not confined to the physical sense of hearing. Beethoven, though deaf, heard harmonies sublime that neither you nor I nor other men are sensible of. His soul was vibrant with the music of eternity, the real music whereof his symphonies and sonatas are only expressions, and though every masterpiece of musical composition be swept away, though every painting and statue be destroyed, the real thing, God's eternal laws of beauty and of harmony existing on, would come to light again in the souls of inspired genius somewhere and somehow on this planet The real things are impalpable; the significant facts of life are intangible. Eye has not seen them, nor ear heard; they are the permanent things, whereof the examples that we with our physical eyes see are but the illustrations. They are the over-soul whereof one of our philosophers wrote.

Holds not the same thing true of the great principles whereon life and society rest? Do not the notions of righteousness, justice, love, present this same quality of eternal principle and transitory appearance? Justice, we say, is one of the eternal laws of the universe, but no one has ever seen this principle of justice; all that we see are the institutions of states and nations, courts and tribunals, laws and codes; finite examples of the eternal principle that rules and without obedience to which society would go to ruin and human life would be impossible. Men, in the course of the world's history, have time and again violated the demands and commands of justice, but not for long; the eternal right has vindicated itself each and every time in the ruin and overthrow of the society whose superstructure was not supported on the pillars—righteousness and justice. And yet who has ever seen this abstract thing, justice, who has ever grasped this impalpable thing, righteousness? Forums, temples of justice, court-houses, tribunals, these are the temporary abiding places of justice, but they are it not. They have passed away, but justice passes never. The grass withers, the flower fades, but the word of God, the eternal principle, exists on forever. The buildings on the forum of Rome, where justice was meted out, crumbled into ruins, but justice passed not away. The temple of Jerusalem, wherein gathered Israel's great law-making body, the Sanhedrin, fell a prey to the flames, but justice lives on. The Areopagus of Athens, where sat the elders in council, has long since ceased to be a hill of judgment, but justice holds high place still in the universe, and so though Capitol at Washington and Parliament House at London and Palace of Justice at Paris, and Rathhaus at Berlin and all great homes that men have built for the making of laws and the administration of justice pass away. The great, permanent underlying principle of justice will live on and new homes wherein its spirit finds expression will rise in all parts of this earth. "Righteousness and justice are the props of God's throne," sang the Psalmist, or, in other words, the support of the universe; the invisible principle is the permanent element, the visible appearance but transitory.

And does not this same contention hold true of kindness and goodness and love? Is not the principle of love eternal, its various appearances in the life of men with one another but transitory? Beautiful indeed are the forms it takes on—the unselfish love of parent for child, the mutual love of husband and wife, the uncalculating affection of friend for friend, but, though these pass away, love dies not. Myriads of mothers have lost their hearts' treasure, in numberless instances life's partner has passed from the side of the faithful associate, frequently love of friend has grown cold, but yet love lives, a throbbing principle of the universe. These appearances are transitory, the principal is eternal. No matter though the special foundations and institutions on earth that men have reared in the name of justice live their day, no matter though love in particular instances be transient as human life, these things in themselves remain the eternal, undying laws of God.

And friends, if this principle of the permanent and the transitory, the eternal and the temporal, holds good in the applications of justice, love, peace, it holds no less true in religion. There are many who will go to any length you desire in the application of the idea of growth in any of the departments of life, but when it comes to religion they would apply the motto *noli me tangere;* they would separate religion from all other provinces of life, and erect an impassable Chinese wall between the so-called secular and sacred precincts. They will grant you that men have had different notions about justice in different ages, and placed different interpretations upon it; that some things which were considered penal offenses in the England of one hundred years ago are not to be so regarded now; that the Spartan idea of wrong-doing does not coincide with our present conception. They will grant you that in the arts of war and peace, of trade and industry, in the provinces of manners and customs, of thought and art, expression has changed, and should change with time, but in religion they will not grant it; what was must remain; what has become must be guarded. And yet, if there be one province wherein this law of the permanent and the transitory, the eternal and the temporal, does hold, it is in that of religion, for religion is not alone a matter of thought; it is also a matter of custom, not alone of speculation on the eternal verities, but also the clothing of these verities in forms that appeal to men and women. Now, if men's minds grow with the passing of the ages, it stands to reason that what appealed to one generation may not appeal to another. Bloody sacrifices once appeared the meet and fit form of worship of the Most High; us of this day this mode of worship would disgust. Religious forms and expressions, as all others, are the temporal, the transitory elements; the eternal principles lying at the root of religion are the permanent elements. . Among us, in Judaism, this has come, or should have come, by this time, to be particularly understood, but ever and anon a wave of agitation sweeps our Jewish life that indicates the contrary. Such is the occasional demand for a definition of Judaism. Such is also the periodic cry bewailing the condition of affairs within the pale of the faith. I believe the best answer that can be given to all such outbursts is the lesson which I have drawn from this day, *viz.:* The fact of the existence everywhere and in all things of eternal, permanent elements and transitory, temporal appearances. Two points, and only two, are essential in the definition of Judaism, if definition there can be and must be, and these are the monotheistic principle and righteousness in action, God and duty. So taught Moses, so taught Isaiah and Amos, Jeremiah and Micah, Hosea and Zechariah; so taught Hillel and Akiba, if authority we require. Ethical monotheism is what Judaism, in its essence, is. These are the eternal principles.

Now, of course, like all other systems of thought and practice, Judaism has passed through various stages of growth and development. Among whatever people the Jews lived, from them they adopted customs and forms, many and various, so that the students who have given themselves to tracing the origin of customs and ceremonies among the Jews have found that many of these had an extra-Jewish origin. Customs, forms, ceremonies grow. Doctrines, too, have their day, and pass away. Men's minds, thank God, stand not still. The glory of our faith is that it cannot be confined within the narrow lines of a creed, for "every creed is arrested development." Judaism is too broad an experience to be limited by any phrase of definition, for to define Judaism properly one would have to tell its whole growth and history, all the stages through which it has passed, all the thoughts to which it has given rise.

Judaism is not confined within the covers of the Bible, for Judaism made the Bible, the Bible made not Judaism. The grand words within the Book of Books are the result of the working of the spirit of Judaism, of the ethical monotheism among men; so that even though the books of the Bible were to be destroyed and disappear, the spirit of Judaism would still live, for it is the eternal element whereof the Bibical books are the expression. Judaism is broader than its literature, for Judaism made it—it made not the faith. Judaism is broader than its history, for Judaism made its history; its history made not it. Judaism is broader than any forms, ceremonies, customs; for Judaism made them when they were needed, and when they are no longer expressive of the needs of its worshipers they must pass away; they are not necessary for the preservation of the faith. Judaism is broader than any prayers and prayer-books, for Judaism gave rise to the prayers and the prayer-books,—not they to it, and though every prayer that has been spoken or written should disappear, the spirit of Judaism should call forth new prayers and aspirations to the throne of the Infinite. Judaism is broader than any language, even the Hebrew language, and even though that language should disappear entirely from the face of the earth, the religion would not disappear, for the Hebrew language made not Judaism; it was its first vehicle of expression, but the spirit of the religion was not bound to it. Judaism is broader than any institution, custom, prayer, day or tongue and, therefore, because it is so broad it cannot be defined in a few pat words or phrases, as a dictionary would do. Our religion bases on ethical monotheism; this is the foundation; all else is growth, development, that must be properly understood.

Is not this eternal element in our faith broad enough, sufficient enough for any one to go on? The belief in the one God of justice and love, and right action among men, the development of these principles being evidenced by the long past and the growth of the faith, the expression that the religion has taken on among us being but another stadium in its growth. No man can tell what the next one hundred years will bring forth, but this we do know, and of this we can rest assured, that the eternal principles will live on forever, while the human growths and institutions, developments and customs will pass away and give way to others proper for their day and time. This in every department of life; whether we will or no, the eternal realities, which though not seen of us are yet more real than the appearances we do visually perceive, compel us; ours be it to so shape our lives and actions that they shall be on a line with the undying verities of justice, love and truth.

What a glorious faith this is to take with us from our worship on this day that preaches the reality of permanent good and right despite the transitory and temporal character of appearances. Unto him oppressed by injustice its voice rings out its cheer, despair not, the world is governed by justice, the right triumphs ever; unto him from whose life the light of love seems to have vanished, its voice says in soothing tones, look up, love dies not, love is eternal, ruling now and forever, unto us all it sounds the good tidings, though grass wither and flower fade, though things pass and are no more, life is laid on the everlasting foundations of right and justice, in the end there is compensation for all things. God's word is tried, enduring forever; God's justice is sure, righteousness reigns in His world, God's grace abounds, His love o'ershadows all. Amen!

THE MESSAGE OF THE NEW YEAR.

BY RABBI LEON HARRISON, TEMPLE ISRAEL, ST. LOUIS.

Text: "The grass withereth, the flower fadeth: But the word of our God shall stand forever."— Isa. xl. 8.

It is the season of transition. . The soil is carpeted with the cast-off clothing of the forests. Like Oriental mourners stand the trees, with garments tattered and autumnal dust heaped upon their heads. Nature is disrobing for her winter sleep, and soon a winding sheet of purest white will be spun for her by those ancient weavers, frost and snow, and ice and wintry tempests. The summer is ended. The world's scenery is being shifted, and between the acts is heard the slow music of the winds, chanting funereal dirges,— Change, the theme, Destruction the composer; and from the oldest libretto of the nations, the words, graphic in statement. severe in simplicity, yet triumphant in promise, "The grass withereth, the flower fadeth, but the Word of our God shall stand forever."

The words are apt, the thought rich, the lesson timely —for the season is the text and nature the preacher.

Nature is an illustration of man, and man of nature. Nature is more than half human, and man more than half natural. Do not brooks sing, and the sunbeams dance? Are not the waves cruel and the heavens kind? And similarly man fades, his youth withers, he enjoys his spring and his winter, he has roots and branches. Nature is the dictionary of man; man the vocabulary of nature.

My text describes vegetation on its death-bed, as its most characteristic phase, most suggestive to us. We are called mortals because we are mortal, because we must die. We are all under sentence of death—the time, the place, the details as unknown to us as to the slayer under the new laws. All things earthly must perish. Birth, implies death, the coming of the new, the departure of the old. Therefore I speak to you this morning, on this solemn holy day of Israel, concerning its two-fold meaning as end and beginning. Over the new gateway of time that we dedicate I write the prophetic verse, as epitaph and exhortation. I take a time-worn theme because it needs repetition. I preach to you the religious arithmetic of division instead of multiplication, of subtraction instead of addition. I know that this is a familiar message. I know that you have heard it before. But when the sexton rings the Sunday church bell to notify pious attendants of their devotions he does not ring one peal. He is not satisfied with one chime. He ding-dongs the bell into their ears; its iron tongue repeats the same clamorous call until all must hear. The preacher is the church bell of the pulpit. He is a wedding bell and a funeral bell. He is also an alarm bell. When men drift and do not steer, he must warn them. When they live as if they would never die, when they pursue shadows instead of substance, when they clean forget the statutes of eternal laws, he must cry out to them, splendid in their corruption, like the autumn leaves in decay and dissolution: "The grass withereth, the flower fadeth, but the Word of our God shall stand forever."

There is here no needless repetition. The clauses are independent thoughts. The sentence is a code of morals and a system of religion. It covers the whole of human life.

I. Verily "The grass withereth." Yet for a season it feeds cattle—though only cattle. And human herds, heedless of the butcher's knife, greedily browse on grass—grass, the emblem of material things. But they must buy their grass for money. And how the crowd scrambles for money! What balances are these I see blind Fortune holding in her uncertain grasp? On the one scale of the balance are yellow coins, and on the other human sweat and blood and toil and tears and groans, yea, life itself, and death. New weights and measures! The equivalent of wealth! The tragic price of current cash! The valuation of grass!

What keen thought, what intense labor, what ungrudging sacrifices are expended by men for gold! They are the martyrs of money. The market is their rack, the exchange their prison house, and before they die they are buried—in business. Natural sympathies decay, poor relations are cold-shouldered, right and wrong become rights and wrongs. Good is exchanged for goods. A new disease is clutching moneyed America. We are suffering from fatty degeneration—of the purse.

You have all more than you actually need to live and make life worth living. Consecrate some of your superfluity to ideal ends. What do you live for? What are you toiling for? The limit of purchased happiness is fixed. You cannot buy more than a certain amount of pleasure, of food, shelter, clothing, physical enjoyment. And they are no permanent investment. They are transient. The draught of pleasure contains its own emetic. You will, every one of you, be bankrupt and poverty stricken—when six feet under ground. Your gold eagles will spread their wings and fly away. Your enjoyments will nauseate you. Pleasures pall, gold melts, youth fades, the body decays. "The grass withereth."

II. And "The flower fadeth." Yes, cattle raisers may value grass as the only staple, but in the garden of humanity cabbage heads are not the only product. Grass and cabbage heads are the democracy of vegetation.

Flowers are its aristocracy. Sunflowers flame, roses blush at their own beauty, lilies toss their proud white heads above their rivals, each blossom a stanza in the fugitive poetry of nature. The flowers are the stars of the earth, even as the stars are the flowers of the heavens.

But they are only shooting stars. Their bridal drapery is soon stripped off by that boisterous wooer, the harsh east wind. They make their debut for a season only to retire and die. They are types of the flower of mankind.

We are full of intellectual pride. When we have earned grass to live, we try to blossom. And this century is the summer of civilization. How we have annihilated time and space; how we have fastened a bit in the teeth of the winds and chained the lightning to our chariots! Science has torn off the veil of nature; art has painted her portrait. And we are supremely happy, because we fancy we are supremely wise. I am glad that we are not. I rejoice that mankind is yet weak and ignorant. There are still fields to conquer, there is still work to be done, and there is still humility to be learned. We blunder into knowledge. Copernicus, Galileo and Newton advanced by contradicting each other. Philosophy has been a series of battles, and religion a bonfire of martyrs and prophets.

What do we know to-day? Not much more than how to label our ignorance. What do we do to-day? Not much more than enjoy more comforts during the same term of years as our ancestors.

Our boasted knowledge is fragmentary, changeable and unsatisfactory. Yet it is invading religion. It is turning your heads. When Disraeli was contesting a parliamentary election he spoke at a turbulent public meeting as an independent candidate to the voters. They were dissatisfied with his independent principles, and the cry arose, "What is your platform? Where do you stand, sir?

Where do you stand?" "On my head," was the quick reply of Disraeli, "on my head." His platform was his head. He took his stand upon his brains. And this generation as a whole is trying to stand on its head; to plant itself upon imperfect information, to substitute thinking for feeling, and facts for faith.

It cannot last long—this insane self-reliance, this turning our back on the past, because we know more than our fathers. I have shown you that knowledge is only one crop from the harvest field of truth, that it fades and must give way at new seasons to new growths. And vague as it is by very nature, it is even more unsubstantial as a basis of life. Figuratively, as well as literally, human beings cannot walk around on their heads either very long or very happily. You can think and speak from the brain, but you must live from the heart. Do men ever boast that they have a big head? But they pride themselves on their big hearts. Are we drawn to a good head half as much as to a good heart? What a world of difference there is between being headstrong and being hearty.

Care and sorrow may scribble their signatures all over your faces, but the heart has no wrinkles. It is young when men are old and lives after their death. O, immortal elixir of youth! how it smiles on withered features! How it endures when wealth and strength and wisdom all pass away. O, treasure of humanity! that can never be squandered, though banks break and business fails, though hand trembles and brain weakens. Though knowledge is a shadow and philosophy a sham, the root is strong—the trunk is sound, though "The flower fadeth."

III. Go, then, wealth, like the grass, and the pride of knowledge like the flower; let the major key succeed the minor, silence wailing strings amid the reverberations of the trumpet: "The Word of our God shall stand forever." O Israel, slothful Israel! Thou wast the guardian of the word. The Jewish people have been, indeed, the trustees of civilization. "Like a ghost," wrote Heinrich Heine. "Like a ghost keeping watch over a treasure that had been confided to it during life, so in its dark and gloomy ghettos sat this murdered nation, this spectre people, guarding the Hebrew Bible." The ghost yet walks the earth. Its mission is not yet ended. But its first duty is to learn its own truths, is to practise its own precepts. How can the Jews be the missionaries of the world, when they themselves so sadly need attention?

Do away, the text thunders at us, do away with, abolish and destroy the fraudulent weights and measures by which you estimate each other, and measure men by the yardstick of right-living. What are you doing for your fellowmen? What are you doing for your religion? What is your rating on the books of God? Oh, if men were valued according to their personal worth and not according to their pecuniary worth, what a revolution there would be in Bradstreet's and Dun's commercial agencies! The rich poor; the poor rich; millionaires, beggars; and tramps and peddlers, our new Rothschilds and Vanderbilts. Have you ever examined yourself as you do your fellowmen? Have you ever condemned yourself as a spendthrift of time? Have you yet laid to heart the awful fact that on this New Year's Day you are, every one of you, one year nearer to the grave?

I ask you now to consider this appalling truth. There is an imperative law. It is the law of God. It is an eternal law. I appeal to you, weak men and women, skating on the thin ice of life, to think for a moment what you are and what you are doing. Have you a plan in life? Have you a fixed purpose? Have you an ideal? When tried before the throne of the Infinite

Mystery of the ages, do you merit acquittal or conviction? O, men and women, my brothers and sisters, the iron gates are closed upon the past and it is unchangeable. But a new year is opening before us with promise and hope and boundless opportunity. Some of you may never see another. Some of you may long with bitter agony for the past to return, for the unchangeable to be changed, for your lives to be re-written. You can now anticipate that awful moment, you can now realize the holiness of duty, the eternity of law. That though the world passeth and its splendor fades, though life is a fleeting and its pains linger longer than its pleasures, though all things human are dissipated into ashes, yet "The word of our God shall stand forever."

Many have passed from among us during the past year. Many familiar faces we shall never see again. Many a living voice has died into silence. Some of you are bereaved, are heart-sore, grieve and grieve and long in vain for the touch of a vanished hand, for the love of a heart that has mouldered into dust. They have become to us only a memory. A memory of what? Of their wealth and luxury? Oh, the smitten soul cares but little for the thought of such paltry baubles. "The grass withereth."

Or do we weep for the dead because they were wise and shrewd and knowing? Oh, what a desecration of grief is the bare supposition! Let pride perish. "The flower fadeth."

But lovingly and tearfully we remember their kindly acts, their tender words, their unspeakable beauty of soul. And round about their shadowy heads we weave as a garland of eulogy the ancient words that have entered our hearts, and will, God grant, guide our lives: "The grass withereth, the flower fadeth, but the word of our God shall stand forever." Amen.

SEEING GOD.

A NEW YEAR'S SERMON BY RABBI MAX HELLER.

A child is leaning against his mother's knee. He looks into the calm, faithful eyes and a solemn hush as in the presence of something great and holy, settles upon his eager, inquiring mind. For his mother, the good, earnest woman, is telling him about the mighty God high in the heavens who gives to young and old very beautiful and pleasant things, for whom nothing is too hard to bring about, who is everywhere, high and low, and who sees everything, the dark as well as the bright, the locked and hidden things, as well as the free and open ones. "And does God see me, too?" the child asks. "Yes, indeed," answers the mother. "He sees you and he watches over you, so that no harm can come to you." "And does he see me when it is dark, too?" continues the child. "Yes, darling, He sees you in your little bed when all the lights are put out, for no darkness can keep him from seeing." "But will He see me when I am way down in the cellar, or when I go far, far away, can he then see me, too?" "He can see you, child, wherever you are; for wherever you may go, there He is, there He guards you and there He blesses my little boy." "Mother, if God can see me all the time and in every place, if He is always around me wherever I am, why don't He let me see him? Mother, why can't I see God, too, only once, if He sees me all the time?"

That simple question of the child, I have no doubt that numberless little ones have asked it and that numberless mothers have been baffled by it. For, simple as it is, it is not a mere child's question. It sounds one of the deepest notes of longing that vibrate through the human heart; in the ambitious dreams of the young, in the lofty flights of poetic fancy, in the endless struggles of the hero, in the burning words of the prophet, in every soaring, high-aiming life, there is pulsating, in each renewed onset of effort and inspiration, that noble prayer of Moses: "O grant me that I might see Thy glory!" And what the child expresses as a mere surprise, what all the great and the high-minded follow as the pole-star that guides their wanderings, it eats into the heart of the feeble, of the lowly and of the unfortunate as a gnawing doubt, when the flame of faith, once pure and steadfast, is flickering dimly amid the glooms of defeat and exhaustion. "Why cannot I see God, if indeed He sees me?" This torturing question is asked not only in the hovel, but in palaces, too, not only on the bed of suffering, but often on the luxurious couch. "Why cannot I see the proofs that God knows of my life and of my pain, if, indeed, He sees me as I am. If He is looking on here now, and if He knows what I feel, better than my dearest friend can know, why then, O God (to use the language of the Psalmist), wherefore, O Lord, dost Thou stand afar off? hidest Thou Thyself in times of distress?"

And here, this morning on the day of remembrance, we ask ourselves with all these thousands of wondering children, of aspiring toilers, of stricken sufferers and exhausted strugglers: Cannot we see God? He sees us, He can be mindful of us, on this day of remembrance as at any other time; but if we are to remember Him, how can we, if we have not seen Him? Can a man remember that which he has never known? Tell us first how we can see Him, then it will be possible to think of Him, to remember Him. Let us go back to our text; it gave us the assurance that God sees; it will tell us also, no doubt, whether God is seen. "And Abraham, it reads, called the name of the place God sees, as it is said to-day: On the mountain the Lord is seen."

I do not know, if I should have understood this passage at all, I do not know, whether I might not have passed it without any particular emotion, had I not had an impressive and memorable explanation of it this summer when I was given a respite from the trials and duties of my sacred office. I would have known what the word mountain stands for and I could have understood the statement that "on the mountain the Lord is seen" as a statement; as a majestic, profound truth I could hardly have accepted it. For I had scarcely ever seen a mountain. On a mountain I had never been. Now our text makes no such sweeping assertion as it would be to say, that *only* on the mountain the Lord is seen or that on the mountain the Lord is seen best or clearest; it calmly says, without going into ecstatic superlatives: On the mountain the Lord is seen. The truth is, the Lord is seen everywhere, and what the prophet Isaiah says so forcibly to King Assa (II Chron. xv., 2) expresses it precisely.

The spectacles with whose aid God can be seen are of many different shapes and hues; the withered leaf, the common pebble, the creeping worm as well as sea and land and field and forest, all may be windows by which a glimpse can be caught of the lordly eye and the master hand of an exalted and incomprehensible Spirit.

Of course, people differ greatly in the various things that appeal most directly to their sense of wonder and admiration; some have no such sense whatever; they feel their own importance, the vastness of their experience and their general smartness and knowingness too much to be surprised, not to say amazed at the most wonderful things; that, they think, may be good enough for young people, who haven't seen much; they'll get over that, too, in the course of time. But I am not thinking now of these people who are so proud of the degree to which the digestion of their senses has been spoiled; but of such only who have to plead guilty to the possession of health and open senses; such people can learn to love God in many surroundings, on many widely different occasions, they can draw a joyful gratitude for this beautiful world, from many sights and experiences; but I doubt not that the greatness and the majesty of God in His creation can be seen no more impressively anywhere than they appear from those towering "domes that lift their heads into the sky," the mountains.

As for me and my own limited experience: I have seen the Eternal on the sea when it roared, when the vessel was lifted to the dizzy top of the wave only to be swept down again into raging abysses, when far and near, under the frowning sky, the mighty waters everywhere were lashed into seething fury; I have seen the Eternal in the peace of the golden fields, when the bended ears were like waving banners in the breeze, when in the calm of the ending day the sun went down, a glowing ball, amid a blazing glory of fiery cloud-shapes; I have seen the Eternal in the tiny insect with its glistening wing and its little limbs; He appeared unto me in the thousand beauteous forms of flower and tree, of rock and ruby; but never did the entire grandeur of His creation so burst upon my eyes, nay upon every sense that could open to the scene, as when I stood for the first time to look upon the abodes of men from one of the high places of the earth. It stretched before my vision for miles upon miles, a carpet of green in all shades; here the dark forest, there the fresh meadow, yonder the waving field; to the right a placid lake like an eye looking into the heavens; before me, though miles away, the river like a band of steel stretching from one end of the horizon to the other. Into this carpet, save where nature made a way for the water-courses, man had wrought irregular designs by marking field from field in figures of all sizes, by streaking the plain with his roads and dotting it with his houses. But how small he was, the Lord of Creation who ploughed these fields, where he had hewn down forests, who made his paths unto the mountain and rode in his little craft upon the winding stream; tiny ant that toiled and struggled down below, the naked eye could not see him; and were it not that houses and fields spoke of his work, of him nothing could be discerned. And what was he indeed compared to all the vastness around him, what was he compared to the tempest that raged in yonder corner, or to the cloud that drifted over another, what was he to the blue-veiled hills in the distance or to the rainbow that spanned the entire glorious landscape. And thus like myself, thousands upon thousands had stood upon that entrancing spot; with a cry of admiration they beheld it at the first and with beating hearts, awed and fascinated, they looked on and on. How they came away, with what feelings, whether they soon forgot or whether they enshrined the hour in their memories, who can tell? but while some, it is true, stood there cold and examining, to by far the most there was revealed in those moments a particle, precious, if small, but a radiant and unforgetable particle of the glory of God.

And thus on the mountain the Lord is seen; imagine at its foot one of those restless human bee-hives, where the shouting and the hurrying, the whistling from factory and steamer, the clattering of hoofs and the rattling of wheels over the pavement do not cease for a moment, what would you hear of all this on these silent heights? Hardly the faintest sound. As little as the smoke of the countless stacks of a busy metropolis could befoul the pure air of the summit, so little can the paltry noises of a man disturb the dignified peace of God's rock-rooted towers. No hurry, no confusion is here to disturb; in that vast prospect God is seen reigning alone and man must dwindle to himself into absolute nothingness.

"On the mountain the Lord is seen." The soul has its mountains, as the earth has; but it reaches them not with clumsy feet or on creeping conveyances; the wings of thought, of impulse, of inspiration lift it with swift or with measured flight to higher and higher pinnacles of manhood and ripeness. Now some can never rise to the summit; their paths do not lead upwards or not high enough; they find some orchard in the valley with tempting fruits or they stretch their limbs in some cool, shady grove; or they even follow some dancing brook down and down till it dashes itself against the stone in some dark grotto; their soul is not strong enough to look up and toil up the steep mountain-side, and thus they remain in the shadow, they see less and less as the years go on and lose forever the grand revelations which await the others on the mountain.

Meanwhile the stronger soul, filled with happy anticipations of the scene at the summit, mounts undaunted along the winding path. The thinker and observer stores his mind with truths and experiences so that his eye becomes clearer and catches glimpses of the view through the trees and shrubbery of daily work and daily pleasure; at first, indeed, he has to look down upon the path lest he should lose it and go astray; he must note the trees, where overhanging branches threaten his eyes or fallen trunks are barring the way; he cannot see God yet, while he is striving and fighting to keep the path; he cannot walk erect, his eye is on the ground; thus it is with you, busy, restless men whose thoughts are filled with business, with the ebbs and tides of the market, with the chances of new openings, with the hopes of profit and the risks of loss; no one will blame you; it is your ambition for yourselves and your families; but in all this toil and bustle and weariness you cannot see God; the woods of care and worry are too thick about you; the underbrush threatens to entangle your feet and it is slow work rising higher on the mountain of humanity though it may be a rapid enough rate for growing rich. The experience and training which one will gain in this contest and in this progress is not the kind which lifts the soul to greater heights; it sharpens ones shrewdness, it gives a knowledge of men and of means for obtaining ends; but it rarely widens the glance or elevates the soul. It is a different kind of experience that leads to the wide outlook, to lofty standpoints and to the beholding of God; the searching trial of a sorrow manfully borne, of an affliction bravely met; or the throbbing sympathy that looks affectionately into many lives and many hearts, the wondering thought of the strangeness of providential happenings, all these bring nearer to the summit and to God.

And then after years and years, when you stand on the summit of rich experience, when you have seen and studied life in every form, under every chance, when your eye is no more fascinated with the spinning of wheels and your ear buzzes no more with the hum and rumbling, when you can look calmly upon the whole, then you see God in every smallest portion of the entire vast machinery; when on your heights of ripened thought you hear no confused noises but only the sweet glad harmony which they form, then, on the mountain is God seen by you.

"On the mountain God is seen;" on other mountains also besides that of the instructed, broadened, ripened mind. From selfishness and smallness, from envying and coveting, from weakness and unruly passions, up to a generous, self-respecting, dauntless manhood, that is a climb too, and at the end of the climbing there also the view opens grandly upon the wonders of creation. You think you ought to see and understand God while you are wading to the knee in mud and foulness; as well might you be allowed to enter the king's ante-chamber, while you are reeling drowsily in a fit of drunkenness. Why, if one of your nobler fellow beings, the pure and upright man, was to present himself to your observation, you would not be able to see or understand his nobleness, mortal though he be like yourself. And do you then expect, in your slimy depths, with fogs and shadows hovering over you, to see God in His greatness and perfection? The God-like alone can see God. But climb ahead over many a stone of hardship, walk firmly on many a slippery path, cling obstinately to the narrow trail, hold yourself erect by your staff of virtue, and as you travel on, the sweet air of the pure heights will fill your lungs, your breath will come freer and easier, with a quiet, unspeakable happiness you will feel that you have been a conqueror and that the rest on the summit with the wide expanse before you will be the sweeter and the more enjoyable. Fight out your way to an honest, fearless, rounded manhood, raise yourself nearer to God and to His heavens—on the mountain of the strong, brave life, on that mountain also God is seen. "Seek ye the Lord where He can be found, call Him where he is near." Draw near to him in your deeds, He will be near to you in your heart.

Thus, as you may conclude from what has been said, the mountain of old age ought to bring us nearer to God, as the declining days bring the aged man and the aged woman ever nearer to eternity. They stand there, on the summit of their many years; stand there alone and more and more deserted, as one friend of their youth after another leaves before them. Down in the valley of their youth everything looks so bright and sun-lit and yet so small; around them, on the lonely mountain-top of age all is so calm, the passions are silent, life flows along slowly and without excitement. Happy they, if they find the summit clear and the air mild and pleasant; woe unto them if they can only see fogs and shadows in the valley and feel only mists and chilling winds on the heights; but if they can glance with a clear eye upon the valley beneath them, then on the mountain God is seen; and then they can say to themselves with the psalmist, 'Though father and mother have deserted me, yet the Lord will gather me in."

And this holiday, the land-mark between two years, is it not a mountain, too, on which God is seen? A mountain with a backward view, all clear and sharply outlined and with a forward view from which the mists are lifting slowly as the winds of time drift them up the mountain-side. On this mountain, as we stand on it to-day, we should see God and remember Him; we should remember Him in gratitude as we look back and see his kindly hand in every day of the year that is gone; we should think of Him in awe and silent adoration as we look forward upon the veiled destinies of the year that lies before us. But if we can realize how we are here together, lifted into a realm of silence and peace above the confusion of every-day life, if we can shut out the noise of the valley, its fumes and noxious gasses, we ought to draw deep breaths of reverence and of manly strength on these heights; it ought not to be a mere visit or excursion, but an invigorating change of climate that widens our charity and deepens our faith. And while we are on the mountain of this solemn season we ought to listen reverently and with sacred thoughts to those far-off mysterious sounds of the ram's horn. Think of the mountains and hills on which this venerable shepherd's music resounded; think of the seers and sages, of the kings and law-givers of Israel, of Jacob and David, of Moses and Amos as they sat alone among their herds, looking now upon the grazing animals, now into the starry sky; think how the simple music of this horn resounded through Palestine's hills and plains all these thousands of years ago. And now the ancient sound will vibrate again through the air admonishing us to remember! How many memories it brings of great men and holy deeds! And better your lives, that is the burden of its mysterious song.

Mother, if God can see me everywhere and at all times, why cannot I see God! oh, how I should love to see God! thus asks the child, thus prays the man. We have discovered the answer here in our text; it reads "on the mountain the Lord is seen," and it speaks to us and it tells us: art thou clambering up breathlessly, with hardly a rest on the little mossbank, art thou only plucking here a fern, there a berry, there a flower, but yet striving onward and upward; though thou mayest bruise thyself against the thorn and strike thy knee against the rock, though thou art panting and hot and weary; if thou seest nought but the rocks and pines about thee, the road is leading thee on to the summit without fail; and through all the toilsome climbing thou canst never see the goal of thy journey and the rewards of thy persistence until the end and the rest, yet on the mountain shalt thou see God; and if thy last dying breath, if the last beating of thy heart be the step that lifts thee over the precipice up to the free view of the top: on the mountain of death surely, God is seen. And after my skin is cut to pieces this *will* be and freed from my body shall I behold God.

And do you ask me how you should remember this great truth on the New Year? By a humble thoughtfulness and by abiding resolves. Let "your righteousness be like the mountains of God and your acts of justice like the great deep." There have been men in history such as our Moses and our George Washington whose entire life is one majestic mountain-scene; men whose skirts were never soiled with the mud of vulgar desire or petty spite; men who lived in the clear air of noble aims and lofty thoughts; men, who could truthfully pray: "Lord, by Thy favor hast Thou caused my mountain to stand in strength"; mountains like these, it is true, are not often to be found; neither are the Mount Everests or Mont Blancs so common; but as they are outlined against the sky for miles and miles they beckon to us; to the noble-minded such lives have a fascination; we turn to the story of their deeds, we climb up with them and as we are borne up on their strong shoulders we feel ourselves nearer and nearer to God. Who, then, would live otherwise than nobly? By these examples, as God has placed them conspicuously upon the undulating plains of history, let our ambitions and our conduct be guided; and while we pray unto the Eternal for all His blessings of the outer life, let us not forget this wiser prayer also, "A pure heart create unto me, O Lord, and a firm spirit do Thou establish within me." Amen.

OUR REFUGE.

BY REV. DR. GUSTAV GOTTHEIL.

Amidst the many and often conflicting feelings which this day awakens, it is a relief to find a word that offers a resting place for our restless thoughts. Such a word is that of the psalmist: בידך עתתי "In Thy hand, O God, are my times."

I.

"My times," that is: the good and the evil. Our life on earth does not flow in an even course; like a river it passes now through green meadows, now through dreary wastes, and now amidst rocks, where the shadows of night cast a dark veil over its face. Only the foolhardy trust in the constancy of earthly things. If nothing else changes, we do; the passing years deepen the furrows, not only on our faces, but on our minds too. It is neither pleasant nor reassuring to remember this, but it is wholesome nevertheless. For whilst a general should go to battle with the feeling that he will surely conquer, he still must prepare for defeat and keep his lines of retreat open. So must we go to the fields where we have to encounter times and conditions with a strong hope of victory, yet not burn our bridges behind us, for some day we shall surely suffer defeat. In the recent storm houses were swept away which the owners thought were beyond the reach of the waves. How glad they were to find a shelter near, whither they could flee for safety! Who can tell when his own habitation shall be invaded or overturned? Knowing this, what refuge have we prepared for our hearts? Oh, it is pitiful to see people in affliction, with no spiritual resource to sustain them—no God near to look up to, no prayer possible to relieve the oppressed bosom, no ray of hope shining into the gloom, nor any idea present of the wider uses of adversity. Only the stroke is felt and not the hand that dealt it. All went so well with them that in the pride of their hearts they said to God: Be thou far from me!

Religion, they say, is only custom. I might agree with this if the "only" were left out. Customs are the flowers of civilization. You can tell a man's education, yea, even much of his character, by his habits. Morality, ethics, *Sittlichkeit*, are words derived from roots denoting that which is acknowledged and adopted by the people as right and proper. There are foolish customs, many and not far between; but these apart—manners and usages are the silent compact, the unwritten law which preserve the proprieties of civilized society. So piety is the fruit of religious customs. What gives this day its sanctity with that numerous class, who hardly share any of the beliefs on which it is founded, but the impressions of their younger days? Religion will not come to our aid the moment we call for her; she must be loved and cherished at all times if she is to prove our true friend in need. Much of the present indifference of our young people is directly traceable to the absence of all religious observances in their homes. A prayer taught by a devout mother is worth all the liturgies of the Temple. A Sabbath or Festival coming to a family with something better than an extra good dinner but bringing devoutness and especially charity with it (as the good old Jewish custom prescribes), will leave a more lasting impression on the heart than the most eloquent sermons. And so with all-religious truths. Remember, O parents, the future of your children; do what you may, leave them as large a fortune as you can, and give them the best of mental education, you cannot change the course of "times," your love must dictate to you the duty of implanting in them a real faith in the fact that those "times" are all in God's hand.

II.

But is this so in reality? Or is that idea merely an invention of the inventors of religion? Let us see.

One thing is certain: the reign of Law is absolute; there is no escape from it; to be is to be in its power. If its rule is friendly to us we prosper; if hostile, we perish. That lead is heavy is good for us, so long as we need weight, but when it falls upon us that very quality makes our death. Electric discharges purify the air, then they are gracious to us; lightning strikes us and electricity becomes our ruin. Or, as Plato states the fact: If there is love between the forces of nature and ourselves we are happy; if hatred, we succumb and they triumph.

"Denn die Elemente hassen das Gebild der Menschenhand."

We can rule over nature only by obedience to her inflexible will, and wisdom consists in the fullest recognition of that eternal fact and the avoidance of challenging her to the unequal contest. And she sends into the field her auxiliaries from the most unexpected quarters. A single hour may change the world for us from a beautiful place to live in, into a hateful scene of woe and a very valley of tears.

Now the question arises: How are we to regard this inexorable condition of our existence? But two answers can be given. These laws of nature are either purposeless and unreasonable or designed for a purpose in accordance with eternal reason. There is no middle course open for us. Which, then, shall we choose? If we accept the former alternative, how comes it that I have reason enough to recognize its absence from the laws of nature, and that my whole being revolts against her blind tyranny? How is it that I, who did not make those laws, can yet, within a certain circle, play with them at will? Can say to steam, be my horse; to lightning, carry my messages; and to water, turn my wheel? In the midst of this incessant whirl of blind forces that shall one day engulf him stands man, protesting and protesting, yet all in vain! How came he here with his reason, his heart, his hope reaching beyond the world of "times," with his love "stronger than death"? Whence his thirst for knowledge, his joy in finding truth, his gladness in doing good to others; above all, with that mysterious voice that tells him: This thou shalt do and that thou shalt leave undone? What is it that drives men and women to pest-breeding houses and the more loathsome scenes in the haunts of vice, so that by their purity and self-sacrifice they may save one single soul? If this world is indeed but a soulless mechanism and no trace of a God to be found anywhere in all its immensities, then man is God; but, alas, not an omnipotent, but an impotent one. Woe to him that he should feel and think godlike, yet be at the mercy of a stone, an insect, a microbe. Then reason is a curse and the tenderly-feeling heart a calamity. But all is changed the moment we say to our soul: Be still, my times are in God's hands. Then you see the source whence our own soul-life flowed. Over the dark horizon breaks the central sun that illumines the world and brings light and rest to our own mind. Without that light our superior nature only confounds and bewilders us; with it we shall be able to feel after the poet, when he sings;

> Know well, my soul, God's hand controls
> Whate'er thou fearest.
> Round Him in calmest music rolls
> Whate'er thou hearest,
> What to thee is shadow, to Him is day,
> And the end He knoweth;
> And not on a blind and aimless way
> The spirit goeth.
> Leaning on Him, make with reverent meekness
> His own thy will,
> And with strength from Him thy utter weakness
> Life's task fulfil.

Here is the true philosophy of "trust in God," and is there a sweeter and more heroic feeling in the human breast than this? Let the scoffers scoff, let the doubters doubt, let the haughty boast—those who hold to that redeeming faith have surely chosen the best part. No better prayer can I offer for you at the beginning of the new year than this. May you be blessed with that strength that shall enable you to say, amidst all the chances and changes of life, "My times are in God's hands."

III.

Need I guard myself against the mistaking of my words, that this surrender of our "times" into God's hands should not take them entirely out of our own? I mean, that we might fold them and let God do all for us? That it is enough and seemly for us beggarlike, to open our hands toward heaven and wait for His alms? No sane mind ever so understood trust in God. The grandeur of human life lies just in this combination of the two factors—human energy and initiative and the inexorable fate under which he plies his hands and his brain. Hence man's joy in his successes and hence also the tragedies of his failures. He confronts the universe with its tremendous forces and awful indifference as to results;

and fights them all so that he may maintain his foothold in it and make it beautiful and strong and safe. And whether he conquer or be conquered the reward of his brave struggle can never be snatched from him. Here again he rises superior to fate and the blind tyranny of natural laws. His soul holds the sweetest fruits of his endeavors, and nothing can annul his rights to them. The soul can only be disappointed by its own faults, its own false and baseless hopes. Duties faithfully done are always faithful in the fulfilment of their promises; only we must know how far they reach and wherein they consist. Trust in God is no narcotic to lull our senses to sleep; it is, rightly understood, a healthful stimulant that energizes all our faculties. Our own activity is a vital factor in God's providence, and in His order their is no substitution, no voting by proxy, no casting of burdens upon other shoulders! You cannot be made contented by God if you make yourselves dissatisfied with yourselves, nor can you ever have a happy home if you sow and nourish the seeds of unhappiness. He cannot, with all His infinite mercy and forgiveness, blot out the memory of our sins if we do not substitute for them the sweet memories of virtue, justice and kindness. If we make gold our god, He will let us do so, but gold will be our tormentor, and we his miserable slaves. He cannot make us respected and beloved by others if we ruthlessly wound their hearts with the sharpness of our tongues or behave meanly toward them. All this seems so very plain that I fear you are growing impatient with my speech; but it is the plainest things that oftener reach highest and are, therefore, of far greater practical value than those for which we climb high, sometimes only to find out how much better it would have been for us had we remained nearer the earth. When you are vexed or injured by men do not always brood over the wrong you suffer, but try to find out how much of it is your own fault; whether you have not provoked it and positively misled your offender into his wrong-doing. Just try this the very next time you are angry at a brother, and I am confident you will not let the sun go down over your anger; nay, you will rather feel as though you had to go to him and say, "Forgive me," than to exact a confession of sin from him.

Happy the man in whom God-trust and self-trust are rightly balanced and who lives in the blessedness of that faith that said in peaceful joy, "My times are in God's hands."

RELIGION'S CALL.

BY SAMUEL SCHULMAN, RABBI CONG. BNAI JEHUDAH,
KANSAS CITY, MO.

Text: Jeremiah vi., 16. "Stand ye in the ways and see, and ask after the ancient path, where is the way which is good, and walk therein; and find rest for your soul."

All religious observances and institutions are creations of the human soul. They have been called into being because there was a deeply felt need for them which struggled through dim feeling and found expression in the clear thought, the powerful word or striking symbol. I have no sympathy with that spurious rationalism which with its cheap wit is ever ready to tell us that our divisions of time are merely conventional, and hence, they would argue, have no significance; that our festivals are matters of indifference to the prolific source of life; that our religious beliefs are but idle projects of our own brain. These critics, who pride themselves upon their reason, are flippant, but not rational. They overlook the facts, the experiences of the soul, the depths of man's nature, from which prayer and festal day naturally emerge. The sages in the Talmud showed a deeper insight and truer wisdom when they said: "The court of justice is not opened in heaven before the court of justice on earth has sanctified the new month." What a profound, critical and beautiful remark. In a flash of intuition they revealed the bridge which unites earth and heaven. They anticipated these critics by voicing their belief in the humanness of all religious institutions. At the same time they asserted the validity of all religious beliefs in so far as they correspond to and body forth the essential facts of human experience. They intimated to us that we only speak in material language of a court in heaven, because there exists already a judgment seat in our own soul. And we testify to this fact by emphatically bringing it home to our minds with the help of the institution of sacred days and solemn moments of reflection.

And so for us to-night a new year begins because our soul wants it so. Emerson says: "Our faith comes in moments; our vice is habitual." Such a moment is this to-night when standing at the parting of ways, taking leave of the old year with its full harvest of joys and sorrows, of success and failure, of possible spiritual triumphs, perhaps of moral defeat and degradation, we stand anxious, looking toward the future, seeking to penetrate beyond its veil. It is a moment exalted by the centuries of history in which Israel, our spiritual mother, used it to turn to her Maker. It is endeared and transfigured for us by the memory of loving parents who clasped us to their hearts and gave us their blessings; it is a moment made holy for each one of us by its recall of the high water marks in our own past life. The inspiration of Israel's historic career, the love of that which is most touching to the human heart and the consciousness of that which is divinest in ourselves unite and concentrate themselves on a New Year's eve, and by the voice of religion proclaim to us its solemn message. This voice may be considered in the words of Jeremiah to have a three-fold purpose. This prophet, who in many phases of his ministry proved himself to have sounded the most ethical and spiritual sides of our faith, has here struck off, in a few words, the function of religion as a call to man, to properly direct his life. Religion calls upon man to see his life as it is; to ask for a rule of guidance and to aspire to an ideal which will give satisfaction and peace to his soul.

Stand on the ways and see. The first step in knowledge is the cultivation of the habit to see things as they are. Science is but the organized and well-sifted series of observations, of instances of true seeing. The characteristic trait of the scientific thinker is that he is able to see important facts and connections where the ordinary eye will see nothing of striking significance. So also the cultivation of our feeling for beauty finds a natural aid in the training of the eye to see the subtle shadings, the graceful contours, the poetic symbolism, in a world of things which through habit have become commonplace. And thus also in the facts of the moral life of man, the world of the soul, the first requisite is to see ourselves as we are. We are to learn to take a comprehensive and penetrating look into the mechanism of our characters, to detect its flaws and injuries, to learn the direction of its tendency. In the world of action we become used up, warped, stained. In thought and reflection we become aware of our nature, and we inevitably judge ourselves. "Stand ye in the ways and see" means study your history, scrutinize your ambitions, look into your memories, and criticise your hopes.

This moment, therefore, asks us to look into the mirror of sacred self-scrutiny and see what our lives look like after a year's wear and use. What do you see there as a man of the world? Does your life present to your eye but the picture of a restless, striving, pushing, fretting egotism? Is it only an intense, unabating pursuit of business whose monotony is relieved by the parallel chase of pleasure? Or does there mingle amid the kaleidoscopic views of the year's experience some colors from a diviner region than the realm of trade? Amid the struggles, victories and disappointments of commercial ambition, is there visible some effort of freeing yourself in spirit from the slavery of toil; some reaching out after the possessions of the soul, some triumphs of conscience in its conflict with temptation; some vindication of a higher thought amid the variety of animal satisfactions, not to speak of ignoble moral surrenders.

Woman, relieved from the rougher contact with the struggle for life, consecrated by her position and opportunity to be the guardian and inspiration of a view of life that shall act as counteracting force, that shall uphold the ideal of duty, of tender sympathy, woman, created to be more sensitively receptive to the appeals of our nobler nature, she ought to ask herself in such a moment as this: How looks my life? Have I used my exemption from the strain of toil but for the more lavish indulgence of indolent, wasteful pleasure? What sacred aspiration, what love of culture of mind and heart, what nobler outlook, what sweeter influence, what regenerating deed can my past life show up as having cast a redeeming and transfiguring light upon the life of the family? As parents you feel in this moment that nothing is more precious than the darlings of your heart; you feel that your souls are knit with those of your children. A spontaneous outburst of gratitude must well up from your hearts in the knowledge that they and you are together, and that the outgoing year, whatever it has brought, has been truly blest in that it has not separated you from them. Ask yourselves what share you have had in the molding of their characters. Scrutinize your work; see what impress you have made upon their plastic souls, which have been entrusted to you for the forming and perhaps decisive influencing of their whole future. Have you risen to the height of your position? to the solemnity of your responsibility? and through patience, self-denial and increased self-scrutiny, have you made yourselves what you ought to be, true representatives of a holy authority, an ark of divine law, a fountain of moral inspiration? Or must you acknowledge that frequently passion and caprice, selfishness and inordinate self-indulgence have combined to vulgarize the home and rob it of its sacredness, because there was not in it the rule and sway of any impulse and ambition that went beyond the satisfaction of purse or pleasure? The young, they who stand in the critical stage of transition, between childhood and maturity, they who are not supposed to lean exclusively upon the aid of parent's advice, and yet in whom the passions are working and fermenting; they who are men and women in the making, let them on a night like this stand on the parting of ways and see whether the year has been one of progress for them, and in what direction. Have they grown not merely in the sense that they see and know and take part in more experiences than children? But what new idea can they point to? What new knowledge won? What virtue cultivated? How many instances of manly triumph over alluring vice and folly can they call their own? What ideal have they attained, and what practical illustrations of it in their lives?

"Every moment," the sage remarks, "should be, and no doubt, can be made, a vantage ground from which to view and judge our past"; but we would miss the significance of the hour and convict ourselves of slavish superstition if in this thrice sacred evening we did not experience what true religion is. We stand, all of us, loving and pleading for life. This tenacious clinging to life we share with the instinct of the brute. Let us ask ourselves how we have made life worth living. After seeing ourselves as we are, which every one is able to do, the question arises, where is the way which is good? Let us walk therein and find rest for our souls. The prophet here tells us that the ancient ways are well known. Among them one is easily recognized as that which leads to the goal of rest and satisfaction of the soul. He assumed a knowledge on the part of his hearers because this way was identified in their minds with a doctrine preached for centuries and known as the way of righteous life, the way of God.

And so we can recognize what the true way is by consulting humanity's conscience as it speaks out of its inspired records, out of its literatures and philosophies, out of its laws, out of the simple dictates of every man's heart. There is a wonderful unanimity as to the theory what the good way is. However various and lasping the modes of conduct may be, however devious men's methods may appear, what different passions may urge them, what winding ways they may use to execute their desire, in the midst of the motley crowd of human characters, two ways may easily be distinguished under which all these may be grouped. From time when man began existence the motive and purpose of his actions regarded either himself, his own interest, or something, some idea, some person beyond himself. Self-regarding conduct and that which has reference to the not-self, these are the two ways upon which the will of man may travel. These are the opposite poles between which the moral life of man oscillates. They are the keys with which to read the characters of his soul and decide from them its worth. One need not exclude the other, but the latter must overshadow and dominate the former. Conduct which has regard for some purpose outside of self alone gives true satisfaction and peace of mind, because it conforms to the innermost law of our being. Selfishness under whatever form, even the most graceful and refined, eventually brings disillusion, a conviction of emptiness, because it conflicts with the highest law of our nature. The difference between the two ways is clear, simple, easily grasped, though its applications may be many sided. Our life is a battle ground upon which these two principles struggle for supremacy, and according to the issue are we blessed or cursed, lifted or degraded, purified and made triumphant or cast in despair.

The most striking phase of this contest is revealed in the realm of conscience. There the issue is clear cut, perceivable, even to the dullest. It is the contest between moral law and self-interest of any form. The moral law, while part of ourselves, yet places itself against us as an authority above ourselves. It seeks to govern us, to circumscribe our actions. It hems us in on all sides by the "thou shalt" and "thou shalt not." To our self scheming it opposes the straight way of righteousness. Our greed it wants to restrain by justice. Our passion and inclination it attempts to overawe by the stern commands of personal purity and self-restraint. It is the watchman ever ready to remind us that in the pursuit of self-indulgence we are in danger of transgressing the laws of right living. It preaches to us the authority of the law which is higher than self. We may wilfully disregard its injunctions, but we do so at our peril. It pursues us unrelentingly like a shadow darkening our life. The retribution it imposes is shame and self-contempt. It argues a false psychology, or rather it overlooks the underlying principles of human nature when it is asserted by many well-meaning men, even in the liberal pulpits, that Judaism is inferior as a religion because it emphasizes the sternly legal aspect of morality. I think, on the contrary, it is a merit of our religion that it has so emphatically announced the authority of the moral law.

The law speaks truly out of our own hearts and not in a strange, arbitrary, transcendent language. But in so far as the moral law is not the same as our personal whims, caprices or fancies, it must be acknowledged to be the great divine power and authority besides which the personality shrinks into insignificance. In so far as we obey the moral law we are acting from a motive that regards a power not ourselves. We are unselfish. In the life of the young the revelation of the authority of the not-self is particularly made through the conscience. The young especially must, as their nature is unfolding, be on their guard, lest they do in folly what is positively forbidden. For they can hardly realize what a significance, what an influence, what an all-shaping effect upon their future the easy habit of transgressing laws may have.

But it is not merely in questions of what we ought to do and what not to do that the contest between selfishness and not-self is revealed. The difference of these two ways is shown in the deliberate purposes of our life, in the things we aim at no less than in the things we keep away from. While it is true that the first condition for becoming saintly in character, for winning the luxury, if one may so express it, of spirituality, is disciplining oneself in obedience to the practical, every-day commands of morality, a man must not remain negatively good, that is, not bad, he must aspire to become positively good. Man may think he obeys the moral law in so far as he does not transgress it. He may be scrupulously observant of every rule of conventional morality, do nothing which will entail the condemnation of public opinion, and yet he may be traveling on the wrong way through his life; he may be utterly selfish. The question for man must always be what is my ideal in life? Is it pleasure, wealth, power, honor, happiness; all these things are essentially selfish aims, and history, as well as the sad experience of thousands, proves how little satisfaction and peace for the soul such things are capable of bringing to a man that determinedly pursues them. They may be used as means, never as the last end and purpose of existence. The true way of life for a man is devotion to some noble purpose, to some inspiring cause, to some idea that makes him forget self altogether. Whether we love truth and seek it, whether we love our fellow-men and serve them, be it culture or philanthropy, or both, the loftiest combination of character, only in having such ideal purposes do we truly serve God. We are on the right way, the way of the not-self. But both culture and the widely spread philanthropy may be, in so far as inspired by motives of vanity, only more refined forms of selfishness. In a word, we travel on the right way when we love some good in life for its own sake and not as a means of some personal gratification.

But do you know what is the highest and sublimest example in this our human life of true unselfishness? It is the surrender of our own claims to the disposition of Providence. How often does it happen in life that a man who has scrupulously to the utmost of his ability obeyed the commands of conscience, who has proven himself capable of lofty enthusiasms and active, unselfish sympathy with his fellow-men, yet becomes a victim of a seeming heartless fate. How the catastrophes break one after another over his head! Out of the depths of suffering he cries out in agony, where is my reward? But this very cry, justified as it seems to our human view, sympathize with as we must by our pity, yet condemns itself in so far as it betrays the last lingering traces of the happiness of self, as a purpose in life. Therein we find the secret of man's position in the world that he is to recognize that he has no absolute claim on Providence. If we ask reward we undo in a moment of despair a whole lifetime of morality and philanthropy. There is a most impressive figure in human life. It is when a simple man or woman, in the very midst of suffering, can still, in heartrending resignation, say with Job: "Though He slay me yet I will trust in Him." This is the height to which human selfishness may rise. The good way, therefore, is the subordination of selfishness to law, of gratification to a holy purpose, of personality to divine Providence. And when we have found this way we have found rest and peace for our soul. We have been able to read the riddle of life. We may not avoid trouble, worry and care, but we have obtained an insight into what is the deepest law of our nature which gives us a faith and power with which to go through life and make it worth living. Not for ourselves, but for something outside of self, for law, for humanity, for truth, for justice, for God. It may have appeared to you strange that I did not identify the way of the not-self with charity or philanthropy. The reason is that charity or philanthropy, understood as practical almsgiving, helping others, is only one form of unselfish life.

The Talmudic sages say "The handful of meal cannot satiate the lion." This means: petty personal gratification has never satisfied any human soul. Our life is and remains a failure, until we have learned to go out of self, humbly obeying, lovingly helping, joyously clinging to God, who is to be for us the very essence and perfection of what is true, good and right. The good way is to do justice, love mercy and walk in humility with God. Paraphrased, it means avoid what is wrong, unjust, impure. Do to others what is helpful, lifting and encouraging, and with all be ready in humility without any claim for thyself even to offer thyself entirely to God.

Religion always has been and is to-day this call to man as man. To observe the facts of life, to study its tendencies, and find the way which brings rest to the lacerated heart, the troubled conscience, the aspiring soul. It is not merely creed, although man, being intellect, must necessarily make one. It is not merely good deed, although this is its noblest fruitage, and most solid proof of its genuineness. It is not ceremonial and symbol, although these are helps. Religion, daughter of heaven, organic to man, has created them all. It is that which out of the depths of man's being calls to him saying: "Stand on the ways and study your life; seek the right way, and walk in it, and you will find rest." Who, in reviewing his life, does not find the need of faith, of a principle higher than that which he is wont to use in his thoughtless daily experience? The happy need religion to save them from hard indifference and pride; the virtuous need it to protect them from self-righteousness, the cause of moral corruption; the sinner surely needs it as an inspiration, a promise of help to rise from his degradation. Those aspiring to a higher life obtain renewed conviction from its message; the suffering and heartbroken obtain peace and rest. So, friends, let us seek our God while He is to be found. Let us call on Him when He is near. Seeing you all here to-night, the familiar faces, the strange faces, to all of you I give the greetings of the new year. May it bring to all those within the reach of my voice, and those not here to-night, life, prosperity and happiness. But as we pray "Remember us to life, King desirous of life, for Thy sake, O God of life," let us be filled with the truth that this prayer brings not to us, the needful help, unless it is supplemented by that simple petition of the divine singer: "O make me understand, that I may live." Let us learn that to truly live we must forget self. Let us ask the ancient ways, find the way that is good, the way that turns us from indolent, thoughtless self-indulgence, from impure thoughts and vicious deeds, from cruel and heartless want of sympathy, from futile pride and narrow egotism. Let us walk the way of God, and find rest and bliss, peace and happiness. Amen.

THE GLORY OF RELIGION.

SERMON FOR THE EVE OF THE DAY OF ATONEMENT,

BY DR. K. KOHLER.

Welcome ye angels of light, bright messengers of heavenly peace and love, blessed Sabbath and Yom Kippur Eve! Come and fill our souls with the glory of divine life, with the sweet incense of devotion, with the elevating thoughts of God's grace and mercy! Which of the thousand and one sentiments that play with such melodious strains on the chords of our hearts to-night shall I single out for brief reflection? Dare it be other but an expression of joy and satisfaction at the sight of the multitudes of devout worshipers that throng the house of God in his solemn moment? Will a friend who meets the longed-for companion of former days again after years of neglectful absence, will the mother who feels the despaired-of son retrace his steps to the well-nigh forgotten home to be quickened to the new life on her burning bosom, mar the happiness of the sweet hour of recovery by angry rebuke and bitter words of complaint? A tear sparkling in the eye washes the soul clean of every guilt, and as though there had never been a separating cloud, the hearts are cemented and brightened anew. "Return my children, saith God, and I will be like dew to Israel, and he shall bloom as the lily." May we all realize to-night how far more precious is an hour spent in the courts of God than a thousand elsewhere. Let me in the brief moments granted me, speak to you of the Glory of Religion.

There is a peculiar charm about a religious devotion at night. The luminous stars of heaven whisper into our ears the glories of worlds which the proud ruler of day hides beneath his robe of light.

The day lures the intellect on to penetrating research, the shadows of evening fill the soul with wonder and awe. And is not religion, are not the sublime thoughts of God and Immortality, sin and destiny, the greatest of all wonders, unfathomable objects of human speculation, immeasurable, impenetrable, like the dark deep nightly heaven? Speaking of his initiation into his prophetic task, the seer Ezekiel says: "As the appearance of the bow in the rain cloud, so was the appearance of the bright throne, the glory of the Lord; and as I saw it, I fell upon my face and heard the voice of God." Why did the sight of the rainbow in the clouds suggest to the prophet of the exile the idea of God's great throne in heaven? I might answer with the psalmist: Cloud and darkness are round about Him. Yet why not rather find Him in the light of day and hear Him proclaim: Seek me and you will find me and live! Friends! Think of the old legend of the flood: When the world was wrapped in darkness, and sin had deluged the earth, there also the men looked up from the floating ark and beheld in the light that pierced the night, in the belt of beauty that arched the sky, a pledge of God's presence, a sign of peace in the handwriting of the Most High. What is the meaning of these strange hieroglyphics of the Bible? Out of the darkness of despair and disaster, out of a desolate temple there, out of a world in ruins here mortal man looks up to heaven to find God, peace, order, the gleam of hope for the future, and what does he see? The orb of day is hidden; dense blackness has covered the firmament; but far more lumi-

nous and effulgent than the light of sun and stars is the
splendor seen on the clouds, a combination of rays and
colors so wonderful that neither sky nor earth have anything to match it. Surely this radiance emanates from
some majestic source of light concealed from human view.
Here are hidden the sun-beams of divine love. Thus
argued man before he knew the nature of that marvelous bridge which spans the heaven with beauty. And
with his deeper insight into the mysteries of God, the seer
beheld there in the truth conveyed: "Mountains may
depart and hills be shaken. Yet my mercy shall never
depart, and my covenant of love shall never be removed,
saith the Lord who hath compassion on thee." And is
this grand lesson not still the same for us?

With a mind eager to drink in the glory of the universe,
we look out through the windows of our soul to perceive
the truth, yet just as our eyes will at the end droop fa-
tigued and dazed by the rays of the sun, so must our
spirit stop in its onward flight when searching for God.
We may advance from age to age, scanning the deep and
scaling the heights to penetrate ever closer into the secrets
of creation and with ever sharper weapons dispel the
clouds that overhang the process of nature's work. We
may succeed in unraveling all the causes and laws that
govern the world. Yet the Master above remains forever
hidden in his innermost sanctuary. We behold but the
hem of His garment; His being is beyond finding out.
Shall we therefore deprive the Universe of a Ruler and
Father, and, with the agnostic, doubt, with the atheist,
deny, that life has a purpose, a harmonious plan and call
existence a mere chance, the world—a failure? Shall we
decry religion as folly, prayer as madness; God a phan-
tasmagoria, an empty dream? Why behold this manifold
beauty and grandeur of the cosmos, follow these laws
which lead from pebble to planets, from mineral to man,

from sun dust to solar systems. Are these not the broken rays of God's wisdom reflected upon our little brain, luminous foot-steps of His glory seen in the clouds?

Yes, reason manifests the plan and order of the finite. Religion unfolds the beauty and glory of the Infinite. The intellect with its ever-progressive, restless inquiry after truth fathoms the immensity of the visible, but stops breathless, hopeless, helpless before the cloudland of the unknowable. Religion, beholding the arch of splendors stretched over the dark abyss, points to the glory of the Father who is enthroned in the light above and makes us bow down in adoration, to join the seraphs in their cry " Holy, holy, holy is the Lord of hosts !"

But there is a much loftier truth expressed in my text to especially befit our emotions to-night. Why was this rainbow, this golden ring uniting earth and heaven, first beheld by man after the flood? We enjoy the brightness of heaven only after black clouds have for days obscured the view. We prize health and happiness only after some peril or grief has brought home their inestimable value to us. Tears make the smiles of friendship all the more precious to us. We are children of the moment, and continual sameness of life tires us. A voyage under a cloudless sky and on smooth waters, however pleasant, wearies us at the end. And the same holds true of our inner life. Our covenants of love and friendship are often best cemented by tears of anguish, by severe tests, by trying moments of wavering doubt and of dissension. A treasure lost but recovered becomes dearer to us than when we never missed it. This was the significance of the sign of peace hung up in the sky after the storm. It betokened regeneration to a race doomed, forgiveness to a world flooded with sin. It spoke of a harmony restored, of happiness recovered, of life rejuvenated.

Is this not the privilege and prerogative of religion?

The law of justice, the code of ethics says: Be just, be good, be brave, and as long as you live up to the dictates of the stern rule of conduct, no matter whence it emanates, you are tolerated, cheered and spurred on. Your success, your honor and social recognition depend on your pursuing the straight line. But woe to you when fate and passion bestir and unman you, when fortune and friends frown on you. What will hold you up when your conscience and your honor condemn you and surrender you to the world's scorn and pitiless shame? Behold, there shines God's majesty upon the very clouds, smiling graciously to offer new courage to the shipwrecked and new strength to the fallen. Through the tears of grief and compunction strikes the light of God's love. However black with blame your past life be, look up to the sky to find God's arm outstretched in all the brightness of a new creation to lift you out of the whirlpool of despair and renew His covenant of love with you. What if men scold or scorn,—rise to hear the angels sing their welcome to him who has struggled hard but won at the end.

This is the greatness and glory of Yom Kippur: we are not perfect, not free from guilt and shame ; and yet we need nor priest nor mediator, nor blind surrender of reason or vicarious sacrifice to obtain God's pardon. When we cast our sins into the sea and throw ourselves upon our Father's bosom, heaven is opened anew unto us. The lost paradise of childhood is regained. We become God's children again, and greater is the joy in heaven over him who has fallen into the snare, but sins no more, than over him who has never been tempted?

But as yet I have not dwelt on religion's greatest glories. People often say: you have too many fasts and fetiches, forms and formulas of faith which do not appeal to my reason. Why? Is it not exactly the mixture of sun and cloud, of light and darkness that makes the rainbow so rich with charm and splendor? Naked truth is for God alone, not for frail mortals. Religion is but a sigh, a longing for light and perfection, and its glorious response thereto. Earth and heaven, the human and the divine, blend harmoniously therein.) Without showers, there is no rainbow. Nor is there the brightness of comfort and hope, of sympathy and redeeming love without the torrents of woe, without the storm-doings of suffering and death. //You cannot have life made out of sunshine alone. There must be night and blight, trials and tribulations. But behold the bridge of heavenly grace which religion builds over the wide chasm to turn night into light, and blight into blessing, trial into triumph. However loud the alarm of despair was Prince Guadama Buddha sounded forth, his religion reared the first hospitals and houses of refuge in pagandom, to give the lie to Nirvana's gloom. However certain the followers of Jesus were of the approaching downfall of the world, faith in his God regenerated the ancient world and rebuilt it on helping love and charity. Religion, the spirit of God, says the Hebrew prophet, is hope for the despondent, strength for the failing, comfort for the sorrowing, relief to the distressed, help to the needy, joy for the cheerless. The lower down the sun is, the grander the golden arch of the rainbow. Science, art and industry gave man all the comfort and wealth of the earth; religion displayed the beauty and glory of heaven—made man benevolent, generous, kind-hearted, forgiving—God-like, bridged heaven and earth by the works of love and philanthropy. Need I single out to you what wealth of light and what beauty of holiness religion was to the Jew in the time when sin and cruel barbarity deluged the earth with blood and, like the dove of the ark, he searched for a place of safety, but found it nowhere except in his own home? Need I emphasize to-night what the Jew did and what he is still accomplishing in the field in which he stands out unequaled throughout the ages?

"The temple is in ruins, but the sacrificial flame of charity and beneficence will forever burn brightly upon the altar of the Jewish heart," said the great master, Ben Sakkai, and eighteen centuries have been at work to fulfil his grand prophecy.

Nor has it grown dimmer in our age, or in our country. Dark clouds have arisen on the Jewish horizon in the years past, but we beheld the majesty of divine love and sympathy shine out of the darkness to imbue the heart with greater fortitude, with heroic self-abnegation, and cheer and spur them on with greater hope for the future.

What of the shadows that rise over the east? What of the doubts that overcast the faith of the Jew in the west? I see, above all the quarreling sects and races and classes and opinions of men, an arch of silver and gold, of purple and violet, of all the colors of the rainbow, spanned over the future—and above it the words inscribed in letters of fire: "Yom Hakippurim—Day of Reconciliation and Peace between all creeds, all sciences, all systems of truths, and all men." Centuries will come and go, empires will rise and vanish like bubbles, philosophies will spring up and dissolve like smoke, and the Jew will partake in all the strifes and vexations, in all the hatred and love of man, but that bow of the covenant made between God and man, shown in the Bible, that religion of humanity proclaimed by Israel and built up of all the precious light that gleams through the ages of history, through the progress of man in all the colors of the prism of human intellect, will form the canopy of the new heaven and the foundation of the new earth. Sinai's covenant will overarch the ages and re-unite man with man, the creature with his Creator. Israel, thy God is the hope of mankind!

Brethren, let us clasp hands for friendship and for fellowship, for granting and asking pardon, for hearty co-operation in the work of love and charity, for the re-awakening and up-building of life in our midst, in our congregation. And whatever tears, worries and clouds of cares the years past have brought, let us wait for the brightness of the Glory of God to appear and illumine our coming years with hope and peace and life. Amen.

SIN AND FORGIVENESS.

SERMON FOR THE EVE OF THE DAY OF ATONEMENT.

BY RABBI I. S. MOSES.

The night has come, ushering in Israel's most sacred day. Wherever the descendants of Abraham dwell on this vast globe—whether on the sun-kissed soil of liberty, or under the leaden sky of despotism and poverty—everywhere this night has the magic power to bring together the scattered members of Israel, to weld for one brief day the remnants of a people into one holy community. What a wonderful charm does this day hold, to thus spell into awe and reverence the most callous and indifferent of our people, and to arouse within them those solemn thoughts and sacred emotions characteristic of this day?

There is no day in the calendar of any other religion, ancient or modern, that ever exercised a similar influence upon men's souls as the Day of Atonement does upon the people of Israel; nor has any other religion embodied in any of its festivities the principle which lent name and character to the day we celebrate. Whence this strange anomaly? Is not every religion based upon this deeper need of the soul, the longing of the heart to be reconciled to that Power it worships as ruling its destiny? To meditate atonement between the sin-laden mortal and his Maker; to reconcile the insulted majesty of the supreme Being with the guilt-covered but repenting child of dust; to hold out to the erring and suffering man the hope of forgiveness and to bring him the message of pardon, has always been considered the chief function of every religion. And still the fact remains that none but Israel's faith has erected an indestructible monument to this idea of forgiveness in the institution of the Day of Atonement. The reason for this singular exception must be sought in the radically different notions of *sin*, as held by Israel's teachers and those taught by other religions. In all heathen religions sin is not a product of man's free will, but an incidental occurrence arousing the anger of the gods and bringing down their vengeance upon the head of the guilty. The divine wrath often pursues the offender with a bitterness and persistent cruelty quite out of proportion to the wickedness of the deed. Neither sighs of regret nor prayers of repentance are of any avail; the anger of the gods can be pacified only when full restitution for the harm or the damage done to them has been made, or the equivalent paid in sacrifices or sufferings. Therefore heathenism could not produce a day of atonement, for it was not man, the repenting sinner, who was to be reconciled, but the angry and vengeful gods were to be propitiated. Man, according to the heathen notion, has no other relation to Deity but that of the weaker to the stronger. Christianity, though solely based upon the principle of atonement, retained the heathen conception of sin: Sin disturbs the equanimity of God; his anger is aroused, it must find vent in punishment of the offender. Only when justice has had its sway, and the wicked has received the full measure of the divine wrath, will the nature of God be satisfied. In spite of the consoling doctrine of the grace of God, and the belief in God's infinite and all-embracing love, this fundamental conception of sin rendered a reconciliation of God to man impossible. Punishment may be postponed, but it is inevitable. The consequence of sin is death. Through the sin of the first man, the lives of all human beings are tainted; redemption from this hereditary evil cannot come from man. Nothing short of a miracle can save him. To escape this dilemma and to save mankind from utter destruction, Christianity introduced the idea of the substitutive sacrifice, the office of vicarious atonement, or the voluntary offering of a sinless being for the wickedness of others. The divine wrath has been appeased, justice has found its object, punishment has been meted out, and now the full stream of God's love and mercy may roll its cleansing and refreshing waves over the repenting soul. Such a plan of salvation implies a *continual process of atonement*, and cannot be satisfied with the ministration of one day to effect that divine reconciliation.

What is the attitude of Judaism toward this vital question of sin and pardon? What are the means which Israel employs to bring to man the assurance of divine forgiveness?

A quaint legend of the prophets, a precious gem of thought, hidden beneath the rubbish of historical happenings, will best illustrate the position of Judaism to the problem of sin, the high estimate it places on man, and the means it employs to reconcile him to God.

"The men of the city of Jericho said to Elisha: Behold, we pray thee, the situation of this city is pleasant, as my lord seeth, but the water is evil, and therefore the land casteth off. And he said: Bring to me a new cruse and put salt therein. And they brought it to him, and he went to the spring of the waters and cast salt therein and said: Thus saith the Lord, I have healed these waters; there shall not be from them any more death or disease." (II Kings, chap. ii, 19-22.)

There was an older tradition that Jericho had been cursed, never to be rebuilt. Disrobed of its mythical and mystical drapings, this little legend is but a description of the difference between the Jewish conception of sin and atonement and that of other religions. There is, on the one hand, the older doctrine of man's inborn wickedness and sinfulness. His flesh is a cesspool of vice, a juniper swamp of corruption. Man cannot help sinning; his very nature is evil; death is his only cure. If redemption is to come it can be only by supernatural intervention. But Judaism declares: The situation of the city is pleasant; man's nature is good; he is not the curse-laden creature groaning under the load of some original sin. Behold the infant, smiling in gratitude for a kind word or caress; does its face bear the stamp of innate wickedness? The evil influences of life poison our disposition and corrupt our character. To be healed of our moral evils no miracle is required; we need no wondrous cure. We must but like the prophet go to the source of evil and with the means which he symbolically suggests, heal ourselves of our spiritual sickness.

Judaism teaches a doctrine of atonement, the chief interest of which centers not in the nature of Deity, but in the heart of man; the change to be brought about is not one in the temper of God, but in man's own soul. Man is to be reconciled, not God. Therefore, Judaism knows of no miraculous, no supernatural means of atonement. The sacrifices offered at the Temple at Jerusalem possessed no vicarious quality; they were part of a priestly ritualism shared by all ancient worships. Nor was the High-priest's office that of a mediator between God and man; he was but the representative of the people, the chosen, appointed or hereditary religious chief of the nation in whose name and behalf he acted. It is man, and man alone, in whom this process must take place. To this end Judaism has chosen the simplest possible means and methods. It has set apart *one day* in the year, on which man shall give

himself up unto himself and shall find himself again.
Left alone with his better self, secluded from the world
and its turmoil, and bidden to examine his conduct, to
search his sins and confess his failings, man will soon
discover that within him alone lies the source of his
misery, and that, as no one can be held responsible for
his good or evil disposition, so no one has the power to
lift him from his degradation except he himself. To such
solemn thoughts man is not susceptible in the hurry and
noise of life's toil; not every day can he hold such holy
communion with his soul; ואל יבא בכל עת אל הקדש
Only once a year may he lift the veil screening from
profane eyes his innermost sanctuary, and there behold
the light of a larger self than is stored in his narrow
frame, and there to be *reconciled unto himself.*

Sin, according to Jewish conception, is not an incidental
act or series of acts arousing the fierce anger of God, but
a *condition of human temper.* Good and evil are not occurrences, but modes of existence. They affect not in the
least the nature of God; their potency lies within us,
working for our weal or woe. In other words, evil is a
pathological process; *sin is sickness* of the soul. The
patient must be cured, not the physician. Nor will it
be of any avail to the poor sufferer if any one else,
from motives of pure love and compassion, will undergo
the painful treatment intended for the patient, or suffer
the pangs and tortures of the disease, and even lay
down his life for the unfortunate one. No! the patient
must conquer his sickness. The physician does not heal
the patient, and the medicine does not destroy the
disease; the one indicates the nature of the disease,
and the other helps to speed or retard the natural
functions of the organism until the normal condition is
regained. Sin is sickness. How will you act if any
one of your dear ones be taken ill? Will you grow

angry and lose your temper or even strike the child when sickness has befallen it? Will you not rather with patience and prudence apply all proper means to restore your child to health? And can we believe that God is less tender and merciful to His children than poor, blind and blundering man? Is it not blasphemy then to utter this libel upon Deity, to repeat this inane assertion that God's anger is kindled at man's spiritual sickness; that He is wreaking vengeance upon the sinning soul, and that He must be appeased by presents or prayers, by ceremony or sacrifice, if needs be, by the life of the innocent for the guilty? "God is punishing me for my sins!" is the outcry of a despairing heart, often uttered in the agony of some fresh bereavement. No! God is not a cruel tyrant and merciless executioner? Not He punishes us for our sins, but our own misdeeds carry the penalty with them. It is to ourselves that we must turn, pleading before the tribunal of our conscience, testifying before the majesty of our convictions, that we have been false to our trusts and our truths, low in our desires, selfish and insatiable in our cravings, cruel and ungrateful in our dealings with others, and by such confession so arouse and stir up our better self that our soul shall regain its resilient power, triumph over the insidious disease, expel from our moral system the danger-breeding germs, and thus restore within us the healthful activity of our spiritual faculties.

Is it not clear now, even to the dullest mind, that the service of song and prayer can only be that of arousing our own heart from its wonted lethargy, touching the strings of our soul and making them vibrate in response to the words of our lips? Of what value, then, are meaningless and unintelligible utterances, spoken or chanted, as if by them we meant to charm God into yielding to our wishes, or to persuade him by the multitude of our prayers to take away from us our sins and make undone our misdoings?

What now must we do, you ask, to obtain forgiveness and atonement? We must follow the example of the prophet, go to the source of evil and cast into it the salt that shall cure our fountain of life. Salt, in the physical world, is that element which, though itself lacking any nutritive quality and bitter of taste, helps to preserve the meat against corruption and lends sweetness to our food. Salt is the indispensable spice of all viands, without it our choicest and costliest meals would be tasteless and insipid. In the moral world there is *one virtue* which, like salt in the physical, serves to sweeten our lives and give to our nature that strength and consistency enabling it to withstand the corrupting and decomposing influences of lust and greed and of overbearing pride.

That virtue is called humility; it is one of the cardinal virtues of all ethics, but it is particularly a growth of Jewish moral and religious experience. The word is derived from a root signifying lowliness, poverty, dejection; and indeed, it must be confessed, that originally it referred to that condition of the heart produced by the severe blows of outward misfortune, that humiliation of the soul consequent upon the destruction of earthly wealth or happiness, even so as pride and arrogance were considered as the baneful fruit of undeserved success. Yet, though born of worldly misery, it rises to the uplifting thought that God will not abandon the unfortunate, that as He has sent these visitations, He will also have compassion upon the stricken one and bring him again to honor. Poor and wretched, he looks up to the perfect holiness and justice of God, and then discovers that his sufferings must be the result of his own sinfulness; therefore, instead of arraigning divine Providence, he accuses himself, and contritely implores God's grace and forgiveness to create within him a pure heart and an upright spirit; to look upon his broken and contrite heart as upon an acceptable sacrifice, a sacred pledge and promise of the thorough change in disposition, his joyful readiness to do God's will. Thus this prayer brings to the humble heart the blissful consciousness of peace with God, the gladsome assurance of divine forgiveness.

But humility is not exclusively the virtue of poverty and misfortune; it is no less the crowning glory of wealth and happiness. You remember the touching words of the patriarch Jacob when mustering his strength for the coming battle: "O God, I am unworthy of all the love and mercy which Thou hast shown to Thy servant; for with nothing but this staff I passed over this Jordan and now I am the possessor of two camps." This is the language that beseemeth him blessed with earthly goods: "I am too small, too insignificant for this great success; it is by God's grace and blessing that these things are mine, and from Thine own I give to Thee." Not only wealth and prosperity, but also intellectual greatness, is ennobled through humility. The wisest of all law-givers, the deepest of all thinkers shrinks in the presence of God and hesitates to accept the divine charge, because he feels his insufficiency. "Who am I," he exclaims, "that I should accomplish the great task to liberate my people?" All true greatness is humble, doubting its own strength and ability, and attributing its success to the love and wisdom of God. Intellectual greatness without meekness, genius without the tempering and sweetening grain of humility, is unbearable and unenjoyable as the most inviting meal is tasteless without salt.

And even so the virtue of humility is the true preservative of our moral relations; it alone protects us against the extravagances and aberrations of our desires, the corruption of our passions, the poisonous seeds of hatred and revenge, the deadly germs of greed and covetousness. Can he be swayed by low desires who is conscious of the greatness of God surrounding him everywhere, who feels that he is in the presence of that Power whose nature is holiness, whose being is justice and whose existence is truth? Will he not tremble in all his being at the mere thought of evil, and choke the wicked inclination at its very dawn? Or how can he lift himself in overbearing pride above his fellow-men, whose soul is humbled by the thought of the majesty of God, compared with which man's most glorious achievements are but images of dreamland? This thought is a true petition for spiritual help and is sure to be answered. It has found expression in one of the oldest prayers, appropriately recited at the close of the Day of Atonement. "What are we, what is our life, what is our strength, what our virtue, what our loveliness? Our heroes are as naught before Thee, our wise men as if without knowledge, for most of our actions are vanity, and life is but a fleeting breath, sweeping away man like beast." But not despair but uplifting hope is the response to this humble confession. In spite of his lowliness, or, perhaps, because of this sense of his own insufficiency, man rises to God's glorious heights and brings back the assurance of his own God-like nature. In jubilant strains the worshiping soul breaks forth, "And still Thou hast distinguished man from the very beginning, and hast destined him to stand before Thee, and recognize in Thee the ideal which he must reproduce and realize in himself!" Thus the sense of his meekness, his deep-felt humility before God lifts man to the dignity of his priestly mission, consecrates him to the service of humanity. Oh, how the dark clouds of passion, of envy, selfishness and greed vanish before this brilliant image of man's true mission!

And, finally, the fact must be stated that humility alone can vest with true value our works of charity. The proud man may *give* of his means to the poor, the humble heart alone *helps* the needy. Overflowing wealth may throw a few crumbs from the table of affluence, but meekness alone puts the tear of tenderness in our eye and makes of us messengers of divine compassion and mercy. Humility will constantly remind us of the time of our own poverty and need, and thus will temper into sweetness and amiability the harshness and heartlessness of private or corporate almsgiving. We must remember, too, that by giving to the poor, or contributing toward the maintenance of our philanthropic works we do nothing more than an act of justice, not of grace; that we only pay back to mankind in another form what we have received from humanity. Wealth, wisdom and power are products not of the individual but of the common life of all men. Therefore, the poor, the weak and the ignorant have a claim upon those who have been benefited by the common labor, the common sufferings, the common sacrifices of all. Charity given in this spirit is righteousness. Such charity is the mark of true religion, because a child of true humility; it is the essence of Israel's faith, as stated by the prophet: What does God require of thee but to do justice, love mercy and walk humbly with thy God?

This thought is especially appropriate at this hour, when, according to the beautiful custom of the Jewish community of this city, the annual collection for the United Hebrew Relief Association will be taken up. I have been requested to bespeak your generosity. Twice the amount collected during the last year is needed for this year's work. Our numbers have increased and our poor have grown with us, our means have increased, but our hearts have not grown richer and deeper in mercy with the needy. It is simply a matter of justice and right if in the name of religion we ask you to double your contribution this year. Whether these words will have any influence upon you or whether they will remain but empty sound, the result of this hour will show. I have done my duty; now you must do yours.

But if, as I trust, I shall not have spoken in vain, it will be to me a blessed sign that, not only in this particular respect, but in all my teachings and exhortations, I have found the way to your hearts, and with the prophet of old have cast into the fountain of your life the healing and preserving salt of true religion. Yea, take this צלחית חדשה this new form of the ancient legend, and apply its truth to all issues and conflicts of life. In your trials and temptations, in your failings and in your victories, may there never be wanting the healing elements of humility, meekness and modesty; then will the spring of your existence be cured of the impurities of outward influences and of death-breeding germs of an evil and vicious temper; then will our prayers be answered, and in the sanctuary of our soul we will hear the echo of the divine assurance, "I have forgiven according to thy word." By thy own strength, thou art reconciled unto thyself, thy fellow-men and thy God. Amen.

SIN AND PENITENCE.

BY RABBI STEPHEN S. WISE.

TEXT, Psalm li.

The story is told of Voltaire, that he set out to parody and burlesque this psalm, which we have read, a psalm sung by David, after Nathan had pointed out to him his iniquity by means of the touching parable and the dramatic application, cited in the Book of Samuel. In order to acquaint himself with its spirit, he read it over and over again. While doing so, a reliable historian relates, Voltaire became so oppressed and overawed by the solemn devotional tone, that he threw down the pen and fell back half senseless on his couch in an agony of remorse. Aiming to ridicule David's conception of a "broken and contrite heart," he had not finished his reading, ere, overcome with a sense of shame and guilt, he fell down "broken of heart." " A broken and contrite heart"; Jean Paul has said, " Man is never so beautiful as when he begs pardon, and when his heart is penitent and contrite." How beauteous and welcome a sight must we present unto our Father in Heaven, as He, looking upon us and within us, beholds our hearts throbbing with but a single hope, our spirits swayed by but one wish,—to obtain His pardon. God hath said, "I pardon according to thy word." Let our contrite heart speak the word: God will forgive.

We ought to feel to-night that this is a season of actual atonement, this is the one holy day of the year, whose meaning we may entirely grasp. In the end, the New Year's day is an abstraction; it is an imaginary line, separating two worlds of time, as little real as the distant horizon, which looks to be the meeting-place of earth and sky. Similarly, it may be said of the approaching " Feast of Booths," that though it be our duty to carry out the observance of this festival, according to the rules laid down in the Bible, we are simply maintaining a custom suited to another, long past, greatly different age. The Sukkoth aimed from the first to be a season, when the tillers of the field might, in token of their thankfulness to the Giver of all gifts, bring a tithe of their fruits and flowers to the house of the Lord. The second, the later element of the Sukkoth appeals to us with still less force than the former, for even those, who in the present time, piously and complacently leave their handsome mansions to dwell for a whole week in a little hut, think not of the years in which a smaller and meaner hovel was their sole home, but obey the law, which calls for this deed, in a half-hearted impersonal way, as though Israel had never had recourse to tents since the march through the wilderness. The Passover is a great national feast, calling to our mind that series of wondrous events, which resulted in the freeing of the children of Israel from the old slave shackles. We may cordially cherish Israel's festival of freedom, nevertheless, it is only from the standpoint of those who are so wholly free as to be unable to realize the significance of bondage. In the same way, we dutifully remember and keep the Day of Revelation on which, in addition to being, like the Sukkoth, a festival for husbandmen, the Torah was first given to Israel; but three thousand years of secure possession naturally render men heedless of the choicest treasures. Loyalty to our past and love for its heroes may lead us to a cheerful regard for Chanukah and Purim, severally marking as they do the triumph of Israel over Israel's foes. We may wax enthusiastic over the account of the recklessness displayed by the Maccabees in defense of their land or the unflinching manliness of the Persian Jews when their existence was imperilled. At the same time we are but witnesses, dumb hearers. Our attitude to these holy days is purely objective. We merely review and applaud, we admire and commemorate—we do not act. Therein this day differs from all other days. The Atonement Day has no victory to recount, no triumph to recall. It is a day for you and for me, for us and for God; it is a day for the individual, it is a day for the present. We have the making of it in our own hands, we are to determine what it shall be. We come to God unconditionally "with a broken and contrite heart," not to parley or to treat with Him, but relying on His never-failing mercy, to throw ourselves at His feet, to leave our past in His hands, to entrust our future to His care. "The sacrifices of God are a broken spirit"—this offering He will gladly accept from us. He hath said it, in the words spoken through His messenger Isaiah. "O Israel, thou shalt not be forgotten of me. I have blotted out as a vapor thy transgressions, and as a cloud thy sins: return unto me; for I have redeemed thee."

"Israel thou shalt not be forgotten of me,"—the very words we have come to hear this night, words more dear and welcome than the tidings of the greatest fortune, "Sweeter than the honey and the honeycomb." Israel, with all thy short-comings and despite thy sinfulness, thou shalt not be forgotten of me. The world may deny thee shelter, I have room for thee: thou mayest reject and scorn thyself, I accept and pity thee. It is the cry of a father who loves his children most, when they least deserve his love. The daintiest flower, once plucked from its parent stem, must die; naught can save it to life. We tear ourselves away from our Heavenly Father, flee from Him and avoid Him; to-night we creep back within the cover of the old home,—no reproaches, no rebukes, no threat, no punishment, no question, no anger, await and appall us. The doors are open: we, who may have been morally dead, are summoned to life in the words, "Thou shalt not be forgotten of me, O Israel." The author of one of the best works of fiction, written in recent years, develops this idea very happily. He portrays the inner struggles and soul-conflicts of a man who has committed a frightful sin. He is arraigned before the law of the land and convicted of the crime with which he is charged. Later he is released, and another, who is adjudged guilty, is doomed to finish the prison-term which the former had been sentenced to serve. But the matter is far from ended. For now he must face another Judge. The workings of his spirit, the writer skilfully shows to result in his making an absolute confession, because he knows that God will not desert him and that His grace will save him. Friends, thus might we hold up our heads in brazen-faced hypocrisy, for you do not know of my secret sins, nor can I gather the story of your concealed errors. There is no inquisitor with rack and thumbscrew to torture us into confession. But this night, when to our sin-stained souls there comes the word of God, "Thou shalt not be forgotten of me," "Though your sins be as scarlet, they shall be white as snow; though they be red like crimson, they shall be as wool," every unrighteous resolve hies itself away, the desire to *appear* guiltless before the eyes of the Lord disappears, the heart that was grimly stern and hard-set becomes softened. "A broken and contrite heart" is the sacrifice we can no longer withhold from Him, dazzled as we are by the glory of God's great goodness.

"O Israel, thou shalt not be forgotten of me." To all of us, this is joyous news, causing us to face the future without fear or misgivings. "O Israel, thou shalt not be forgotten of me." Upon hearing this, a murmur of doubt and dissent rises to our lips, which dies ere it is born. For it seems to be belied by the experience of the past. "Israel shall not be forgotten by me." Your innermost thoughts are disclosed to me. You are asking yourselves —how else shall we explain the evil that has befallen us? God must have forgotten us, or else we would not appear before him to-night robed in the sable drapery of woe. God-forgotten and God-forsaken were we, or else He would have heard our prayers and spared to us the dear life, whose untimely end we deeply deplore. "Thou shalt not be forgotten of me." Surely God is not taunting us that during the past year He remembered us only with sorrow and suffering. "Thou shalt not be forgotten by me, O Israel," reminds us all of the occasions during the past year when in the throes of agony and the depths of despair we cried, "O God, why dost Thou forget us?" On this night of nights, thrilled with a hope of perfect pardon, we turn about as it were to exchange confidences, to tell each other of the new-born joy—the *other* is gone. Wife weeps for him who at this moment is standing before the Heavenly throne, and she prays, "God have mercy upon him! Reward him for all his goodness and his love and his devotion. Bless me by pitying him." Some of you strong men, seated before me, are weak, this night. Your faith is not sure, and the voice, which might have allayed every anxiety, is hushed and still. Yet, do you not hear seraph-tones from afar, pleading with you, "Loved one, have patience: bear with Him who has borne with you." Parents petition that the words "Thou art not forgotten by me," may be true for the sake of some little one. This is their only comfort: "Far from us, may our child be near to God. Having parted with earthly parents, may it be united to its Heavenly Father. Having forsaken us, may it not be forgotten of the Lord!" The prayers of some children to-night are strangely solemn, for at God's right hand standeth the absent father, whose humble petitioning will be mingled with the grief-begotten entreaty of his children. For some of us, Heaven and the hereafter have ever been a will-o'-the-wisp: they are realities, now that they enshrine a new angel, the mother, whose gentle and kindly glance as of yore would bid us refrain from all complaint and make peace with our God. Thus it is not to-night alone that we offer unto the Lord the gift of "a heart that is bowed and broken." In the few years of my pastorate, I have seen many homes ravaged and many hearths shaken to their very center. But to-night in response to our offering, the gladsome message peals forth, "Thou art not forgotten by me." Verily, he who can forgive will not forget nor forsake, will not abandon our souls to death.

God saith more than "Thou art not forgotten by

me." He supplements the simple promise with the ampler assurance, "I have blotted out as a vapor thy transgressions, and as a cloud thy sins." A moment's earnest consideration of this utterance will impart to us perhaps the most valuable lesson to be drawn from the belief in the principle of atonement. God speaketh, "I will blot out as a vapor thy transgressions, and as a cloud thy sins." Let me ask you, can vapor and clouds be blotted out? The first and simplest law of nature treats of the "conservation of energy," which means that in the household of nature no power is wasted, no forces are destroyed. To what, then, can God refer in saying, "I have blotted out as a vapor thy transgressions, and as a cloud thy sins?" A vapor may be scattered, the clouds dissipated, but blotted out, never; their inevitable end is to descend to earth in the form of rain or snow or mist or hail. Thus God blots out our sins and transgressions. He forgives us, not really declaring our sins void of effect, but simply blotted out. We may be cleared of them, still they exist. Earth and dust are none the less earth and dust after the precious metal has been extracted out of the rough ore. In truth, in the very first instance where God is described by Moses as "Gracious, Merciful and Pardoning," we also find the expression, "Visiting the iniquity of the fathers upon the children and upon the children's children unto the third and to the fourth generation." This idea ought to be the means of making us more truly penitent. Has it ever occurred to you that the word penitent is derived from the Latin *poena*, meaning pain, punishment? Pain, punishment, are the preliminary requisites to penitence. These lend earnestness to our repentance, and sincerity to our contriteness. As we reflect that the evil we do lives after us, the thought, that our sins are not to be blotted out, will make us pause. It will spur on the "broken and contrite heart" to sin no more. As we consider that the sins we commit perpetuate themselves in many ways (and according to modern science nothing is more definitely proven), we do resolve to return to God, worthy of His love and deserving of His confidence. Thus ours become "a broken and contrite heart," which God raises from the black earth of tears and terrors and lifts to the blue sky of tender trust and firm faith with the words, "Israel, thou art not forgotten by me; I will blot out as a vapor thy transgressions, and as a cloud thy sins; return unto me, for I have redeemed thee." Amen.

A DEFINITION OF JUDAISM.

MORNING SERMON FOR THE DAY OF ATONEMENT,
BY RABBI I. S. MOSES.

Text: Deut. x, 12.

It is with considerable misgiving that I approach the subject of my discourse this morning. I desire to speak of Judaism, its nature, the reasons we have for maintaining it. What is Judaism? What are its requirements? What our duties to it? Is there a more befitting theme for us to discuss on the Day of Atonement than this? And yet I fear that I am somewhat out of touch with my audience in selecting Judaism for a subject. I am well aware of the fact that with Jews Judaism is not a fashionable subject. They are not over-fond of the name ''Jew.'' They are not given to discussing religious topics, least of all one which concerns them most. Nor do they require or expect the minister in their pulpit to call their attention to the stern, inevitable, and, withal, not altogether pleasant fact of their being Jews. Still, if I rightly understand my position and the name of my office, to be a rabbi in Israel, I feel it my bounden duty to at least once a year, when I have the pleasure of seeing you all before me, bring near to your hearts the reasons why we should remain faithful and loyal to the religion which we call Judaism.

A DEFINITION OF JUDAISM. 75

It is not a very pleasant experience to be told, often with a sneer, that no one exactly knows what Judaism is. The term is surrounded by a haze, an indefiniteness, that puzzles even the scholars and the students of religion, if required to define with exactness the line of demarcation that divides off Jew from non-Jew. Were we to ask the large majority of the civilized world, the preachers, teachers and professors of the creed by which we are surrounded, what Judaism is, the answer would not long be wanting. "Judaism," they would say, "is the religion of the Old Testament: Christianity that of the New. Judaism is the old dispensation; Christianity is the new covenant. Judaism is the religion of law and ceremonies: Christianity is the religion of love. The Jew believes in the Great Jehovah, the awful, angry God, who revealed Himself amidst the thunder and lightning of Sinai, and gave to the people of Israel a number of laws, promising His protection as long as they would keep these laws, and threatening dire vengeance and destruction if they should venture to abandon or to change them. These laws," they will tell us, "were only tentative, they were meant as an education of the people for a higher stage; they were only a preparation for a faith that was to come. It was a torch that should guide in the wilderness until the larger light would arise to illumine the world."

Judaism, then, was only a preparation for Christianity. This having come, the old dispensation was made superfluous and ought to have vanished 1800 years ago. All of it which has not disappeared is merely a survival, not of the fittest, rather the unfittest, form of religion. It clings to the poor, misguided, self-deluded Jews like a hereditary disease. It follows them from land to land, and from nation to nation. It singles them out as belonging to a peculiar people. It makes them exclusive, narrow and, to a certain extent, proud of their past, and disables them from amalgamating with, and assimilating the larger religious life that is moving all about them. Judaism is an anachronism; it is out of date and place in the modern intellectual world. Strenuous efforts have been made, and are continually made, to persuade the Jew to give up his old-fashioned, worn-out kind of religion. That he is unwilling to do so, and, despite the disadvantages it brings to him, despite prejudice and persecution that it draws upon him, he still continues to cling to his time-beaten form of faith, is evidence of something more than obstinacy and stubbornness on his part. As a class the Jews, both by heredity and by training, are mentally alert, quick to see the fallacy of a position that cannot stand the test of reason, and are not easily held in mental or spiritual subjection. If, therefore, the Jew persists in holding fast to a religious system which is declared to be superceded by a new dispensation, he must have cogent reasons for doing so. These may not be always clear to his consciousness; they may he latent, dormant in his mind, or cluster around his affections and emotions. It ought, therefore, to be of the utmost importance to us to make clear to ourselves these reasons for our adherence to Judaism.

Were we to ask a number of Israelites to give us a definition of their faith, we would receive as many different answers as there were persons to whom the query was addressed. Let us ask a staunch orthodox Jew to tell us what his Judaism is. If he does not belong to the ignorant, uncultured class—he will tell us, that Judaism is the covenant of God with Israel, made first with Abraham, repeated with Isaac, confirmed with

Jacob and completed on Mount Sinai; that the Torah, or the law of Moses, is the unchanging and unchangeable constitution of the Hebrew people; that on the basis of it they built up a commonwealth, established themselves in a land of their own, with judges, kings and prophets, with a consecrated priesthood and a national sanctuary; that all subsequent literature was simply an amplification of the Mosaic code, that the laws and enactments of the rabbis as laid down in the Talmud and the later casuistic literature, are the outflow of the Mosaic spirit, and are binding on all Israel, and that to deny or neglect them implies denial or rejection of Judaism. Through the destruction of the Temple and the collapse of the State, Israel's political life has not been annihilated; it is only in suspense, and will, at the gracious time known by God, be revived in its pristine beauty and glory. The Messiah, the son of David, will lead the dispersed of Judah back to their country, and re-establish the kingdom of Israel on Palestine's soil. I shall not indulge, however tempting the opportunity, in argument to refute this position.

For me Judaism is not a polity, but a faith, not a contract or covenant, but a living inspiration, not a survival or tradition, but a development and continual growth of an original thought. However misunderstood by the outside world, however caricatured by many within the fold—Judaism is neither steppingstone or foil for Christianity, nor is it racial distinctiveness and national pride, clustering around bygone glories and shattered dynasties. Judaism is a *spiritual force*, a *moral movement*, a *social mission*. It came into this world not as an invention of priests, not as a policy of kings, but as a moral guide, a spiritual illumination.

The difficulty in understanding and defining Judaism does not lie in any mystery inconceivable and unfathomable, but in its very simplicity. Because Judaism is a growth, and not an invention, because it is life, and not theory, it requires a different measurement than dogmatic faiths sprung upon the world to meet a temporary need. We need not go far in search of a definition of Judaism. The Master-Builder who erected the magnificent system of Israel's religion, has given us also the key wherewith to open the portals and to enter the sanctuary. Listen to the words of the Great Teacher, the foremost of all prophets, and you will receive the desired information,

> "And now, O Israel, what doth the Lord require of thee, but to fear the Lord, thy God, to walk in His ways; and to love Him, and to serve Him with all thy heart and all thy soul."

These are the elements of true religion, these the essential requirements of Judaism. To know a religion we must examine the three great divisions of which it is composed and which have here been indicated: *Reverence, Love* and *Service*. We may translate these theological designations into terms with which the modern thinker is more familiar: *Philosophy,* *Ethics* and *Humanity*.

As to the philosophy of Judaism, it is contained in its God-idea, in its spiritual attitude to the universe. The charge that is often made by Christian thinkers against Jewish theology is that of its extreme poverty and fewness of thoughts. With some ancient Greek philosophers modern theologians assert, that the Jewish mind was unable to rise above the thought of one God. The Aryan mind was more prolific, and peopled the heavens with armies of deities. Christianity reduced them to a trinity. It fructified and deepened the barren monotheism of the Jews by bringing God in human shape nearer to the heart of man. And yet, whoever follows the currents of thought as they flow through history, whoever watches the intellectual struggles of to-day, cannot fail to notice that the battle of modern theology rages around those very doctrines that are so proudly placed in opposition to the Jewish thought; that despite the alleged closer kinship with human nature, the dogmas of the trinity, the incarnate God, the vicarious atonement, are more and more abandoned by the intellectual portion of Christianity, and that the highest Christian thought as represented by its great thinkers, poets and writers, runs in the direction of Hebrew monotheism. The literature of to-day in the lands of modern civilization, in Germany, France, England, America, betrays but feeble affinity to trinitarian theology. It is saturated with the Hebrew conception of the One God, who is Father of all men. And to-day science comes to corroborate this ancient view. There is no room in this universe for more than one spiritual force. Unity is the principle underlying the whole cosmic order : unity the purpose of all human development. "If I were asked," says Zangwill in his famous essay on the "Position of Judaism," "If I were asked to sum up in one broad generalization the intellectual tendency of Israel, I should say that it was a tendency to unification. The unity of God, which is the declaration of the dying Israelite, is but the theological expression of this tendency. The Jewish mind runs to unity by an instinct as harmonious as the Greek's sense of art. It is always impelled to a synthetic perception of the whole. This is Israel's contribution to the world, his vision of existence. There is one God who unifies the cosmos, and one people to reveal Him, and one creed to which all the world will come. In science the Jewish instinct, expressing itself, for example, through Spinoza, who seeks 'for One God, one Law, one Element:' in æsthetics it identifies the true and the beautiful with the good; in politics it will not divide the Church from State, nor secular history from religious: for Israel's national joys and sorrows are at once incorporated in his religion, giving rise to feasts and fasts; in ethics it will not sunder soul from body: it will not set this life against the next; this world against another; even in theology it will not altogether sunder God from the humors of existence, from the comedy which leavens the creation. *Unitas, unitas, omnia unitas.*"

Will the world ever outgrow this conception of God? Or will science substitute for it an impersonal, unconscious force guiding and directing the life and destiny of man? As the human mind is constituted, we can conceive of no higher view of the principle of cause and effect than the Jewish postulate: One God, the Creator of all. Before this God of the universe the mind bends in adoration, for it feels its kinship with Him. It knows itself to be a part of this great life of God. For this God, so Judaism teaches, is not an abstraction dwelling in some remote part of the universe; His temple the human mind; His sanctuary the human heart; His seat of glory the soul of man. No inseparable gulf yawns between God and man: God the Creator, man the creature; God the Father, man the child; God the King and Sovereign, man the subject and servant. "God dwelling in man," what does it mean? It means to make man's life divine, to lift from the dust the lowly, to crown him prince of creation; it sanctifies his life by making it a part of the divine life, and thus blending dust with Deity plant heaven on the earth. In a word, God revealing Himself to man in order that man may lead a moral life. Ethics is the purpose of religion—sanctity the outcome of the fear of God.

Every religion is judged by its code of ethics. Israel need not fear to stand this test, for if sifted to its very root, Judaism is by its very nature an ethical movement. It sprang into existence in opposition to the immoral practices of the religions around it. The very first call to Abraham and the promise that he shall be a blessing, is based on the assurance that he will teach the way of God to his children and to his household, to do justice and righteousness. What are the requirements of true religion? asks the Psalmist: "Who shall ascend the hill of the Lord, who shall stand in His holy place? He who has clean hands and a pure heart." Or listen to the Prophet's creed, "Wherewith shall I come before the Lord? bow myself before the Most High? He has told thee, O man, what is good, and what God requires of thee: to do justly, to love virtue, to walk humbly with thy God." Study the history of Israel. The stages of his growth are the mile-stones of his moral development: intertwined and interwoven with his political life is the growth of his ethical ideas. Even his ceremonial laws and precepts were but symbolical of moral obligation. The morality of Judaism has often been contrasted with that of Christianity and declared to be on a lower level, and resting on selfish motives. If there be traces in the Old Testament and Talmudic teachings of a doctrine that makes reward the incentive of a moral act, the whole life of Israel is a refutation of this charge. For a whole nation, during hundreds of years, to pursue a path of duty in the face of almost insurmountable difficulties, to bear the persecution of the world and suffer unparalleled martyrdom, does not betray a selfish nature swayed by mercenary motives. The love of God and the love of virtue did not bring to the Jew the compensation craved and promised. For, let it be remembered that the rewards mentioned in the Old Testament have reference to this life on earth only, to temporal happiness and well-being, to the permanence of national life: there is no allusion to celestial rewards, to heavenly banquets, enlivened by angelic music. Yet in the face of facts, what were the rewards of the Jew for his faithfulness and his virtue? If he did not crave heaven, he certainly did not win the earth; the joys and pleasures of the world were not his share. Nor is the charge of inadequate morality true even if judged by the current of his literature. The present generation of high-minded Christians would declare it a misstatement of facts were their morality to be judged by the standard of the New Testament only, or by the practices of the mediæval church. They claim progress, not only in thought, but also in morals. Does not the same law hold good for us? Has Israel not progressed ethically as well as intellectually since the last two thousand years? The Talmud, that oft-maligned book, is full of passages breathing the most unselfish morality:—"Be not like hired servants that work for reward. Be, rather, like slaves that serve their master without thought of compensation." And another rabbi said,— "The reward of a good deed is another good deed, and one virtue brings another in its wake: and the punishment of sin is sin." Is this not a higher standard of virtue than the leering glance toward a crown in heaven? To do good because God commanded it, is a nobler incentive than to do God's command in order to save one's soul. Whether the soul of man is immortal or not, is a matter of theological speculation and faith: with the Jew it never enters as a motive of morality. As God is merciful and kind to His creatures out of His infinite love and compassion for them, so must man fulfil the moral behest out of his deep love for God—for God's sake and not for his own sake,—neither here nor hereafter,—shall man love virtue and practice it. This theory of ethics has been fully exemplified in the life of Israel. His morality has not been closed up in a book and read as devotional literature on the Sabbath Day while the week days testify to a different system; but his whole life was permeated by the feeling of moral obligation, to do the will of his Heavenly Father. That will is a righteous, just and holy one, which demands not of man anything that is unreasonable, unjust or unholy.

And what is the purpose, the aim and goal of this morality? What the higher plan of Israel's holiness? Does obedience to the will of God and carrying out His behests close the circle of man's duties? No one who is acquainted with the history and literature of Israel will charge him with such narrow view. As to Abraham, so to the whole people, the promise applies—"I shall bless thee in order that thou shalt become a blessing." The moral life of Israel, his entire ethical code—yea, his whole history,—it is a preparation, yet not a preparation for Christianity, but for Humanity. The way out of Judaism leads not into any sectarian faith, but into a larger life which includes all men and all faiths. And here we strike the major key of Israel's Mission —"Israel, the servant of God," means "Israel the servant of humanity." The theme, "The Mission of

Israel" has often been derided and ridiculed as the presumption of arrogance, the vaunt of impotence. If it be possible to represent to our minds the history of mankind without the presence of Israel and the contribution which this people has made to the wealth of the world; if it be possible to construe the course of events in a manner as to leave out the currents and influences emanating from Palestine: it certainly transcends human imagination to picture the state of society to-day depleted of the spiritual and moral elements derived from the treasury of Israel's thought. If the Jew had rendered to the world no other service than to have given it that great book, the Bible, written with his heart blood, punctuated with his great national experiences, emphasized by the soul-hunger of his noblest sons, and sealed in the dungeon and on the scaffold with the last breath of the dying martyr—this alone would entitle him to the gratitude of all coming generations. But he has done more. He has given to civilized nations two religions which have become sources of salvation, remodeling their national character. For in this lies his secret of strength, that Israel is more than a religion, more than a theological system, that it is a *social force*, a national corrective. If Feuerbach's dictum be true, that all religion is anthropology (that is, the study of man), it is still more so in regard to Judaism. It is not only anthropology, it is sociology. It is an attempt, and a successful attempt, to regulate the relation of man to brother-man, of nation to nation. That all men are born equal; that they stand on a level before God and before the civil law; that they ought to have an equal share and opportunity in the field of toil; that high and low, rich and poor, learned and ignorant, priest and layman, stand in the closest inter-relation and inter-dependence with one another, and are equally accountable for their actions before the moral law; in a word, a Common Humanity,—this truth did not wait for the eighteenth century savants to announce it to the world; it was the foundation of Israel's commonwealth, the life principle in Israel's history. It made possible the survival of the Jewish people during centuries of persecution. His very suffering for the sake of liberty of conscience, his frugality, his thrift, his commercial circumspection, his inter-nationalism, his freedom from theological bias and dogmatic bickering, made him a valuable instrument in the service of mankind, enabled him everywhere to become the teacher and the inspirer of a larger and broader society than existed around about him. Is it mere accident that during the middle ages, up to within recent time, the Jews were the bankers, the physicians and often the statesmen of Christian and Mohammedan nations; that Jewish philosophers in the persons of Ibn Gabirol, Maimonides, Spinoza, Mendelsohn, gave impetus to new thought; that Marx and La Salle, both Jews, were the fathers of modern socialism; and that the latest religio-ethical movement has been inaugurated by a rabbi's son? The most powerful book of to-day, the latest addition to sociological literature, is the product of the Jew, Max Nordau. This seems to be the tendency and the drift of the Jewish mind—the prophetic spirit of old revived in the latest descendants, seeking to re-adjust and re-arrange the distorted relations between man and man. If out of the chaos and confusion of the present, there should arise a new form of faith that shall offer to mankind the bread of life and the water of health, that new faith will not deny its origin; it will bear in form and features the semblance of Israel, its parent. Israel, the servant of God, Israel, the servant of Humanity, is yet to become the Messiah of mankind, bringing the new message of social regeneration, of moral re-birth, of spiritual unity.

Will you now ask: What is Judaism? Is it race? Is it ritual? Is it feast or fast? Is it language, dead or living? Is it orthodoxy, reform or radicalism? Away with all these petty distinctions, these belittling divisions! Rise to the height of prophetic outlook. Judaism is Reverence for God, Love of Virtue, Service of Humanity. Are you ashamed of such a religion? Will you hold in light esteem the name that binds you to such a faith? Shame on the coward and the craven that forsakes the flag which has witnessed these glorious battles in the service of God and man! No more precious heirloom can you bequeath to your children and children's children than this honorable name "Jew!" Live up to your faith, sanctify by your life the name of the God whom you profess and who, through you and your history, has been working for the salvation of mankind. Yea, help to bring nearer the time when the barriers will fall, and divisions will be removed, when there will be no distinction between Jew and non-Jew, but all men be known and recognized as children of God, exclaiming with us the inspiring words of our confession: "Hear, O Israel, thy God is my God, thy people is my people. Hear, O Israel, the Eternal is our God, the Eternal is One." Amen.

I AM A HEBREW.

A NEILAH SERMON, BY RABBI LEON HARRISON.

Text: Jonah i. 8-9.—"Then said they unto him, 'Tell us, we pray thee, for whose cause this evil is come upon us? What is thine occupation? And whence camest thou? What is thy country? And of what people art thou?' And he said unto them, 'I am a Hebrew.'"

Some words palpitate with life. Great sentences are immortal. A proverb may contain a century's experience. A motto may be the crystallized code of generations. A battle-cry may inflame armies with furious valor and change the map of a continent. The tongue may be a two-edged sword. Catchwords have ere this decided political destinies, made and unmade parties and proved the most potent weapon of controversy. Religious strife hinges upon words, differences of opinion are mainly verbal. And often by one striking statement, by one clear-cut sentence, curiosity may be satisfied, questions answered, and history symbolized. Our text is such a summary. A series of searching and exhaustive questions is answered in one plain and pungent phrase. "What is thine occupation and whence camest thou? What is thy country? And of what people art thou? And he said unto them, I am a Hebrew."

The speaker, the prophet Jonah, is the most notorious character in the Hebrew Bible. His name has become a proverb. His remarkable adventures have amused the sceptic, alarmed the faithful and confounded the theologian. He is the bug-bear of orthodoxy. And yet in spite of general derision, this startling narrative has been embodied in the liturgy of our holiest fast. It is read on this day in every synagogue throughout the world. Is it to encourage credulity, to foster a belief in the miraculous, to force a holy Munchausen down our throats when we assemble with earnest purpose to speak and to hear the truth? Or is it that our sages have wisely discerned in this tale, a parable of mighty meaning, that concerns you and me to-day, and shadows forth the tragic story of a nation's pilgrimage?

I see in this storm-tossed prophet amid the threatening crew, a type of Israel, the wanderer. He has fled the home-land. He has embarked upon the treacherous tide. He has committed himself into the hands of strangers. His danger, his risk is at least equal to theirs. Yet they cast him out even from that frail shell to struggle in the pitiless waves. They charge him with their calamities. They punish him for their misfortunes. And finally they ask him those eternal questions that have been re-echoed from age to age and from land to land, to justify hatred, pillage and massacre, and to serve as the sanction of inquisitor and Czar, "What is thine occupation? And whence camest thou? What is thy country? And of what people art thou?" And ever the answer is flung back at them with pain, perhaps, and tears, but proudly, exultantly, defiantly, the answer rings out through the world, "I am a Hebrew."

For centuries these inquiries were a taunt and a sneer. They were the mockery of gratuitous offense. Why need they have been asked? Why should the world inquire, "**What** is thy occupation?" when trades, professions, opportunities and reward were all cut off from the friendless exile. Why ask, whence comest thou, when the answer would indicate not his home, but simply his last point of departure. Why ask, what is thy country? had the Jew a country? And when met with the query, of what people art thou, how need he respond save by pointing silently to his garments with their yellow badge of shame; to the squalid ghetto his home, the prison of his people; and to the changeless features of his countenance that advertised to the casual eye, his tribe and his descent? And if articulate statement were needed, then "I am a Hebrew" decided at once his trade, his origin, his country and his people.

That time, thank God, has passed away in almost every land, where the Hebrew was indicated by the evidence of material degradation. But so powerfully had the centuries moulded the national character, so intensified was the Jewish type by ages of isolation, that deep in the brain and heart of all Israel, the Hebraic characteristics were imprinted. It is startling to note how even renegades from the ranks, in spite of themselves, proclaim: "I am a Hebrew," by their very genius and achievements. I have in mind four illustrious apostates, Jews in spite of themselves, saturated by their ancestry,—Mendelsohn with the passion and witchery of his songs, Heine, a Jewish blending of wit and melancholy; Disraeli with his Asiatic dreams of empire, and Spinoza with his gigantic system of monotheistic thought. The children of their brain were born of Israel, their intellectual progeny could not disclaim its origin.

And now to-day on hospitable soil, in the spacious cradle of a new civilization, we are loosening the ties that formerly made us strong. Lulled by favoring gales we float smoothly with the tide. We are breaking away from our ancient moorings. We are forgetting the past, with its terrors and nightmares of horror. And children have been born to you on these gracious shores, who can hardly realize the events of our sad history, nor ever had burnt in upon them the meaning of the verse that is our text to-day.

We need an awakening. American Jews have been more fortunate than faithful. They have been swept away by the currents of a busy life, and though dowered with a mission and divine message unto men, like the prophet called to Niniveh yet fleeing to Tarshish, a richer province, they have swerved from their appointed purpose, and taken ship for the Harbor of Fortune.

And to-day at the time of such dire need for many of our faith, the old battle-cry should be heard in no uncertain tones. The old question used to be answered silently by the garments and the ghetto. Then even in happier ages we could point to Jewish poems, songs and noble thoughts. Now we need the answer to these curious inquiries to be made manifest in our homes, our children, our religious life. Each one of them should be an illustration of the eternal motto, "I am a Hebrew."

The home should be something more than a bed and a table. It should be something more than a social center and a lounging-place. It moulds many lives, it decides the destinies of the rising generation according to its prevailing spirit. It is a nursery, a school, a source of life-long influence. The work of the teacher, the words of the preacher may be neutralized or emphasized by the fireside. There it is that principles are formed, fidelity is fostered, and habits of thought as of action are fixed forever. What is the influence of your homes? Does the charm linger there of the ancient Jewish life, the tender customs, the affection, the reverence that made it a paradise for our fathers? You, parents, are preaching Judaism, not the ministers in the pulpits. You are deciding our religious future. You are determining whether the Hebrew faith shall be a colorless imitation of other creeds, an outlived antiquity, a mummy to be scanned curiously and then passed by, or a living reality entwined with sweet recollections in the hearts of the children, endeared to them by the memories of the old fireside and the example that you have set them. The Hebrew spirit that has been extinguished in the home will never be rekindled in the schoolhouse or in the synagogue.

And after the home in importance comes the school. The education of the young should be inseparably associated with their religious training. Jewish children are not taught sufficiently the meaning of the word, Israel. Their history, the records of their race, the leaders of their people in the past, should be engraven upon their susceptible minds. The Hebrew language that has been a vital bond among Israelites in all lands should be more widely studied. I would favor the establishment of schools in which secular education should be combined with Jewish training. Why should it not so be? The great colleges of the country are supported by religious sects. The Unitarians, the Episcopalians, the Presbyterians have each their pet institution of learning. Reverence is fostered with enlightenment, integrity with intelligence. The Catholic Church is the mightiest organized power in the world to-day, because it secures the young, it surrounds them with its influences, it makes religion a second nature to them, and binds them for life to be soldiers of the church. We need a similar policy, if we would perpetuate the spiritual power of the synagogues, and make our children proud of their descent by understanding its historical significance.

And finally let this same ringing declaration characterize your allegiance to your religion. Is it simply race-pride that attaches you to your brethren, is it simply the bond of blood? Is Israel a nation to-day imbedded within a nation? Is the cry of Jew-baiters justified that we are simply a class, united by the freemasonry of common interests, but pledged to no principle, bent upon no high purpose? There is no calumny that has wrought us more harm than that, no hateful libel that is so generally believed in by the world. It is for you to stamp out this false aspersion by proving your fidelity is rather to your religion than to your race; to the race when persecuted for their religion; but chiefly to the religion in its purity are we attached as a unit by our belief in its sublime excellence. When charged with exclusiveness; when assailed for being a peculiar people; when accused of arrogance in refusing inter-marriage with the people of the land, what justification have we in this policy of isolation, if it be not the guardianship of an hereditary trust that cannot be committed to strangers? The un-Judaized Jew, the mongrel type of half-breed that is so common to-day, has no reason to stand apart and preserve his separateness. Nay, but it devolves upon those chosen out for a high mission among the nations of the earth, to either live up to their calling and stand by their flag, or lose their useless identity and merge themselves into the population of the world.

This is really the alternative presented to each one

of us. It is a choice of extremes, a necessary choice of extremes as history will ere long demonstrate. The Catholic Church has been suffered by mankind to seclude herself behind triple barriers because she had doctrines to preach, a purpose to fulfil, an ideal to further. The Jewish synagogue can claim the same high privilege, if the motto "I am a Hebrew" be made manifest in faith, in practice, in fidelity; by the fireside, in the halls of learning, and in the house of God.

This is the great lesson of to-day. This is the wisdom that history teaches. This is the mighty inspiration that surges into the hearts of multitudes in a wave of flame, when they hear that their kinsmen have suffered cruelly without cause, and that they must protest against the atrocity by their loyal lives as by their burning words.

It would be much if on this day, the high, old spirit could be rekindled, the same grand fervor glow in our blood, warm our hearts and arouse us to passionate devotion towards the wonderful old cause. I see all round the world millions of an ancient race assembled for prayer to-day. I see upon their shoulders white garments. They are wearing shrouds as they pray before God. It is as if this were a ghostly people that had risen from their graves in their winding-sheets to fulfil a solemn charge, and verily they have risen from many graves, they have emerged from the raging deep, they seem, indeed, to be an enchanted race that not water, nor fire nor weapons can destroy.

We receive now upon us the inspiration they breathe. To-day when we commemorate our dead, to-day when we bury our dead past, may we be moved by the same mighty spirit. May loyal hearts be ours, and tender sympathies, the love of God and pardon from His throne of mercy. Amen.

THE HARVEST FESTIVAL.

BY EMIL G. HIRSCH.

Pessimism and Judaism, friends, seem to lie in different planes. But rarely does the carol of Jewish hope and aspiration, the song of Jewish thought and Jewish conviction, run in the minor scale; unresolved discords and passing chords are exceedingly rare in the score of the Jewish symphony. The reader of the Bible understands this without further proof, for the diapason of its melody is joy. Even when prophet or bard remembers the darker outlook, when the disappointments that burden his heart and the forebodings of evil that oppress him crowd to his lips, he never neglects to accentuate the hope that after the somberer notes shall have rung their measures, a brighter movement shall round out the message glorious in the golden certainty of victory and of peace.

And the same is the case with our post-Biblical literature, when indeed there might have been provocation for the harp of Zion to be attuned to the dirgeful vibrations of pain and grief, of lament and woe. Certainly to no other number of men did ever come what befell our fathers in the fifteen centuries designated in history as those timing the triumph of Christianity. Whatever human ingenuity could devise to degrade brother man was utilized for the subjection of the children of Israel. They enjoyed none of the rights, they had to discharge all the obligations allotted to the sons of God. Even the air was measured to them with stingy hand. Huddled together in their ghetto they were forced to invite the ravages of plague, and their physical life was intentionally so conditioned as to be exposed to the insidious attack of cowardly disease. It was their buoyant spirit allied to the prophylactics of their religion which set to naught the plans of their demoniac enemies. To speak of the intellectual advantages meted out to them would indeed be calling darkness light, the wanderer was not granted either the natural or artificial means to set ablaze the torch to point out to him a track in the dreary waste of hatred.

The government and the churches conspired to rob Israel of that which Israel loves, the light—the light of the soul and the light of the mind. Their intrigue failed ignominiously, for the Jewish notes that fill with sound those fifteen centuries were but rarely freighted with despair and lent themselves only unwillingly to gloomy despondency. Certainly one or the other of those gifted poets whose divan even to-day constitutes the wonder of the students of mediæval literature, at times poured out his grief in rhymes dedicated to Zion in ruin, or wrung from his heart by Israel writhing in pain. Yet even he loved and longed to win from his harp the stronger notes of hopefulness; to sing in joyous confidence of the day when from the dust will rise again what the flame had reduced to ashes, when from slavery once more Israel will scale the heights of liberty, physical, national and intellectual. So even in that long dark night of tears, the song of Israel was quick with the fire of joy and gladsome confidence illumined by the rays of a pathetic hope and a prayerful trust.

This festal tide, which we this year celebrate with such dignified symbolism, is monument to the joyful spirit, very warp and woof as it is, of Israel's conviction. Behold, it follows immediately upon the solemn days. Israel will not tarry long wrapped in reflections upon the gloom-lined clouds of sin—Israel is indeed of a serious temperament, but its seriousness never savors of the bitterness which is the condiment of hopelessness. Its solemnities are void of the sting of despondency. The broken notes of the ram's horn on the natal day of the year were not the echo of hearts torn by doubt, of souls drooping for want of light, and the day that we celebrated a week ago—the most insistent in the cycle of the synagogue's appeals, is, according to the old rabbinical conception, a holy day and a holiday. It is not a mate to Good Friday—an hour when church is hung in somber curtains, the lights extinguished on the altar, when ashes alone are eloquent and gloom and doom wield the brush to quench with nightly ghast all that would glow and would be glorified. No, our Day of Atonement is flushed with light, even when its message clarions the appeal of most earnest moment.

And as a child of these two solemn days, greets us this festal tide with its invitation: "Thou shalt be joyful—surely be joyful." The Biblical ordinances iterate this in such an emphasis that no one may read the passages without being struck by the stress and anxiety quivering through every phrase that this week be made one of genuine joy and universal joyfulness. As such a harbinger of good cheer this hour is, however, not a strange visitor to the synagogue. Joy is not a transient guest in the household of Israel. The old pagan religions, too, had festal tides when pleasure asked for the hospitality of heart and home. But theirs was the joy which is a rare respite from sullen servitude. No wonder that its visit was signal for riot and revelry—its main preoccupation, for a brief spell, to ignore all bounds of customed decency. The Saturnalia of Rome filled the streets of the eternal city with drunken bands of ribald carousers, and woe to the woman that durst brush against the throng of pleasure seekers! They were slaves attempting to forget their chains in the illusion of masqueraded freedom, yet haunted by the certainty that the morrow would fasten around their ankles once more the ring of rankling, grinding bondage.

Not so this festal tide in the Jewish calendar. It is not a season of riot, because it is not a passing guest. It comes not as a short measured interruption of the chain-gang's dreary degradation; not as a flitting sunbeam on its hurried passage from night to night. This is not a festival sacred to Bacchus or to Dionysius, whose symbol is the flowing cup that cheers, but engenders by its very exuberance and assumed gaiety emptiness of heart, and racks with its consequent uneasiness the very frame of its votaries. No, because joy is a constant attendant at the table of Judaism, this day spells a chaster, a healthier mood than debauching pleasure of tickling and tingling senses. Its legend is hope, its lesson, to be well laid to mind, to be profitably applied in our daily doings, in the round of hourly duties, is trustfulness in Him from whom all blessings flow.

It is true, for us this day has no longer the significance it held in the symbolism of the fathers. For the Biblical age this tide was vocal with gratitude welling from the hearts of the farmers. The Jews are no longer farmers. That they are not such, is not their fault. From platform and pulpit, in press and in private prints, especially in these last years of anti-Semitism, the charge has been hurled against us that we are vultures following the caravans of pioneers that go forth to spread culture and civilization, waiting for the camels to fall, or the weary wanderer to sink, in order to swoop down upon them and to fatten upon the rotting carrion. A proof of this accusation is always our alleged disinclination to handle the plow, to draw the rake, to scatter the seed, to break the sod, to woo and win from the earth that which sustaineth man.

Certainly we are no longer farmers; but there is no natural instinct ingrained in the Jew which would turn him away from agricultural pursuit. There is nothing in his religion that would tend to arrest the hesitating inclination to be a tiller of the soil. To the contrary, the natural bias of the Hebrews and Jews in Biblical days ran toward the plow and the hoe and the rake; and the religion of the Jew, if it encouraged any tendency, engendered and promoted the slumbering leaning toward agricultural life, and discouraged the exceptional predisposition of its adherents to engage in mercantile pursuit. Interest is condemned by the social economics of the Pentateuch—agriculture is the skeleton, the back-bone around which grows the flesh of Biblical religious ceremonial. Sacrifices had to be offered in the temple—whence were they procured? From the pasture and the fields under high cultivation. The law of the land religiously proclaimed and religiously sanctioned, rooted in the presumption that the people as a whole were farmers. More than one third of the ordinances that fill the Pentateuch deal with subjects of vital concern to the tiller of the soil. Poetry borrowed its symbols and eloquence its metaphors from the farmer's life, and when the prophet wished to paint the future in colors of peace and plenty, he knew no other way to press home his vision than by predicting a time when everyone shall rest under his own vine and sit under his own fig-tree. Again remember that the early compilation of rabbinic maxims and regulations, the Mishnah, has one sixth of its bulky mass inscribed to the elucidation of laws relating to agriculture—to the farmer's vocation! And in spite of these facts, our enemies to-day shout with lying lips—"The Jew by nature and by religion has a strong, an irrepressible bias against handling the plow—he is a merchant, dealing in money; he is the usurer—vampire like, sucking the blood of his victims—the nations that, in a weak moment of theirs, prompted by a mistaken humanity of theirs, allowed him to tarry in the midst of them and to strike the roots of his Upas tree into their very soil." It is a lie blacker than which there is none. This festival is the best proof that the calumny has not even the shadow of an historic excuse. If we ceased being farmers, Christian church and Christian state must trace the blame to their own intrigues. To-day in Russia, a sample of the Christian state—Christian to the core, I suppose—to-day in Russia, the Jew is not allowed on equal terms with the non-Jew to own land. And so it was throughout the world—landed estates were by law prohibited from being under the control and from being worked by the hands of him who proclaimed as his creed twice each day the unity of God.

And that God—was he not a farmer in the beginning? I know Mr. Ingersoll and others play upon this string to evoke a salvo and volley of laughter on the part of their rattle-brain hearers, "Why! the God of the Jews planted a garden, walked about among its fruit trees, cut the trees, bound the hedges, he worked in a vineyard." This poetic metaphor is a patent of dignity to the God of Israel. It reflects the feelings and the convictions of the Jews. A people that in its mythology could make its God a farmer, was a people alive to the nobility and to the necessity of the farmer's vocation.

To-day we could not render Judaism a better service than by, if possible, combining to lead once more the young men and the young women into the channels of agricultural pursuits. A blot on American Israel are the ghettos arising now in our cities. Against that sea of misery our relief societies cope in vain. Its frothy billows rage and bring to surface muddy sub-sediments. That day's would be a blessed dawn whose sun would shine on concerted action to wean the young—not merely of the Russians—the young of all Jews in due proportion, from mercantile life, to win them for the noble duties of the farm. Yea, not merely the Jew should heed the lesson of this day. The whole of the American people might lay it to heart. There is something unhealthy in the growth of our city centers. The cities are the seat of culture—who would deny this? But city culture is often fringed by shame and sin. The city is the home of learning, it is also the cover of the slums. These slums should be cleansed, and out into the freer and nobler air of the country should go the waifs of our streets and others, and our nation would be all the stronger for a deeper appreciation of the value of the farmer's station in the economic conditions, and as a factor in the financial prosperity, as a power for moral redemption, of the whole community from ocean to ocean and from the lakes to the gulf.

Those societies that make it their business to plant the children, lost in our great cities, on the opportune soil of a western farm, do more for humanity than we do in our orphan asylums and other institutions for the preservation and education of our children.

I do not wish to be misunderstood. If the system be

granted good, there are no nobler institutions than our orphan asylums, but with all this, I say that the non-Jewish societies that are organized to find homes on farms for dependent children, do much more for humanity than we do by clinging with the tenacity of fanaticism to a system which has its limitations, to a plan that, by many of the best philanthropists of the world, has been condemned as falling short of the ideal within reach.

This Sukkoth-tide should call out to American Israel at least: Make efforts that your slums be cleansed and your ghettos be thrown down! Let there rise, as was visioned by prophet and psalmist, once more all over the country, Jewish farm houses; let us rear Jewish tillers of the soil, blessing by the pearling sweat of their brow all humanity!

Another thought our fathers laid to heart when this Sukkoth-tide gladdened their homes. The oriental emblems, the waving palm branch reminded them of the sky of Palestine, and the traditional fruit of the "splendid tree" also spoke of the land of the rising sun, of the days of their rising faith.

In the Middle Ages this symbolism meant much to the wayfarers in the desert of persecution. They had no country. Edward Everett Hale's story, pathetic, stirring, awful, sublime—of the man without a country, has been lived and lived in sorrow, lived in pain and lived in tears, not by one alone, by millions. But while the exile from country who never heard name of flag or mention of fatherland had brought this doom upon himself by his own folly and the fanaticism of his own stubborn sympathies, those millions, expatriated and treated like outcasts in the dark centuries, had done naught to deserve such cruel treatment, such dehumanizing ostracism from the privileges that go with man in the very hour of his birth. They were in the eyes of the law strangers, without country, and still they loved the land where they were born—still they loved the soil which covered the ashes of their fathers. Let them say what they will, even the mediæval Jews—not allowed to be citizens under the sky that welcomed them into life, were patriots to the last. They clung to the language of their home-land with an attachment wonderful.

To-day even, the descendants of the Spanish Jews in the regions of blighted Turkey, speak Spanish—the Spanish of the day when Isabella of Aragon and her husband signed the decree that drove nearly three hundred thousand men and women from the shores where for hundreds of years their ancestors had been settled—whose songs they sang, whose idiom they spoke, whose loves they shared and whose prosperity they helped to deepen and to spread abroad. To-day the Jew speaks German in non-Germanic districts if his ancestors were German. The international language of the Jews is not as many suppose Hebrew, it is German to this very hour. How justly then do German anti-Semites rave and rant that Jew and German are contradictories!

The Jew in the Middle Ages had no country. The *Sukkah*, the *Lulabh* and the *Ethrog* spoke to him of the distant land that once was his, that was to be his again with the revolving cycles of the speeding suns. This day was prophetic to him of a future national redemption. To us the Sukkah does not herald a national restoration. Thank God we have a country. Ours is a flag, and there is none more glorious than that which waves over this house, a pendant worthy of these Eastern symbols. Let us be asked, which is your country? We answer, not Palestine. We answer, America. Patriotism is part of the Jewish religion and the symbolism of the synagogue has no more sacred sign than that which has borrowed the colors of the sun, and the fields of the sky, and the twinkle of the sentries of the night, to bring home to the people o'er which it floats the duty to be the beacon for the oppressed, the star for the weary and the wanderers. Not of a distant, but of a near land speaks to us the symbolic language of this hour, and thus, as the Sukkah of old appealed to Israel not to forget Jerusalem, so to-day it calls out to us not to forget loyalty to land, not to neglect duty as citizens, as members of the larger community.

And another lesson the Sukkah points out. It is a hastily constructed shelter. It spells the warning that no man on earth is more than a pilgrim, it frames the admonition to remember that in synagogue and in temple there shall always be free access to light—to air, and that Israel shall ever be ready to break up the booth and pilgrim on to build another at a new station, where fresher waters bubble and higher palms wave in the purer air.

Sukkoth is emblematical of the eternally progressive spirit of Judaism. The world at large does not understand this, and the world at home in Judaism, is often ready to deny this. Why otherwise so many born in Israel's household indifferent to Israel's spiritual appeal? That persons should be indifferent who have no higher view of life than pleasure, who know nothing more as a standard of humanity than possession of earthly things, is natural. There be men that are color blind. There be others that are sound-deaf; there are again men that have no eyes for spiritual things, that have no ears for melodies intoned in the higher sky! But it is not always among these that they are found who deny to Judaism to-day the right to be. That men who grovel in the dust cannot understand the poetry and the moral potency of a martyrdom extended over centuries, stands to reason—for what tokens to a man so organized, a defense of principle? Why, certainly, if dust and dross—if gold and glamor of earthly glory be the sum and substance of human life, the Jews are fools for refusing to yield when the world in one hand offers gold and in the other threateningly lifts up the lash to let it fall on the back of him who spurns the bribe. Then indeed the fathers were worse than fools in living the life they did, ever ready to pilgrim on, never sure that they be not hailed with the cruel "Move on, cursed Jew! Thou must not loiter and tarry!" Then they were worse than criminals in denying what they denied and in affirming what they affirmed. But if there be more to life than what is made of dust—if there be a higher glory than that which streams out from shining ducats, if there be more to human existence than the reeling passage from riot to revelry and from pleasure to passion, then indeed there is no record so sublime, no page of history so studded with sparkling diamonds, emblematic of the diadem of human dignity and human royalty than is that tear-stained document telling of Israel's fortitude and of Israel's fortune under stress of bitter, relentless persecution.

What did Israel stand for? For liberty of conscience—for freedom to think. What did Israel deem the highest? Free thought. Who was the aristocrat among the Jews up to one hundred years ago? The man of learning. The richest man thought his daughter happy and enviable if she married the poorest תלמיד הכם, the poorest among the learned. Learning was the patent of nobility. Where is another set of human beings that paid such regard to intellectual pursuits? There is none.

The Sukkah is symbol of freedom; it invites ingress and egress of air, it courts and covets light. Like it always was the condition of Jewish religious thought. We have no trammels, no dogmas. Each one of us can think out his highest problems as he chooses. No synod and no symbolum will tell you what you must believe. Thought is free in Judaism, and therefore the spiritual Jewish synagogue was always a Sukkah— a temporary construction. Those among us to-day, and there be such even among the rabbis, that constantly clamor for a more definite statement, for a stricter and more strenuous organization, for symbolism that is more generally accepted and must be everywhere observed, mistake the spirit of Judaism. They are traitors to this very symbol, the Sukkah. They would shut out light and air. They would rob Judaism of that which is its privilege—to break camp and to move on. The Sukkah, the tabernacle, was the symbol of God's residence in Israel, but it was not a דירת קבע; it moved and was movable; and so did, and so will, and so shall Judaism move ever on. This restlessness is its distinctive genius.

Do you suppose that our organization in this congregation is final—that perhaps to-morrow changes might not be made and must not be made? You are mistaking the spirit of Judaism, if you so reason. There are men of ideal tendencies to-day among us that are cold to the synagogue, simply because they do not understand this. Judaism in the Middle Ages made an alliance with Aristotelian philosophy, because Aristotle then was held to have given to man the key to the riddles of the universe. To-day Judaism strikes alliance with evolution. As then, so now it remains— Judaism.

Was ever Jew tried for subscribing to a new doctrine on the Bible? Was I ever summoned before council because I stated in the hearing of a company of forty-five rabbis in conference assembled that I believed that not a single word of the Pentateuch was written by Moses? I was not. I am a Jew to-day. There is none that can deny this to me, while the Presbyterian church quarrels with Prof. Briggs, and while Baptists look askance at the possibility of President Harper spoiling the young men for good believers in Baptist doctrine. We Jews know that freedom of thought and freedom of expression is the very vital element in Judaism. And why then, be ye indifferent to a religion that welcomes of searching science, the light, and gives to freest thought, so long as thought it is, free access to its ever temporary abode? The Sukkah symbols the progressive spirit of Judaism, which always is a preparation for a higher, a deeper phase and tide of spirituality and humanity.

Again the Sukkah is the silent but eloquent preacher of profound ethical ideas. The farmer's life, what does it teach? It illustrates at least this one truth—that all that man can do is to do his duty, and that reward, or the withholding of the reward cannot affect him, because this must be left to a power higher than his—to a will wiser than his. The farmer may plow—he may plant—he places the seed in the keepership of mother earth, but whether that seed so cradled will sprout into fruit he knoweth not. The heavens must co-operate with him. The sun must be his ally. The dews of the night and the tears of the day-time must come to his aid in proper measure. He may work and work—if the winds blow the hot breath of the sirocco—if the skies be leaden—if too copiously the heavens weep, or if too charily the night sheds the honey of its dew, the farmer's toil is in vain. Thus, the farmer's life teaches dependence, and it teaches trust.

It has been noticed in all times that farmers are more religious than other people—that there is in agricultural pursuits an element which will attune the human mind to religious sentiment. The observation is well founded. For the farmer learns from his daily task the great lesson of dependence and the vital insistence of trust. Science to-day has not robbed the operation of the farmer's occupation of its mystery. Agricultural chemistry can tell us what substances enter into the formation of fruit—it can inform us of the quantities of this element and of the presence of another—it may caution us that without phosphates the soil will not allow the seed to sprout—it may be eloquent about the physiology of the plant, relate to us how the cell develops into the semen, how plant marries plant, in shy timidity as a cryptogam or in bold joy as a phanerogam—it may describe in detail the lacery of the leaves, and nature spins laces so delicate that none of our buyers who go to Brussels and there consult the masters can bring back to us wonders of art such as drop from the skies, so to speak—such as are woven on the looms where the plants are threaded by the hand of creative nature. But all our science does not tell us how from the seed and why from the seed, comes plant or fruit. It is dumb in the presence of this mystery of creation, this great monition of trust and of dependence. The farmer believes in the benevolence of nature. He believes in the lawfulness of nature. He believes in the steadiness of nature.

Bind the ideas I have now described in these common terms together as are bound together the leaves of the waving palm branch in our Sukkah—you have what theologians call God. All the world is one chain of dependence. All life is under law, and all life is under mystery. That mystery no science can unravel. That trust no science can replace; that dependence no science can annul.

Religion is then the doctrine of dependence. Religion is the messenger of trust. Religion is the emphasis on the orderliness, on the rationality of the universe. Religion teaches what the farmer knows—that it is for man to do his part, but whether that part event in harvest or end in drouth, depends upon a higher wisdom, and upon a deeper purpose than we men wot. And thus this day proclaims to us this thought: Do your duty! Do it hopefully! Do it trustfully! Do it in the reverence of the mystery that pervades the all! If you succeed it is not you alone who have wrought the victory. If you fail, and you have done your duty, a wiser economy than you know requires the sacrifice of your failure. Do your duty—the rest is with God.

And now finally another thought.

The farmer's occupation teaches us that men do not work for self alone. The farmer produces what he cannot use up himself, yet he knows that upon his work depend the health and life of thousands of others. There is not a farm but produces more than the owner would consume. Is the goal that leads on the farmer, is the goad that pricks him to his work the hunger of money? The farmer knows that in money his produce brings but little, and still he listens to the voices of the deep that exclaim: "Plant—we are ready to pay our toll!" He knows that if he were to strike, were to lay down his task, thousands that he does not know, millions of whose existence he is not aware by name, will die of famine, of dread plague and of disease. Like the farmer, everyone of us works for another. Like the farmer everyone is responsible for the health and life of others.

In olden days distinctions were made between professions and business. The professions were called liberal. Business was held to have its compensation in gold — the professions to have theirs in honor. But everyone of us should have a profession. The distinction between profession and business is this: Business is indeed for money—profession is for service to others. A true physician will not work for money. It is with him a secondary consideration. And a true jurist—not a lawyer—a jurist, finds his satisfaction in being the pleader for right, and the defender against wrong, in being the spreader of higher appreciations of what justice is. And the minister too, has his satisfaction, not in the gold that is meted to him. Up to the day when you made such generous provisions for me, no minister was, among the Jews at least, paid more than enough to buy his salt, and there are congregations that to-day even do not know their responsibilities to their minister who, hired by the year, may at the expiration of the contract term be told without pity and without shame, to go, if they are not satisfied that he, the drummer has done his duty, the commercial agent has won new customers; until you set the example, the minister had indeed no compensation to expect in the financial sense of the term. His reward was the sweet knowledge that he worked for others, that he meant something in the life of others, that he stood as the sea-wall does, against the inroads of despair into the minds of thousands and thousands— that he was to be the mountain-top upon which rested the sun's light first, and upon which it lingered last when the shades of superstition and of selfishness wrapped in slumber the fog beset and mist hung vales at its base. Now this sense of satisfying honor we all need. The day is past even in this country when our business enterprises will event in a deluge of gold. To-day—and

Americans will have to become accustomed to the prospect—work will not resolve in wealth, but by a painful and a tedious path of self-denial. The compensation of our daily doings must be sought in things suggested by the farmers, in the consciousness that we are of service to somebody.

And here you have the test of what is ethically legitimate. The farmer works. Upon his work others depend. He injures no one. He crowds to the wall no one. He gives bread like God to all. No wealth is ethically legitimate that does not stand for work and for production. All wealth won in any other way is from the ethical standpoint, an injury, and modern society begins to understand that this is the case. All enterprises that, not like the farmer's, are grounded upon the notion of working for others, but upon a merely selfish basis, that result in the crowding to the wall of thousands—bringing thousands to the brink of poverty, to the ragged edge of despair—are from the ethical point of view reprehensible and to be condemned, and this is not among the least important lessons that Sukkoth should teach us.

We Jews, by cruel fate of history have become largely a capitalistic class. In Europe especially the large resources—productions of industrial ventures and industrial necessities, are under the control of Jewish firms. Anti-semitism to-day is not merely an out-cry against religion, a crusade against the race of the Jews, it is as much a protest against exclusive capitalistic organization. Of course, those that crusade against capital do not understand what they are attempting. They, too, have to learn the lesson that one must work for others—that no wealth and no pleasure can come except as the pay for self-sacrificing service. They clamor for their rights and they would not do their duties—but the fact stands that notwithstanding their stupidity and their cupidity, these masses that are now rising in blindness like Samson of yore, have only the power to tear down the pillars of the temple of society, and while they crush themselves, will also crush us. Here is now the opportunity of the Jews to-day, and it is this that the world desires and asks of them. Your exclusive capitalistic fate must now be turned into a source of blessing for all humanity, and until the Jews learn this, there will be no peace.

What can we do? We can do each one more than we deem possible. If you are the controller of labor, give to labor its dues. If you are in a position to fight against the iniquity of our social organization, fight it. If all houses were agreed in a certain line of business which I cannot mention here, they could put an end to the sweat-shop. There is no profit that is God-blessed to which clings human life degraded and woman perhaps unwomaned, and child robbed of its childhood. Give to your working people a chance to work in a Sukkah, free, airy and full of light and not in huddles and holes that you might be saved a little bother, for in these immoral operations the profit is not to be for a moment considered. This may be bold talk, for all I know or care, but if the minister to-day cannot plead for the poor, if he cannot speak for those that have no joy on a day when we say "Thou shalt rejoice and all of thy servants with thee"—if he cannot plead for the weak and the down-trodden, then, indeed, there is no use for him, and should the day ever dawn when the muzzle is put on us, I for one would rather go into the street and earn my living in any manner whatsoever, honorable, than to be dishonest in an enforced defection from the prime duty of my calling. These things must be learned and must be spoken, for the storm is gathering, and unless we come to reason, the blind Samsons of our day will pull down our palaces, though they themselves die in the attempt—and we die with them.

This Sukkah reminds us of our whole life. What is our body but a Sukkah? To-morrow it will be broken, and the grave will cover our mortality. What is our wealth—the ornaments to this Sukkah? The richest man descends naked into the grave as does the poorest. Perhaps a casket has he to shield him against the ravages of the elements—the other but a box of pine board, but his dust is dust, and the dust of the pauper is dust. His ornaments he cannot take along. Yet there is something that is left when the Sukkah is broken up, in the case of him whose life was full of the green garlands of hope and rich in the fruits of humanity and of duty. Let him die—he leaves behind that which is more than gold—a good name and a shining example. Ah, those that have, ought to learn their prerogatives. Those whom God has blessed with the rich harvest might to-day do much for lifting up all, were they to write their name into the hearts of their fellow-men and on the tablets that tell in great institutions of learning and others, that there have been sturdy pilgrims along the paths of life. He who thus makes his whole life a festival of Sukkoth, who gives the hospitality of his possibilities to stranger and to Levite and to the maid servant and the man servant, as to son and to daughter, in his going home in the harvest time to meet the great harvester, death, and then to fall asleep in the realm of light that is divine—leaves a world richer for his life, poorer in his death.

And so let us in this spirit remember this day and its symbol. Farmers we were—farmers we should try and make again of those especially that now herd in slums. Patriots we are. Not Jerusalem is our capital, but Washington. Ours is the flag with the stars and stripes. We must work like the farmer in trustfulness and hopefulness – work one for the other, and in our vocation know that the true recompense for whatever we do, is in the service of our higher purposes. And Judaism is the religion of progress which teaches these things. If we live as a Jew should live, in the last hour, when the Sukkah breaks and the grave opens, we shall be sped home by a melody that will never end, for the angels sing it and men answer it "Blessed is the name of him who has been like the farmer, a joyful dispenser of blessings to others of his kind."

ISRAEL'S RELIGION A MESSAGE OF LIGHT AND GLADNESS.

A SERMON DELIVERED AT THE 25TH ANNIVERSARY OF CONGREGATION B'NAI YEHUDAH, KANSAS CITY, BY REV. DR. SAMUEL SALE, ST. LOUIS.

It is singularly fitting and significant that you should have chosen as the time for the commemoration of the silver jubilee of your congregation this festal hour, bidding farewell to the "Rejoicing of the Law," still ringing with its joyous melody and ushering in the sacred Sabbath, which is in itself the great symbol and exponent of the light and gladness that pervade the religion of Israel. Indeed, this hour must be radiant with joy and gratification for you, when you remember that it tokens for you the devotion of a quarter of a century to the highest ideals of life, of which the synagogue has always been the living embodiment. When to-day you give thanks to God for the rich harvest of spiritual blessings that you have gathered, and praise Him that He has permitted you to witness this day of your rejoicing, your celebration takes on a wider significance. It is not merely an evidence of your faithfulness and zeal in the past, but it becomes an earnest and steadfast of your loyalty and devotion in the future, to the same lofty principles for which you banded together twenty-five years ago. It is a revival of your obligations and your vows to be faithful still to the eternal truths that were the palladium of your forefathers, that were first heralded in Israel, when over the wide world there lay the deepest gloom of superstition and idolatry. You re-dedicate your lives to the religion of light and joy. This is the theme of this hour, as it is the burden and strain of Israel's song. All its message is one of joy and gladness, all its tidings tell of light and inspiration, of hope and courage for the human heart.

On the opening page of the Bible, in the portion we shall read to-morrow, is written with matchless beauty and simplicity the purpose and purport of the religion of Israel. When chaos and confusion reigned supreme and darkness covered the deep, the creative word was heard, "Let there be light." And as its magic note rang out through nature's realm the divine behest, out of chaos came the cosmos, a world of order and of beauty, out of the dreary waste and darkness. The Bible is not a hand-book of science, and it matters little to us whether its narrative concerning the origin of the world meet the approval of the learned or not, nay, grant it to be wrong in its statement of facts, still the truths which it enfolds are such as science can neither displace nor disprove, and which, despite the wondrous strides which we have made, are yet as important to mankind as on the day when first they were proclaimed. Over the portal that leads to the sanctuary of Israel's faith is written in characters that cannot be effaced, the truth which has been the hope and stay of the human race, the source of all its bliss and inspiration, "the fountain light of all our day, the master light of all our being"; it is the truth that there is a central light in the universe, a power that in the past has wrought with wisdom and purposive intelligence the order and harmony of this world of matter, and has shed abroad in the human heart the creative spark which shall some day make aglow this mundane sphere with the warmth and radiance of justice, truth and loving kindness. Let there be light, ye sons of Judah! Open the windows of your souls and let in the sunbeams of this message of gladness! The belief in God, as the power that makes for righteousness, is the beginning and the end of Israel's religion, it is the source and fountain of all law and all life, all virtue and all wisdom, the מקמו של עולם. When the idea of God is firmly fixed in the human mind and deeply rooted in the human heart, it becomes the mainspring of a life of honor and of purity, it is the seed whence spring the flower and fruit of all virtues. As in the beginning all was desolation, thus in the world to-day there would be naught but darkness and misery, unless it were illumined by the faith in Him who spake, "Let there be light."

The human family would have been crushed into dumb despair, were it not for this uplifting force and perennial spring of inspiration and of courage. "The ox knoweth his owner and the ass his master's crib; Israel doth not know, my people doth not consider." The prophet in Israel was of the opinion that it was as natural for man to rever and look up to God, as for the brute creation to regard man as its superior. As the domestication of wild animals was brought about by association with man, thus man himself has continually risen in the scale of creation by lifting his eyes on high, so that we may truly say, the process of civilization is the unfolding of the God-idea of man.

The history of mankind forms an integral part of our book of revelation, for there it is, especially when looking into the past, that we behold the gradual and steady development of man in every province of life and thus become convinced of the wisdom and goodness that underlie all things. "The fool saith in his heart there is no God," and yet there are many in our own days, would-be philosophers, who crave the honor of wearing the cap with the tinkling bells. The air about us is still laden with confessed or implied atheism, and while its apostles may not be as insolent as they were in declaiming against God, nor so heady and foolhardy as those who figured in the carnival of reason a century ago, they have only assumed the mask of agnosticism, which is but another name for shame-faced atheism. The Jew of to-day holds as firmly as ever in the past, to the fundamental principle of all true religion; that "there is a spirit in man, and the breath of the Almighty giveth him understanding." This faith was the joy and delight of his existence, a pillar of cloud by day, a pillar of light by night, and were it not that this belief had become structural in his very being, he would have been swept from the earth by the storms of hatred and persecution. The secret of the Jews' endurance and almost superhuman strength lay in the fact that God to him was no mere metaphysical notion, no induction and no scientific hypothesis whereby to explain the origin of the world of matter, but God to him was a living and ever-present reality, the Deity enthroned in conscience, the Being all holiness who "will not look upon iniquity, and with whom evil cannot abide." While the philosophy of the ancients began with matter and ended with mud, the religious literature of the Jew begins with God, the ordainer of good, the source of light, and ends with man as the image of God, as the incarnation of the divine on earth.

Here we come upon the second announcement of this message of joy and gladness. No matter out of what and how the world was fashioned, suffice us to know that it was made good, and for the realization of the good. At the end of every day's creation the words are repeated as if by way of increasing emphasis, and "God saw that it was good." Our purpose and aim here on earth is "to do the good" and herein we are not hindered, neither by cruel fate, nor a conspiracy of the powers of nature that are superior and opposed to the God-given faculties of man. The world is so ordered and all of its parts so nicely and wisely adjusted, that no power on earth can foil and frustrate the divine efforts of man to make of this world a home of the good and the true, a paradise of righteousness and justice. There be powers of darkness and spirits of evil in this world, that work sad havoc against the ideal interests of man and check his onward course towards the divine goal, but only when man has become estranged from God, and no longer hears within himself the voice of Him, who said: "Let there be light." The doctrine of evil as a positive quantity and triumphant factor separate and independent of God, incarnate in the devil, could never find acceptance in Judaism.

In the book of Job Satan himself sits in the council of God, and all the forces of evil according to the glad tidings of Israel's belief, are but so many incitements to the energies of man to overcome them and make them subservient to the cause of good. Evil is but a foil to the good, as shade to the sunlight, to make its achievements all the more glorious. In a world that is made by God, and in which his light shines forth, God must indwell the devil himself. How quaintly and how wonderfully this inspiring truth is blazoned in the Bible; darkness is in the beginning. It is not the result of God's creative power, as is the light which comes at His command. We are not poor, miserable sinners, and we are not here to sigh and lament and hang our heads in gloom and sorrow. This world is not a vale of tears and the abode and den of vice and wickedness from whose snares no mortal can escape. We are not to make ourselves believe that this life is under the doom of original sin, and that man is by nature degraded and depraved, so that he cannot lift himself up by his own moral effort. This is a world of light, and we are the creatures of the power that fashioned it.

"Light arises for the righteous, and joy to the upright of heart." Light and joy are the very essence of our belief, they are co-relatives in the religion of the Jew. To walk in the light is to lend ourself to the cause of righteousness, and the only joy that is never marred is that which comes from an earnest, conscientious and unselfish devotion to the cause of the right. Do we no longer need the blessing and inspiration of this simple and beautiful lesson of our ancestral religion? Shall we hearken to the ravens of our day, who keep croaking into our ear, the dismal note, that life is not worth living. Indeed, if pleasure and enjoyment and clogging of the senses be its end and aim, it is not worth the pains we are at to sustain it; if it be but a mad foam-ocean of passion, and a wild whirling eddy of getting and grabbing, its price is overpaid, no matter how trifling it may be. But if the principle of our religion old and ever young, still holds good, "Behold, I have put before thee life and the good, death and the evil," then our being here is a golden opportunity and a sacred obligation According to this gladdening message to live is to do good, to regard one's self as an instrument in the hand of God for the working out of the cause of the true, the good and the beautiful.

He who permits the name of Jew to hang loosely upon him, he who stands idly by, when by word or deed he might champion the cause of the weak and down-trodden, and further the coming of the Kingdom of God on earth, by valiantly serving in the army of truth and righteousness, be it in the rank and file, in the van, or in the rear, he is false to the ideals of our household. To live is to do good, to give countenance to wrong actively or passively, is to be dead in the living body.

> Living thou dost not live—
> If Mercy's spring run dry,
> What Heaven hath lent thee, wilt thou freely give,
> Dying thou wilt not die.

Our sages have pithily and pointedly expressed this sentiment, when they said that the righteous are called the living, even after they are dead, and the wicked are called the dead, even while they live.

The Jew who in private or public life soils the fair name of this religion of absolute trust in God, and righteous conduct, is a traitor to his cause. Those who fling their arrows barbed with envenomed spite and prejudice against us cannot harm us. As long as Israel clings to these simple tenets of its faith, it is invulnerable and invincible. Its history is the strongest proof of the superiority of mind over matter, of the absolute futility and folly of opposing brute force to moral conscience and conviction, intent, with single purpose on the worship of the Most High. In the words of Scripture: We have struggled with God, against men, and we have been victorious, and in this struggle our fathers have suffered a martyrdom compared to which that of all the races of man are as a molehill to a mountain.

Thank God, the dawn of the day our prophets foresaw is at hand. The ideals of our past have been gradually finding their way into the thought-life of man, and though dark clouds still lower upon the house of Israel in foreign lands, the sunlight of freedom and humanity will drive them away. Monarchs and monarchies have always been known as ingrates, but here in this blessed land of liberty the Jew, thanks to the genius of our constitution, is the peer of his fellow-citizens. In Europe you must seek the synagogue of the Jew in by-ways and narrow courts; hidden away from public gaze, they are a sad commentary on the standing of the Jew in the past, and partly indicate his social position to-day. In this country the synagogue stands out boldly and prominently. Here above all other lands, we have cause to rejoice and be glad. Arise, shine forth, for thy light has come. Where could we have a better opportunity to unfold the glories of our faith, than upon this soil, and in this age. Armed with the enthusiasm and heroism of our fathers, and wedded to the ancient ideals of our prophets, Israel could carry a new world by storm. Let this be the cause of your joy to-day. Thank God, that He has made you the heirs of the ages gone by, and the richest spiritual legacy in the annals of history, one for which mankind to share with you, must become your kith and kin. Let us rededicate ourselves on this day of your joy, to the God of our fathers. May the fountain of our life be blessed, and may it pour forth its limpid streams of light and law and truth into the broad main of humanity. Come ye O house of Jacob, and let us walk in the light of Him who spake, Let there be light!

THE ANCIENT ANTI-SEMITE AND HIS MODERN SUCCESSORS.

A DISCOURSE BY EMIL G. HIRSCH.

If twenty years ago some one should have prophesied that the day of the Maccabees would in this our broad and enlightened century, ever assume a deeper meaning than goes with a mere historical memory; or should have suggested that this day might ever again take upon itself the guise of an appeal for modern Jews to don their armor of defense and to gather around their flag, he would have been put down as a reasonless grumbler and inveterate pessimist—as one not satisfied even with the sun's light because the sun's disk occasionally shows spots. We all believed that the night of mediævalism had passed forever, and were confident, jubilant, because so many triumphs had been won by the sciences, that the day of religious bigotry had set to rise no more. The whole race stood on tip-toes, every man curiously craning the neck and pricking the ear to learn of some new and marvelous discovery. We were proud of our rulership in the vast and wonderful domain of nature. We boasted that the stars had confided to us the secret of our birth, we were sure that we could command in reality, as Joshuah did in the legend, the sun to stand still, for we indeed know how to lengthen the realm of the day and shorten the terrors of the night. The ocean was at our feet a bound slave; rocks had to yield to our insistence and open admission to their innermost chambers; mountain ranges that divided nation from nation were forced to become bold and noble gateways of union through which the iron rivets and links were laid to bring the laughing south in closest intimacy with the sterner north across the eternal snows of the Alps; and where land interposed its barrier to the free flow of intercommunication between man and his fellow tenant of our globe, our science enabled us to apply the scalpel and the knife in a surgery which became the most signal accomplishment of modern engineering. What for ages untold, ever since the mighty geological forces had ceased to tinker and to tamper with our world, had stood unmoved and uninterfered with, was opened with a bold incision of our instruments, into a new bed for the more willing waves of two oceans. The umbilical cord between Europe and Africa was cut and commerce, white-winged messenger of peace, unfolded her sails and the heavily freighted keels of swimming palaces, gamboled cheerfully and cheeringly on the newly-created nuptial couch of two seas.

And in the domain of literature certainly a new spirit seemed to have coined word and attuned voice. In the arts the lines of race and of nation appeared to have been overleaped. The dream of the federation of man appeared about to become real. In religion the old demon of distrust had at last been chained—one common religion certainly, though rich in varied dialects, called the best among men to one law of life. The old superstitions had had their day and were no more. Twenty years ago, the time for joy and trust did not allow, according to far-spread conceit, any other intonation but that of exultation at this victory finally won and forever in its fruitage made the grand possession of all mankind.

But even at that time, there were those who maintained that this pæan of victory was premature. The captain on his ship, casting a glance at the barometer, can read off the signs of warning, of a gathering hurricane when his passengers are still whiling away the heavy hours of an ocean voyage with unmeaning sport, or dull halting conversation. A quaint old German superstition warns us that ere house is about to fall, weird noises may be heard of spirits at work—night-born spirits running through the doomed palace with feet whose gliding touch over wall and floor is distinctly noticeable to the few chosen ones endowed with capacity to apprehend these mysterious omens. In an old Arab tradition it is writ that in the very night before a mighty dynasty was dethroned, strange sounds issued from the graves which the dervishes and the faithful understood full well to be an alarm sounded by the uncanny tongue of death and the dead. And so there were, even twenty years ago, when all men had been lulled to sleep by the confidence that our age was the age of fulfilment, no longer a century of preparation, those who had heard the voices from the grave, who understood the strange moving to and fro of the spirits of the night in the doomed palace; those who read from the barometer the signs and warnings of an impending tornado—their voices were not heeded; they were held to be Cassandras speaking of evil—the reflection and projection of their own melancholy, but not the shadowed fringe of a possibility about to become real. And yet, notwithstanding the oft-repeated plea that our age need not fear another invasion of the minions and ministers of darkness, to-day we know that Maccabee is not merely a memory to us; it is an appeal that the fight waged erst on Palestine's historic soil is on to-day again, that to-day once more the trumpet of the alarm must sound in Israel that each one of us who believes that not for himself alone, but for humanity, he holds treasures vital, must don the armor and draw the sword for defense, perhaps even for the attack in order to insure all the better the strategy of the defensive movement.

Anti-Semitism, the spiritual pestilence of our day, has gained a foothold on almost every soil under God's sun. There is not a nation but has suffered from one or more outbreaks of this epidemic. It is not merely in Russia, herself a slave to a slave-master; it is not merely in Germany, distracted by internal dissensions; it is even in France, the child of the French revolution and also in England, though there most faintly, where the gospel of hatred finds voices, and often ready auditors. America too is suffering from an invasion. Not only since last week when one has drifted to these shores whose name is too profane to be uttered in a spot devoted to high instruction, but for years and years in this country the prejudice has been alive; it has taken on a form which of all forms in which this distemper vests itself, is perhaps the most despicable, the meanest, and at the same time the most cowardly.

Thus, then, wherever to-day the Jews be,—in Europe or America, in Asia or in Africa, even in distant Australia, the Maccabean contest has an actual interest. But its lessons are those that we need, that we might not despair, but stand our ground.

What is fundamental to this hatred of the Jew now masking itself under the high-sounding name of anti-Semitism? The situation in which Antioch Epiphanes did place the Jews of his day, is to a nicety that is almost appalling, repeated in our own generation. Antioch Epiphanes does in his statesmanship illustrate all the motive purposes, the impulses, the passions of those that to-day would raise the standard of the Crusaders against the Jew, against the Semite, against Judaism. This is the power of history, that it holds up in the figures of the past the mirror of the present, and he who understands what events have been, recognizes his own physiognomy. He therefore may draw from the peep into this glass either encouragement or feel, as it were, the lash of censure and condemnation. Yea, history is the voice of God. If Sinais do not thunder; if Carmels be silent; if Golgothas have no inspiration; if those high mountains from which the prophet spoke have lost their dialect; if the stars do not sing of God, and the oceans do not fall in with responsive amens; if the fields be hushed into silence unsyllabled and the forests have lost their cunning of articulation, it is history that proclaims His one purpose and His guidance upward into ever-developing righteousness. History is the pulpit that has eloquence such as never was given to man, and its is the proclamation which all philosophy can but verify and all skepticism is incompetent to deny. History, by showing in the past centuries the same troubles and tribulations, the same triumphs and the same driving forces (as the Germans say,) as to-day are besetting the child of the most recent hours, does speak in the tones which the prophet re-echoed when he said, "Not by might and not by power, but through my spirit, saith God."

Yea, history is the prophet described in the words of the second Isaiah: "The spirit of God is upon me, he hath appointed me to preach good tidings unto the meek, he hath sent me to bind up the brokenhearted, to proclaim liberty to the captives, the opening of the prison to them that are bound, to proclaim the era of acceptance unto God, the day of vengeance unto our Lord, to comfort all that mourn, to appoint unto them that mourn in Zion a garland for ashes, the oil of joy for their weeping, and that they might be called trees of righteousness, the planting of God Himself."

It is generally the superficial impression in Jewish and non-Jewish circles that the root of this Upas tree is religious prejudice. Antioch Epiphanes, the cultured king of his day, the disciple of Rome, if he had been prompted to issue his decree by religious prejudice, would have been a strange anomaly in the days of old. Ingersoll is correct—this cannot be disputed—classic antiquity is free from the spirit of religious bigotry flaming forth in the unholy fire of religious persecution. Tolerance,—religious tolerance, is characteristic especially of the one people that seems above all others to incarnate the working ideas of the ancient times, the Roman. Rome is tolerant of religious differences because Rome is organized cynicism. The Roman is an atheist by nature and by constitution. He cares not for the gods. The gods are nothing for him, but if others wish to toy with these bubbles of fancy, he will not interfere. When the Romans captured a town they left the gods undisturbed. The Romans never interfered with the religious rites of such as they conquered.

But we are confronted with Antioch Epiphanes, a Greek trained in Rome, where he spent his most impressionable years, issuing a decree of religious persecution! This interpretation cannot be held to represent his motive or to correspond to the actualities of his day. He was not animated by a religious spirit of bigotry. Nor is anti-Semitism to-day the off-spring of religious or irreligious intolerance. Now and then an anti-Semite may cloak his inward motive under the assumed guise of fanatical devotion to religious truth. He may pretend to be anxious that the Jew be saved unto Christ. He may 'parade his impatience at the stubbornness and blindness of the Jew. Christianity as such has naught to do with anti-Semitism. The Christian believes that the Jew is preserved for a purpose, the Catholic church insists upon the Jew remaining a Jew lest the historical proofs of Christian authenticity be weakened by his disappearance. And even so has the devout and resolute Protestant the certainty that the Jew as a Jew must survive. He is destined to return to Palestine that prophecy might find its fulfilment. Moreover, one who believes in the Christ must be actuated, if he be Christlike, by motives of love to the people of Christ. Christ was a Jew, and had to be a Jew, according to Protestant theology. The apostles were Jews, and had to be Jews, according to Protestant doctrine. The Old Testament is the cornerstone upon which rises the new; without the old, the new becomes incomprehensible. It is, then, not true that religious bigotry is the fountain of poison from which rushes out the turbid tide of hatred that now has flooded the whole world and our age.

Of course, unintentionally perhaps, religious instruction is helpful to the ease with which the hue and cry of the anti-Semite is tolerated by our generation. Children have no sense of historical perspective. As the little baby when it makes its first attempt at seizing the far-off object does not calculate the distance, but stretches its little fist as readily to grasp the light in the ceiling as to take hold of the little toy at its feet; so children for a long time after they have outgrown the nursery, put forth their intellectual prehensiles as strangely after the distant occurrences as they might for the nearer events. Centuries have no value for the child's mind. Yea, we, the adults have considerable difficulty in estimating time distances. We may speak of yesterday as a cognizable, realizable quantity of time spent. We may have a distinct consciousness of the gap that yawns between this hour and the corresponding one twelve months ago, but the farther those intervals stretch out their lengths the less vivid remain the distinctions of intervals and epochs. I have no doubt, at the name of Cæsar even many who are educated have to make a mental effort in order to grasp the fact that Cæsar lived so and so many centuries before America was discovered; and when one speaks of the mighty empires of Asia or Africa, whose first king probably ascended the throne four thousand years before our era, or when one reads of the many dynasties that wielded scepter in Egypt, and century upon century is required to measure their passage across the stage of history, there is none of us that without great mental labor, learned though he be, carries away a distinct impression of the great gulf of separation between this hour and the cradle day of the mighty monarchies under discussion.

And now teach a child history. He will not be able to locate an event that occurred or is said to have occurred eighteen hundred years ago at the proper distance from one that possibly may have taken place a few years ago.

It is due to this circumstance that the Sunday-schools of the orthodox Christian, and alas, also those non-Christian liberals—the Sunday-schools of ethical culture—for instance—no less than those of the Catholics and Evangelicals, in teaching that at a certain time the Jews crucified one who represents the noblest, the best that humanity could ever garb in human clay, do prepare the heart of children for the reception of the seed of prejudice. Perhaps evangelical Christianity cannot help teaching this—perhaps orthodox Christianity must insist upon the crucifixion because it is woven into the fundamental dogma of the Christian church. Give up the crucifixion and Christianity falls—the God crucified is a God redeemer, a God not crucified would not unlock the gates of salvation. My quarrel is not with them for teaching what their religion deems essential. There are honest Christians. I do not belong to those liberals who deny the possibility that men may honestly think differently from them. I do not hold, that men of learning cannot subscribe to these dogmas, or if they do that they are hypocrites. I for one will not claim that we are learned for our denials, and that someone else is a fool and knave because he views history and the fundamental needs of the human heart from an angle of vision that we reject as improper. There are honest men that teach the drama of Golgotha as a bitter fact. There are men of the profoundest scholarship that are convinced of its truth. This teaching is a misfortune, from one point of view, for us Jews; from another, it is not.

Trial is not an affliction. Trial confers the messianic crown, and if we are messiahs, as I believe we are,—if we, Israel—the spiritual Israel, are for a messianic destiny and the messianic dignity, we must expect to be tried and to suffer. The child cannot distinguish when it hears the story of Jesus's death, between the Jew that was and the Jew that is. That the Jews did not crucify Christ, is my conviction; but even if they had, what share have I in the deed of my remote ancestors? Of course, in a certain sense, I have. History imputes guilt and imparts merit by the wonderfully mysterious law of descent and historical continuity. Nevertheless the Sunday-school is fruitful of undue prejudice against the Jew, for the child confounds the Jew of to-day with the Jew who is said to have affixed to the cross the "sweet and beloved and blessed Jesus." For a liberal to teach in the strain of evangelical orthodoxy, is indeed prejudice. An orthodox Christian in insisting upon his view of the last scenes in the life of his savior, is loyal to the dogmatic positions of his church.

With all this, it is safe to say that it is not religious prejudice which is the main channel of spreading anti-Semitism. Antioch Epiphanes was not a religious bigot. What cared he for the gods? Religion for him was a means to an end. It was a convenient shield behind which to hide his political aims, to veil the real principles of his statesmanship.

To-day we have various species of anti-Semites, and first is the Russian type. What is at the root of Russian anti-Semitism? The ambition cultivated by the ruling Russian statesmen that Russia shall become a national unit, that in Russia in religion, in custom, in language, in the composition of the people there shall be but one exclusive standard of national life. We call this a centralization on the basis of national unity. That this system which apprehends national unity as possible only when racially, linguistically, in custom and religion, the nation be a unit, should have been born a child of our day, no one who has any knowledge of the philosophy of our times can marvel at. Such a political creed had to be framed in the days, the waning days of this ebbing 19th century. Materialism here draws its direct and inevitable inferences. Blood makes the man. Man is but a beast. The race decides the quality of the brute. Nations are not the outcome of spiritual forces. They are the result of local accidents—of geographical positions, but within the circumscribed limits of national territory there should be racial unity, and whatever resists the intention of so mixing the inhabitants that from the process racial unity shall event, must be ground down into its elemental primaries, that these all the more readily enter into the amalgum to be evolved from the chemical retorts operating upon the theory that national unity is of necessity conditioned on racial unity.

And in the same spirit it is assumed to be axiomatic that language too must be one. A nation must have a national language, there can be no dualism of language in one national home. Nor may religion as one of the manifestations of the national spirit, be other than national and one. All this accords with the orthodoxy of modern materialistic philosophers.

The fanatics of this school have misapplied the Darwinian theory. They have heard something about descent or selection, and because Darwinism, in the lower manifestations of life, undoubtedly strikes the ringing key-note of truth, they would apply its canons to the higher domain of man. Denying that man is higher in the scale of being, they contend that he is under the one law which is typical and autocratic in the lower forms. The Russian statesmanship of to-day is thus the outgrowth of the materialistic philosophy of our age.

On whom now shall this process of crushing all individuality that the desired uniformity might event, be first tried? Naturally on the Jew. Complain not, ye Jews of faint heart! You cannot deny it, and you cannot help it. It is the function of the Jew to be history's field of experimentation, in which is tried whatever of error man would tempt, that by the Jew's experience men may learn the futility of their efforts to thwart God's higher ends and cross His methods.

The Jews are what the Germans would call the "Versuchsvolk," the great laboratory of experimentation with all sorts of political and social doctrine; it is by the Jew that the world has learned the fallacy or correctness of methods tried and of principles applied. It is a pity that so few of the Jews understand their history and its relations to the times. If they did, they would know that theirs is an essential if unique service to mankind, and would find in this the compensation for all that is amiss. Is there higher glory than to teach by one's own suffering, by one's own resistance to error, others the error of their ways? I know of no higher task. I know of no greater dignity—I know of no nobler station and function than this, and so I am gladdened by my burden. So were the thinking Jews at all times. It is merely those that have no thought, that have no knowledge of the wonderful destiny which is theirs by birth, that complain and cry out.

The Russian Jews do not complain. They have the instinctive and unconscious knowledge that they are there for a purpose. They may not have a clear comprehension of this purpose, but they do not lament. We often affect to be the superiors of these Russian Jews. Yet they are true aristocrats! Devotion to principle confers the knighthood in the hierarchy of the spiritual and moral forces of man; and tested by this alkali, these Russian Jews appear to be our better. They suffer. Would we suffer? They do not desert. We do desert. They migrate when the mere pretense of baptism would save them from fate's cruelty – save them? No, would place their foot on almost the top rung of the ladder of honor and distinction in the Russian empire. Here is Russia under the spell of its mistaken notion that a Russian nation can only exist if there be racial linguistic and religious unity, and the Jew must suffer for this conceit of his co-nationalists and must prove as he will prove, as he has proven, the fatality and fallacy of this Russian statesmanship and its ideals.

Antioch Epiphanes, too, was actuated by a wrong view of what constitutes a nation. He aspired after national unity and national strength dependent upon artificial, mechanical, racial and perhaps linguistic unity. He learned the lesson by the Maccabees that his statesmanship was fatal, radically wrong in its principles. Russia will, too, learn this. All accusations against the Russian Jews are mere subterfuges to mask this national fanaticism for Russian unification.

If the Russian Jew were as he is painted by his sworn enemies; if the Russian Jew were the very incarnation of all that is low, vulgar, fiendish, all that is criminal, all that is immoral, this frightful state would be an accusation not against him, the Russian Jew, but against the Russian Czar and his ministers. Are they still men who allow other men to sink so low; who contrive and conspire to deprive human beings of the possibilities of honor and regard for their humanity? Every criminal is the outcry of society's conscience, and, if there be in Russia three millions of Jewish criminals—and they say there are—this sad circumstance is a scathing rebuke of the Russian treatment of fellow-man; and if Russia suffers, I grant for the moment that it does—if Russia suffers from its Jews, Russia has to blame no one but herself. "Mine is the vengeance," saith God, and this is the retribution of God: every social crime, while it may crush one fellow-man or another, does recoil upon the concocter of the scheme.

But is the Russian Jew this incarnation of low and fiendish purpose? The wonder is not that he is what he is—the wonder is that he is, in comparison with others, not worse than he is. You cannot compare the Russian Jew to us, though in many things he is our superior. Let me tell you that among the students at the university, for instance, there are none that in eagerness to learn and in the spirit of sacrifice for learning, undergoing hardships that are even harrowing to tell of—there are none that can rival some of the Russian Jewish students. Their idealism for science is touching. I know some of them that never eat a warm meal from one end of the week to the other—why? Not because they are too lazy to work and win their bread, but because they work nineteen hours at their books to get knowledge, and with a few pennies a day at their disposal, keep the body alive that the soul may feast on God's light.

I say that if our own young men are pedestaled on glory, these Russian boys are on a Mont Blanc of exaltation and transfiguration which none of us would ascend under such trying surroundings. Russian Jews are not brutes. I could tell you a thousand and one things of them that condone for many of their shortcomings; we German Jews make the mistake of which we ourselves complain, to take individuals and generalize from them. For whatever the experience of our relief societies counts, my experience with them counts for a counterweight. If relief societies have reason to complain of what their wards do, and generalize on this basis as to the character of these people, I generalize from those whom I have learned to know, and to respect, perhaps to love. If one tramp stamps them all tramps, one of these students marks them all as idealists. Let us not clutch the mistake so dear to our enemies, of thinking that every Jew is like every other Jew, and taking the lowest among us as the type of the best! No, the Russian Jew, by not sinking lower than he has, by preserving a high idealism, if even only in individuals, shows what Jewish history has always demonstrated, the power for humanity of our Jewish religious inspiration; the potency for uplifting morality and fanning idealism, which goes with the faith in the Jew's election to be God's witness among men. And Russian policy to the contrary notwithstanding, the Jew will teach the Russian empire the lesson that a nation is not a mechanically manufactured thing but an organism of spirituality in which languages may differ, in which habits may differ, in which religions may differ.

But what about the German type of anti-Semitism? What is the motive of the fatherland's anti-Semitic movement? Antioch Epiphanes suggests the explanation. What was he after? Under the parade of the wrong principles of his national policy, he had a main eye to money. He needed gold. Greek life in his time presents a lapse and had taken a tumble from the high idealism of Plato, of Æschylus and others. In the idealism even of its foremost days ran a strong under-swell of sensuality, this had risen now to the surface. The typical Greek young man of those days knew only one incentive, that he must try and get a good time out of life. If he happened to be rich by birth he had no trouble to satiate his appetite; if he was not rich, he resorted to his wits to keep step with the procession. The gymnasium, the club of those days and climes, was the fostering place of all that was low and vulgar under the cover of social recreation and polite indulgences, and the plea for cultivation of good fellowship. And one of these young Greeks was our friend on the throne, Antioch Epiphanes. Let the curtain fall on his vices and the debauchery of his court! But he needed money to carry on this life. Among us a vulgar philosophy has it that "money makes the mare go," so he believed in the primal and fundamental necessity of turning everything into means of money getting. He had heard and the Jews induced him to believe it, that untold treasures were stored up in the temple at Jerusalem. He did not expect resistance to his crafty scheme on the part of the Jews, for the Jews themselves had encouraged him to expect that they were ready for a change. For the Jews did whatever they could to obliterate the traces of their native "curse" of Judaism. Young Jews of those days would not pay respect to their temple, of course not. But they made up a purse in Jerusalem and sent it as an offering to Melkarth of Tyre. Melkarth of Tyre they worshiped, but the God of Israel they knew not. Whatever was fashionable "went," and woe to a preacher in Jerusalem who would have the hardihood to raise his voice against this folly of imitating the way of others.

These gilded yet cowardly Jews had encouraged Antioch Epiphanes to expect that if he made a strategic move to get his hand on the wealth of the temple, there would be no resistance. He issued his decree without religious zeal but with the ultimate design uoon the Jews' wealth and possessions.

In Germany, too, anti-Semitism, is a form of anti-capitalism. Individual liberalism, of which we have heard so much, egotistic liberalism in economics, for instance, which was the dogmatic creed, of the German economic schools, before 1879, has opened the sluices wide for the rush of the turbid stream of selfishness. From England one hundred years ago was heralded the doctrine that all we needed to be men was to be free, and that each one should run his own race at his own pace, that God would take care of all, but that the devil would necessarily take the hindmost; as a result of this system of individualistic liberty has developed in Germany the social conflict, and its deep undertone is the outcry of the people against a selfish system of heartless exploitation. Who is always made responsible for the mistakes of others? The Jew. Fortunately in our country the Jew does not represent capitalism. Those that harp on the rich Jews in this country know not of what they are speaking; if they would only ponder that in our universities, the so-called rich Jews have not erected buildings or endowed chairs; that our only college in this country, the American Hebrew Union College, is always struggling between the devil and the deep sea of depleted treasury and of bankruptcy: they would know that we have no rich Jews. If we had them we should certainly not lag behind our neighbors in munificence and public spirit. That we do, is the best proof that we have no rich Jews. But in Germany through the conspiracy of the mediæval state the Jews were compelled to become the money lenders of their country.

In the handling of money there is nothing disgraceful. The opposite is an antiquated prejudice. Antiquity knew not the social function of capital, nor did it understand the ethical import of interest. Money is power and work as clearly as is sinew and bone and brain. If the Jew has become the capitalist and is engaged in capitalistic ventures in Germany, let Germany blame herself if there is anything immoral in the assigned position; and if there is not, the Jew certainly has not abused of his resources any more than the power which goes with possession has been abused everywhere and by everybody. The individualistic system of economic organization has made one the harvester of the fruit of the common labor and he is the capitalist. Deny it if you will—there is something wrong in our present social organization, if all our inventions, all our great finds, the advances in industry, have fundamentally redounded to the benefit of capital almost exclusively.

In Germany, however, since the days of the new empire, has spread the practical creed that life is worth living only to the rich, and hence all over, the watchword is wealth. The new aristocracy of finance can command luxury which the poor baron representing the hereditary nobility cannot emulate. Yet he must keep up appearances. He would not be eclipsed by the luster, the glory of the new order of things, and thus he mortgages his property foolishly. He has lost the sense that the dignity of a nobleman compensates, in a true nobleman, for all that he has to miss by not being in the "swim" of society, in the debauchery and revelry of wealth displayed vulgarly; and so from the highest to the lowest in Germany, all are possessed by the craze and the greed for money lest the barons of finance be the only ones to feast on rare wines and dissolve even pearls for their daily bath if they so choose.

This greed for money is always the signal for a crusade against the Jew. Individualism has become bankrupt,—it is bankrupted in religious philosophy to-day; it is bankrupted in political science, it is bankrupted in social science. The creed of Adam Smith was a curse to humanity when it was carried further than its legitimate but limited scope. We need to-day the social organization of industry and capital. This view is the true outlook; it will become real ere many more decades will have spun round in space. "The Jew is a capitalist, the money holder," is the keynote to German anti-Semitism. The Jew has thus to-day in Germany to teach the German people the error of its ways, and the best way for the Jews in Germany to fight this anti-Semitism would be to sever their connection with the individualistic political or individualistic economic schools. Professor Lazarus, in the year 1884, raised his voice of warning. Though maligned for his courageous stand, events have shown that he prophecied true. The Jew cannot be in economics an individualist. The prophets' philosophy had a distinctly social tendency.

It is not an accident that La Salle was a Jew; that Marks was a Jew; that Singer to-day is a Jew. Jesus too was a Jew, and in theory socialistic, in the highest sense of the word. True socialism, as the prophets taught it, is not anarchy, nor is it destruction—it is construction, it is building up, it is the broadening of the foundations of humanity, it is stretching the rope of the tabernacle of life. If the Jews in Germany knew what the cause of this distemper is, they would speedily exemplify the better knowledge that as capitalists they have to do the highest duty to society, to show that their capital is ready to become the stepping-stone to a new social organization of humanity on the basis of justice and of righteousness.

But the German government used the Jew as a shield to protect itself. "Let the dogs attack the Jew. They will leave the emperor in peace!" Such was the Bismarckian thought, and wherever there is a German, a similar disposition is engrafted in his heart.

Wherever there is only a little drop of this prejudice against the Jew, it crops out in unguarded moments. Rare is the German that has not imbibed this prejudice because up to the present day Germany has not been industrially trained to self-reliant efforts. The Jews of Germany are the dynamo of the industrial activities of the fatherland. And here is the root of the matter. This anti-Semitism of Germany is child of the social unrest of our age, and the Jew as always must suffer for others.

What about the American variety of this prejudice? It is the meanest of all, for it is spun of the threads of social ostracism. There are Americans, so called, who also would have America be one in religion, with God and Jesus in the constitution. One in language with German suppressed; one in political creed, one in puritanism and the Sunday observance especially, one in many more things, with a straight-jacket for its uniform. They would not tolerate the "foreigner"; and unless one's ancestors have come over aboard the Mayflower, they look upon one as their guest, tolerated merely here by their kindness; but one so admitted must vacate the premises the moment they sue out a writ of ejectment. These Americans are, however, in the minority. In America will continue to live side by side different nationalities combinedly making the great nation of America; in different languages will be sung the great proclamation of liberty and will be choired the chant, "My country,' tis of thee"; in America will be the home of many religions, all teaching patriotism, duty and the rights and responsibilities of man.

Nationalism is not the cause of our difficulty; nor is anti-capitalism distinctly anti-Jewish in this country. We have yet to learn that the Goulds and the Vanderskilts and the Lord knows whatever their name may be, that fix things in Wall street, that know how to build railroads and wreck them and bid them in again; that are experts at organizing trusts and their dissolutions, for the purpose of depressing stocks and then buying them back, and after a long legal battle at again coming to terms to boom once more the securities purchased at a low figure, to fool others with a new bait, and shear the lambs and rake in the proceeds, are Jews. Those engaged in this warfare on society are not Jews. Now and then one Jew is allowed to sail this maelstrom of corruption, but most of the freebooters are members of churches. Anti-capitalism has nothing to do with the prejudice against us. What then is its character? "Society" will not recognize the Jew. This prejudice is harbored especially by the women. One probably a descendant of a good honorable fur-trader, who came to America in the early days when fur traffic was profitable, has become anxious to represent a social nobility, and, as even the common clay of Christian Americans is not good enough for her daughters, she imports at a high price some foreigner to take the daughter off her hands and give her a title. Another is the child of some good honest butcher, who made his money by killing sheep and investing it carefully, through the unearned increment became wealthy. Terribly learned and terribly cultured, she will not mingle with one that may possibly be a descendant of the family that gave to the world Jesus, her own redeemer.

It is the American women mostly that foster this prejudice. What is their excuse? They affect to believe that the Jew is vulgar, that the Jewess as a rule is a walking, perambulating jewelry establishment. The Jew cannot speak English. The Jew is rude. All these ridiculous charges are winged arrows sent to keep at a distance and to do injury to a class of men and women who, to say the least, are as refined as their snobbish traducers. If these Americans traveling in Europe knew any language but their own, so that they could understand what is said of them, they would learn that in Europe the Americans are held to be what these Americans hold the Jews to be. Why? Because probably at rare intervals one American of their set was of this character, and as the Americans in Europe are the minority, all suffer, as every minority will suffer, for the misdeeds of one of their number.

I do not deny that there are Jews that are vulgar. I hold that the Christians have not a monopoly on vulgarity. I do not deny that some of our Jewesses are foolish enough to lessen their beauty by a display of jewels that ought to be in a safe deposit or under the guard of a detective. I do not deny that there are Jews that are rude, who do not remember the distinction between solitude and publicity, who consider a street car a fit place for explosions of all sorts of sentiments, who do not remember that they have a responsibility to others; but there are as many non-Jews that do the same thing. Judaism certainly does not teach rudeness, and the Jew who is a Jew not merely by accident, but by conviction, will repress all superfluity of boisterous sentiment, or curb all barbaric inclination for display of vulgar splendor.

This prejudice is again a phase of, and at the same time a travesty, on our individualism. It looks to the individual, but makes him or her the type of a class. What are we going to do about it? Some of us are terribly anxious that this thing should stop. I am not. Those that do not wish to associate with me simply because I am a Jew, are welcome to follow to the full their bent. I consider myself a gainer by exclusion from their society, for what can I profit by associating with narrow-minded bigots? Their horizon is low, much lower than mine. Their sympathies are contracted. Their prejudices are deep. What matter to me that they refuse to meet me? Let them wait until I ask them to be admitted into their clan! I hold that here is a call for the assertion of the Jewish feeling "I am just as good as you are." What matter if clubs do not admit me? I am better off on the outside. I am much more comfortable on the street than in such clubs. I am the gainer, not the loser. If they do not wish to take me into their hotels—well, is there absolute necessity that I should go to a fashionable caravansery with its frivolities? There will always be men, I believe, that are above these prejudices, and in many a so-called non-fashionable resort one finds much better company than where "plutocracy" convenes. So far as the cultured Jews are concerned, they can endure this sort of injustice philosophically and be proud that their experience is an exemplification of the many things that need yet to be done in America to teach the Americans the lessons of liberty and tolerance; it is unworthy of the American to harbor prejudice in any shape or manner whatsoever. But we should police our own district. We should resent from pulpit and in the press, in our private relations with one another, everything that smacks of vulgarity. We must train ourselves and others to be what we should be, minority as we are, above reproach and without stain or blemish. Another thing we might do. We might take the liveliest interest in all that affects the welfare of the community. We should not be those who are in the rear when something for the welfare of country, county, city is done.

What is the best method of fighting prejudice? This holiday says, light is. These lamps here are a forcible reminder of the power of light to win the battle still raging about us. In light, let our message go out into the world, and teach what the Jew is, and what he aims to be, and half of the battle will be won. Light, by giving Jewish science a home in our great universities. These universities, as far as the state has not founded them, are all private endowments of men of deep religious and Christian convictions, and therefore we cannot expect that they will give hospitality to Jewish science unless the Jews make provision for the maintenance of this branch in the curriculum. Not every university is even willing to give the rabbi place on the faculty, unless the chair be endowed. Here is the opportunity to fight the prejudice. One Jewish professor, whatever his branch may be, and especially if he teaches Jewish science and teaches the history of Judaism and the philosophy of Judaism, does more for the generations to be than all other movements to combat prejudice combined. Do you think that the theologians, the baptist theologians, who will remember me as their teacher, can go into their pulpits and dare fire off the old ammunition? They know better; they are ashamed to use the rusty arms from the old arsenal of bigotry.

Here is a noble work to be done. Let your light shine forth! Let its rays penetrate into the institutions of learning. We Jews of this city ought to have a building in the blocks of buildings at our university. When we visit the campus and look around—and read one name—another name—a third name, recalling the munificence of Chicago's citizens—how long shall we ask in mortification, why is there no Jew in the number? We have no rich Jews, as I have said—but many poor Jews make one rich Jew. Is it not possible for the Jews of Chicago and the northwest to erect the library building, and to call it after Lessing? One hundred thousand dollars would accomplish this. Are there not a hundred or two hundred that are willing to bring this sacrifice? Yea, let light stream out, and the minions of darkness will disappear. I fear not that in the long run Antioch Epiphanes will be defeated. Even now the tidal wave is receding. Russia has learned the lesson—is learning it—that nationality is not based on uniformity, and Germany will, throwing off individualism, come to its own ideal consciousness again, and in America the social prejudice will die out for want of fuel and provocation, if the Jew be in every field the leader toward the height where God's own light kindles the *Menorah*, the holy lamp in the temple of humanity. Amen.

'HANUKKAH.

BY REV. DR. G. GOTTHEIL.

In one of the rocky caverns of the Judæan mountains, Matathias had gathered his five stalwart sons around his deathbed, to consecrate them to the service of their country and their religion. He charged them not to be carried away with those that, either by their own inclination or out of necessity betray the customs of their country and their ancient form of government, but to become such men as are above all forces and necessities, and so to dispose their souls as to be ready to die for their laws; and to be sensible of this, by just reasoning, that if God see that they are so disposed, He will not overlook them, but have a great value for their virtue and will restore to them again what they have lost and return to them that freedom in which they will live quietly and enjoy their customs. As he spoke, so it happened. All the five sons gave their lives to their country; but their blood was not shed in vain. It fructified the soil from which a new life sprang for the nation. Long afterwards the pillars rising over their tomb at Modin arrested the foot of the traveler, and called forth that spontaneous homage which the human heart never denies to heroic souls. We, the heirs to their fame as well as to the price of their death, ought to do more. We ought to reflect on the lesson it teaches.

That deathbed scene points to the primary sources from which flow the inspiration for the ideal life. It is the parents' teaching and example. God has given them charge of the young soul: theirs it is to mould and direct its faculties. If they fail to do their whole duty, it is very rare that after life can repair the injury.

The child that has grown up in a home where there is no religion of any kind will seldom find it in temple or church. Where pleasure and profit are the only gods worshiped, the poorest chance remains to awaken the heart to a love and reverence for better and higher things. The magnet attracts iron because in the iron there is an answering force and disposition; it never attracts wood or stone. Judaism, above all, never was an ecclesiastical religion, never was identified with the priestly function or a consecrated house. One of the secrets of its power of endurance lies in the hold it always had on the home. Because that was a house of God, the House of God became the home of the worshipful heart. True, we may "come to scoff, and stay to pray," but, as a rule, we must bring some religion with us if we are to find more in the House of Prayer; just as we must have music in our souls before we go to the concert hall, or a sense of the beautiful if we would enjoy the productions of art. Our children receive lessons in literature; for what purpose? to create the faculty for reading the poets understandingly. The work of our religious schools must remain incomplete if not supported by a corresponding home influence. The Psalm appointed to be read during these memorial days bears this superscription: "A song for the dedication of the House of David." Yet tradition has it that its real author was Solomon, because he it was who built the first temple, but that he inscribed the dedication hymn to his royal father, because it was by his forethought in collecting treasure and material, that the son was enabled to rear the stately fane on Zion. It is just so in the spiritual building up of the souls of children. The parents must furnish the material out of which it is to be constructed. And this is true not only in regard to religion—character, principles, manners, in fact, the whole life takes its complexion from what the children hear, or see, or silently observe when the parents think that they notice nothing. In times of visitation, in trials that search the heart, children must receive the same impression which the brave Hasmoneans received from the lips of their dying father: to be above all force and necessity and so to dispose their minds as to be ready to sacrifice everything at the call of duty.

Looking at the scene in the cavern from a historical point of view we may well call it a turning point in the religious life of Israel, nay, of the human race. Before that hour Judaism was mainly a divine discipline, a system of ordinances of what was to be done or was to be left undone, weighted with alluring promises for the obedient and severe punishment for the disobedient. But from that moment the power of bearing and self-denying became the test of piety and fidelity. The martyrs crown was first raised over that ever memorable deathbed. Religion, henceforth, became a faith, a conviction, a spiritual possession of infinite significance to the soul. The God that had descended only on Sinai now entered the heart of Israel, where He has dwelt ever since. Before that day only the chosen few had so conceived of religion, notably the great prophets. The fifty-third chapter of Isaiah is not a prophecy of the appearance at same time of a single man, but of man in his highest aspect, the heoric servant of God in all ages. It is an incomparable elegy on the suffering redeemers of all generations and of the manner of their reception amongst men. Surely he has borne our griefs and carried our sorrows, yet we esteemed him stricken, smitten of God and afflicted. The chastisement of our peace was upon him and in his stripes we were healed; yet shall the work of the Lord prosper in his hands. Self-sacrifice is the only creed which can never be questioned, but not self-sacrifice without a purpose and without an end, worthy of our reverence. Every true act of heroism is religious in its very nature, and so considered the world is full of the true faith. The Creator, who planted this impulse into our being, is glorified from the rising of the sun even unto the going down thereof. Few souls have seen God thus revealed face to face; have seen Him in that pure light in which He appeared in the cavern of Judae. The heroism of faith is Israel's acknowledged patrimony. May we ever guard it and transmit it unimpaired from generation to generation. Amen.

SILENCE MEANS RUIN.

A PURIM DISCOURSE BY RABBI MAX HELLER.

The spiritualizing influences of this modern age which have transfused with higher beauty so many of the hoary traditions of Judaism have shed their roseate glow of tender sentiment upon that festival also which to-day we recall, even if not celebrate. The Purim-feast of old in whose diadem glittered the sparkling jewels of charity amid the bright gold of mirth and laughter, a feast of gratitude for deliverance, not undimmed, however, by bitter reminiscences of deadly persecution, is to-day a lovely dream of a fair heroine guided by a patriot's stern counsel and while the Hamans are still with us in the spectre of anti-Semitism, yet is the lesson of Esther's self-sacrifice principally one of Jewish unity, unshaken loyalty and the widest generosity.

As to the story itself, whose freshness of eternal youth would well deserve that we should annually rehearse it even if we should miss thereby the enjoyment of some latest product of ephemeral fiction, it is a moving scene of dazzling descriptions, surprising changes, dramatic episodes. In the fascination of the rapid narrative we are apt to do scant justice to the nervy, terse words at the critical points in the action, words which sear and burn, out of whose white flame shines luminously the majesty of heroic souls. I cannot forget, for my part, and year after year it seems to me more strenuous and adamantine in its firmness, the vivid energy of Mordecai's warning. "Imagine not in thy soul that thou wilt be saved in the king's palace out of all the Jews; for if indeed thou wilt be silent at this time, deliverance and enlargement will arise to the Jews from another place, but thou and thy father's house will perish."

It is not merely the restrained power in these words which moves me so strongly; it is the obvious application with which they beat upon our age which appeals to me with a force so immediate and vital. This is in our very day the fatal error of cultured Jew-dom which needs a rebuking like Mordecai's; that blind error by which the glittering palace of a materialistic civilization is trusted in as the fortress of safety, that error by which the royal splendors of modern refinement are looked to as a safeguard against the power of Haman-edicts, however these might rage amid the dark poverty outside. The royal palace is a treacherous refuge and affords as kindly a home to bloodthirsty Haman as to the lovely queen; the royal palace reverberates with the strifes of brutal selfishness, of insatiable greed; it is in loyalty to the Jewish name, in the glad response to duty, in the brave outspokenness of conviction that safety is found and the preservation of the "fathers' house."

Upon the hollowness of modern professions, upon the continuing danger from savage egotism, upon the unweakened necessity of Jewish solidarity, I have dwelt more than once on similar occasions. To-day, gleaning from the ancient narrative a lesson of more than racial application I prefer to expatiate upon these selected words: "If at a time like this thou wilt be silent . . . then thou and thy father's house will perish."

As a sweet type of shrinking modesty, as a fair vision of womanly dependence and obedience few heroines of history or fiction could contest the palm of beauty with the lovely Hebrew myrtle which shone as the radiant Persian star. Submission, service, the shy constraints which sit so well upon a noble countenance are her principal charms; Jewess, orphan, exile, it is but natural that loveliness and self-effacement should surround her as with a halo of unconscious purity. It is in such as she that aggressive women with their bold claims of masculine privileges might recognize wherein, by nature's immutable law, is found woman's highest beauty and grandest dignity.

To this frail woman it is that Mordecai addresses his kindling words: "Dare to be silent now and destruction will crash over your head; it is a time to speak, to be fearless and bold, it means *your* ruin and your annihilation if now you hold back and shrink from duty." And lo! the light of courage shines from the beaming eye; calm determination takes the place of confused hesitancy, of timid pleading; it is she who gives the command, she who guides and enjoins, her life is her people's either to save them from the threat of doom or else to die for her defiance. Henceforth, though she awaits in calmness the nearing opportunity for the decisive utterance, the words are formed in her heart to spring to her lips on wings of courage, to be hurled like bolts of lightning into the very face of the cruel enemy.

How beautiful a word in season; the cowardly proverb commends in diplomatic counsel that while speech may be silver, silence is gold; as if it had been the silences of cravens and not the words of heroes that have lifted humanity from rung to higher rung, as if the great treasure-house of centuried wisdom was filled with the voids of stillness rather than with the wealth of golden speech. Against the shallow policy of proverb-prudence how much wiser the saying of our sages which commends silence only as the hedge around wisdom. There is a silence of self-restraint which is not shrewd concealment but benevolent moderation, there is an abstinence from speech which proves the strong character, a manly reserve which only emphasizes the timely outspokenness. This silence is the frame for speech, the tranquil background from which decisive action and unambiguous utterance step out more boldly; for the great men of silence, a Grant, a Wellington, a Moltke, have been men, though principally of action, yet also of priceless words.

But in this complacent world of ours, in the pushing and jostling of competition, in the wire-pulling and log-rolling of social and commercial and public causes, in the slavish imitations and thoughtless repetitions of the great herd who are simply echoes, in all this chaos of diplomatic selfishness, supine indolence, flabby good-nature, indifferent carelessness, underhand intrigue and unprincipled lying, there must be some one to clear the atmosphere of all its fog and soot with a ringing word of truth. "In the place where men are not, strive thou to be a man." Where candor and sincerity hide in the corner, there is a deliverance in the fearless avowal, in the puncturing charge.

That straightforward courage redeems is a lesson of manliness which we need at this juncture of a false refinement and an unprincipled social diplomacy more than it has ever been needed before. We are so civil and punctilious in our international relations; when a presidential message rings out its resounding demand for justice the thin-skinned culture of our universities cries shame upon the disturbance; but when a Brazil, a Cuba, struggle for liberty and justice, a finical respect for international courtesy restrains the birthland of constitutional freedom from going as far as even officially recognizing the undisputed reality. Are we not blinking facts with as much cowardice and remissness to duty in our private lives? Does not our silence and our social indifference give the sanction of consent to all the scoundrels and rascals we tolerate as our company? Are we not afraid of the naked truth as of something rude and refined? Have we not dressed her image up in so many circumlocutions and equivocations that we flee from her when she appears unveiled in the beauty of her purity?

And we that claim the title of truth's guardians, we Jews, on what kind of terms are we living with candor and frankness in our social relationships? Not enough that petty business considerations and effeminate society habits keep back from our lips the strong words we have almost unlearned to use, but we are trembling with redoubled apprehensions when it is our own foibles that are to be pointed out, dragged to the light, overwhelmed with righteous condemnation. It is the Gentile's opinion we pretend to fear, the Gentile's judgment we are warned against affecting, but it is our own morbid sensitiveness, our own petted conceits around which we want drawn the protecting fence of a politic silence. To my mind no greater injury could be inflicted by the presence of prejudice, by the threats of exclusion than if it wrought in our characters, in our moral lives the fearful havoc that springs from self-deception, from the secret festering and feeding of ulcers which should be cut out, no matter at what cost of pain and mortification.

We cannot afford to be silent in the presence of evil; and like a magnificent sunburst from out black clouds has come to the world the heart-deep realization of man's keeper-duty to his brother. And if craven governments all over the extent of boastful civilization are observing a criminal inactivity in the presence of wrongs that cry to heaven, with the shrieks of butchered innocents in their heedless ear, the people will speak for Russian Jew, Armenian victim and Cuban insurgent; they feel, in the royal palace of their freemen's privileges, that their existence, that freedom's house should totter, if, at times like these, they should indeed be silent.

There is a speech that is gold, it is the eloquent response of active help. "Money talks" and the silence which is death is often no more nor less than the narrow-hearted refusal to obey the generous impulse. And this speech is at present the only one in which we can speak for our oppressed brethren, our liberal assistance from our means is the only earnest we can give of our sympathy, of our literal Jewish fellow-feeling. It is our duty, our indisputable duty to give to the brothers of the Orient; it is an appropriate duty to perform on this feast of Purim which emphasizes that we *are* their brothers, no matter what radical extremists may prate about our differences of belief and standpoint; it is our duty always, no matter how great may *seem* the burdens of our local charities. Let us at last cease repeating the brazen falsehood that we are weighted down with charity; who of us is suffering from self-deprivation in consequence of charitable extravagance? Not one whom I can point out, myself included. How many are the pleasures which we deny ourselves so we might be able to give to the poor? Very few, very few, indeed.

Again, therefore, as in the years gone by, I appeal to you with the old confidence on behalf of the educational work of the *Alliance Israelite Universelle*.

Let your generous hearts proclaim in golden accent that these days of Purim have not passed out beyond your feeling of duty; and give with an open hand in the reassuring confidence that your seed will be well sown by careful gardeners, to sprout forth in distant lands to blossoms of culture, fragrant with the perfume of the higher life. Amen.

LIBERTY AND LIGHT.

A PASSOVER SERMON.—BY REV. O. J. COHEN, MOBILE, ALA.

On the first page of the Bible we find emblazoned one of the sublimest passages in the whole world's literature; brief in statement, powerful in expression, infinite in suggestiveness, wonderful in comprehensiveness:—"And God said: 'Let there be light!'—and there was light."

That was the first decisive act in creation. The material of the universe, the heavens and the earth, had already been fashioned by the divine power. But this was a rude and shapeless mass, with darkness brooding over the face of the deep. By the august command "Let there be light," the darkness was thrust back, the world was wrested from chaos. By that one stroke of the Almighty Artist, the confused elements ranged themselves in proper parts and relations, the successive stages of created beings appeared; and order, which is Heaven's first law, began its reign;—for there was light. Thus the first word of the divine mouth called into existence that which was the greatest need for the physical universe, and the greatest need, as well as the richest gift, to man, God's co-worker in the development of the world. The ancient philosophers who felt constrained to conceive God under some material form, considered that

His essence was fire, which they regarded as the purest and noblest of all the elements. Likewise in order to express what to them was the highest idea of the human soul, they declared it to be made of fire, an emanation from the divine fire. A similar conception, but in sublimer and truer form, is that of the Scriptures, many verses of which speak of God as light. We have, too, a passage in Proverbs, that calls the spirit of man "a lamp of the Lord"; thus pointing to the essential and best part of human nature as a flash of that divine *light* which shines through the world.

But the primitive light did not remain. The darkness came again. By the command of the Lord who made a division between light and darkness, each had its place and its time, night and day followed in regular succession. In the career of mankind the divine light of truth did not at once reveal itself and act as the all-governing power. The lamp of the soul did not always shine with the divine light that had at first kindled it. It was dimmed by folly and ignorance, and flickered in error. Humanity began a slow, though steady growth, and in its earliest stages darkness predominated.

Travel now in thought through the corridors of time, through the many centuries from the day of creation to the time commemorated by this festival of Passover. What do we behold? Israel in bondage to the Egyptians. A nation, whose early ancestors had perceived some of the light of religious and moral truth, groaning in servitude under the iron rule of a nation that in spite of its advanced material civilization, was intellectually and morally in darkness. But the signal for emancipation had already been given. Inspiration that led to the breaking of that cruel yoke had already descended from heaven and fired the soul of Israel's great leader. Boldly did Moses go before Pharaoh and demand that his people should be set free and allowed to go and worship their God and the God of their fathers. The hard-hearted refusal was met with avenging plagues, which one after another afflicted the king and his subjects; but they obstinately withstood the divine wrath. There came, though, the ninth plague, the one before and preparatory to the last, that of darkness, which hung over Egypt for three days, in the graphic words of the Scriptures, a thick blackness that could be felt. "But," we read, "for the children of Israel, there was light in all their dwellings." That was the decisive occurrence. When the Israelites saw distinctly the darkness of Egyptian idolatry, superstition and folly, and in their souls gleamed the light of truth and reason, they could be restrained no longer. Then it was that Moses made his final audience before Pharaoh and emphatically repeated his demand without the least compromise, and being refused exclaimed to the haughty monarch who forbade his presence henceforth, "thou hast spoken well; I shall never see thy face any more." It was the work of but a short time when the first-born of Israel's enemies were smitten by the last plague and the people, now irresistible, pressed forward and cast their chains of slavery forever behind them. Even the pursuing host could not bring them back. Fearlessly Israel marched right into the waters of the Red Sea and did not stop until, their enemies drowned, they sung on the further shore their triumphal song of liberty.

This was God's second great gift to mankind—liberty. It was given to Israel not only for their benefit, but that they might spread it through the world. Israel was made its apostle, to proclaim it to the world, and to teach at the same time that the two go together, light and liberty. Light needs liberty. To gain the light of wisdom and truth, there must be freedom of search and inquiry; the mind must not be fettered. On the other hand liberty needs light. Darkness and servitude go together; but wherever there is light of reason, the fetters are broken, and mind as well as body will emancipate itself. This is true not only politically, for ignorant slaves with better understanding have risen against their oppressors and gained freedom, but also morally, religiously and intellectually. As long as ignorance was enforced, there was servitude to falsehood and to error; but as soon as the light of reason shone, the people freed themselves from the tyranny of superstition and folly, and proclaimed and followed the truth.

This great lesson of liberty, impressed so early in history upon the people of Israel, has never been lost to them. Already in the days of Moses, a law was made prohibiting a Jew from making a slave of any of his brethren; the Jewish spirit could not tolerate servitude. Through all times they showed the same disposition. All the oppression of the mightiest nations of the world could not enslave them. And even when their external circumstances were made bitter by the hand of tyranny, their minds could not be fettered and their thoughts could not be held down to any enforced belief, but remained free in the great ideas that were their heritage. The same thing accounts for their condition to-day. Russia maintains its barbarous power over its subjects by keeping them in the darkness of ignorance; for that country, it is well known, not only makes little provision for, but even hinders in every possible way public education. Especially against our co-religionists are restrictions enforced to prevent them from gaining education. All the persecution of our people in that country comes from the fact that they have the light of reason and truth from their own ancient sources, and so cannot be made the submissive slaves which the ignorant peasantry certainly are.

Furthermore, the Jews have generally been, wherever they have been situated, the champions of liberty. They have been, and are to-day, the advocates of freedom of thought, freedom of speech, freedom of conscience and freedom of action. In testimony we may mention such names as Cremieux, Lasker, Lasalle and Marx, whose policies, speeches and writings govern and inspire those that are struggling for greater liberty in the still backward countries of Europe. It is the duty of the Jews in all circumstances, on every occasion, in every field, to be on the side of progress and advance. The teachings of their religion and the spirit they have inherited from their ancestors should devote them to the cause of light and liberty.

They have contributed something, indeed much, to the world in this respect. Why, what is the cornerstone of this Republic which is pre-eminently the land of freedom? The republics of ancient and mediæval times were unsuccessful or unsatisfactory experiments of liberty, but here first has the principle of political, social and intellectual freedom established itself and furthered the prosperity and happiness of the people. To what origin must this success be traced? The settlers and founders of America got their ideas not from any text-book on politics or political economy, not from the past experience of the nations of the world; but got their main inspiration from the Hebrew Bible, which is the book of light and the gospel of liberty.

An emblem typifying these principles stands at the gateway of this country. When travelers from the still backward countries of the East, fugitives from lands of oppression, first spy the shore of this abode of freedom, there towers into view from New York harbor the famous Bartholdy statue which its maker has boldly named "Liberty Enlightening the World." An imposing sight is that statue, the gift of the people of France, the most prominent republic of the old world to the people of America, the great republic of the new world, with its colossal figure and brilliant light streaming for thirty miles down the coast. Though it may be presumption to speak even of this triumphant monument of genius and skill as enlightening the whole world, yet it distinctly symbolizes that spirit of liberty and enlightenment which animates this country and will in time govern the world.

Here again the lesson is brought out that the two principles must go together. Either one is worthless without the other. Where there is liberty there must be light. It is dangerous for people to have freedom, without having wisdom to use that freedom. Liberty must not become license, but must be tempered by the restraints of law and order. Hence this country, in contrast to the instance before cited, dwells on the need of education, provides for it, and insists on it; encourages the spread of the light of wisdom; and admonishes that the actions of its citizens, which must have fullest freedom, must nevertheless be governed by the principles of right and justice and truth. When our ancestors were to be freed from Egypt it was not that they might run riot, and pursue any whims and pleasures. The divine voice spoke to Pharaoh through Moses saying: "Let my people go that they may *serve me.*" It exhorted the people, ye shall be slaves to no man, but ye shall be slaves to me. After they gained deliverance, they were but a few weeks on their march of freedom, when they were made to halt before Mt. Sinai, from which in thundering tones were proclaimed the the Ten Commandments, telling them what they must do and what they must not do. After they had liberty, then came from Sinai's summit that light of which the Bible speaks in the words "The law is light." Liberty means not freedom to do what you please, but freedom to do what you ought. So in all our actions, in our thoughts, in our beliefs, let there be liberty but let there also be the light of guidance, of higher principle, of truth.

My friends, the mission of Israel is by no means yet ended. There are still nations groaning in servitude. There is still much darkness of ignorance, error and falsehood. As long as the ideas of freedom and truth are not universally prevalent, we must stand firm, we must lend all possible efforts to aid in establishing them. At least we must aid the cause of right and justice by tearlessly proclaiming their sovereignty; and must encourage the champions of these by unflinching assertion of our faith in their eventual triumph, in accordance with the cardinal doctrine of our religion. This is what we mean by our teaching of a Messianic time of whose approach we have firm conviction. This is the lesson of this festival of Passover. Our sages made the redemption it commemorates, the prototype of the ultimate redemption of mankind. It took time for Israel's release from Egypt: four hundred and thirty years did they while in bondage; but the deliverance did come, though not hoped or expected. So whatever doubts we may have as to the progress and perfection of humanity; it will take time, but it will come. We should govern our actions and inspire our endeavors for reform in every department, by a firm belief in the final enfranchisement of mankind from the dominion of error and wrong, and their devotion to the principles of truth and justice. The world will have *true liberty*, when all nations shall be bound by ties of common interest, when they will recognize the welfare of all in the welfare of each; when strife between them shall cease and all be united in the bonds of peace. There will be *light* when all shall conquer the lower instincts and desires, abandon the follies of ill-informed understanding, accept the dictates of reason and govern themselves by the higher principles of truth, which is a revelation from that divine Power whom all should serve. Let the prophets' picture of that Messianic future be ever before the eyes of your soul and until it is realized make your rule what he appends as his final exhortation: "Then many nations shall go and say: Come ye and let us go up to the mount of the Lord, to the house of the God of Jacob, that He may teach us His ways and we may walk in His paths. For out of Zion shall go forth the law and the word of the Lord from Jerusalem. And He shall judge among the nations and shall rebuke many people. And they shall beat their swords into ploughshares and their spears into pruning hooks. Nation shall not lift up sword against nation; neither shall they learn war any more. O house of Jacob, come ye to let us walk in the *light of the Lord.*"

FOUR SENTIMENTS.

A PASSOVER SERMON, BY REV. DR. MAX LANDSBERG.

After a long winter's season we have assembled in God's house in larger numbers than usual, to celebrate, under the cheerful rays of the new sun of beautiful spring, the resurrection of nature, combined with the resurrection of our ancestors from ancient Egyptian bondage. It is a soul-inspiring holiday. It revives and renews hope and energy, it confers strength and joyful courage to fulfil our work on earth.

Let us understand the full significance of the feast as expressed by the four cups of wine of the *Seder* night. The Jewish religion has always been a religion of the home, of the family. If we wish to cure the evils of which our generation is suffering, we must restore the Jewish house to its old privileges. Every Sabbath, every feast day, private and public, has from olden times been made the occasion of a family gathering. At the table the happy and susceptible mood has been used to arouse and keep alive sentiments of piety, of charity and religion which would exert a sanctifying and lasting influence upon all the members of the family in all conditions. No dinner or supper table was ever considered perfect without a sensible, instructive and pleasant conversation. Without it, the meal was compared to the offerings formerly brought to the dead; with it, the majesty of God himself, as it were, was said to partake even of the humblest meal. No gathering of the family or friends could be thought of, none was complete in its arrangements without a cup of blessing, the cup of wine which gladdeneth the heart of man, and which—so far from leading to dissipation and debauchery—breathed an air of true sanctification over the company assembled. The word *Kiddush* needs no translation for a Jewish audience. Its very sound recalls to our spiritual eye the sweetest pictures which slumber in the sacred chambers of our memory. It carries us back to the happy days of our childhood, when father and mother, surrounded by their children, greeted together the Sabbaths and the holydays in the cheerful room brightened with light; when, after their return from the house of God, the real celebration began; when joy filled every heart, all cares and anxieties of the daily life were forgotten and the father lifted up the cup and thanked God for the grace with which He had preserved us, and for the benefits, worldly and spiritual, He had bestowed upon us; and after having tasted of the wine, let the cup pass around, that every member of the household, down to the youngest child, should partake of it after him. It was, indeed, a *Kiddush*, a consecration and sanctification, not only of the day, but of the family also. A feeling of holiness pervaded every one, and no word or act of rudeness was possible among the children during the meal thus initiated. They all felt hallowed; a spirit of good cheer and kindness had entered and was sure to remain with them during the Sabbath and festival, and not even entirely to depart, when, on the following evening, leave was taken from the holyday again with a cup of wine, in the last drops of which the light that divided the Sabbath from the weekday was extinguished with that characteristic and familiar crackling noise, never to be forgotten. The sweet angels who accompanied our fathers to their home on the Sabbath eves had pronounced their blessing. The holy sensations aroused in their soul remained a living power during the struggles and trials of the coming week.

But, while at every occasion one cup of benediction was considered as sufficient, there was one great and memorable exception on the most distinguished evening of the year, on the evening which inaugurates this beautiful feast of the spring and liberty; when, instead of one, it became obligatory to drink four cups of wine, when every one had to celebrate an unusual feast at the family table, and even the poor, who depend on the gifts of their more fortunate brethren, must for the nonce forget their dependence and enjoy in this *night of watching* the feeling of largess and freedom, when the cup of the father shall not make the rounds of the table, but the women must also have their four cups, and even every little child must have a cup of wine before him of suitable size. Not, however, for the mere enjoyment of a good meal such custom was introduced. Connected with these four cups of wine are the highest and loftiest ideas which the human mind is capable of thinking, and our ancient teachers well knew that, thus inculcated, they would make a deeper impression and be surer to become the common property of the whole people, than by formal religious instruction and by a thousand lectures and sermons.

Four times we are directed to drink a cup of wine at the *Seder* table, but not before the father has offered a sentiment. And these four sentiments let us now consider and we shall understand that they are still worthy being proposed and remembered once every year in every Jewish family, and that we should try to make them the property of the human race.

The first sentiment to which we drank last night was gratitude to God, that our forefathers were set apart to know God and to recognize His will before all other nations, or as our teachers express it, to the memory of our father Abraham.

Kings are proud and noblemen regard themselves as better than others, if they can trace back their family tree a few generations more than their fellow-men. Such ancient lineage, they imagine, gives them a right to boast of better blood of a more distinguished family than the commoners, and even if the ancestor at the beginning of their line was a pirate or a highway man, or one who has reached distinction by trampling under foot the rights of others, or accumulated the wealth upon which the power of his family was founded by grinding down the poor and robbing the helpless. What is the nobility of even the mightiest on earth compared to ours, which dates back four thousand years, what their family tree, if placed side by side with ours, which contains the most illustrious names by which men were graced, the names of those who are honored and respected and held up as patterns and declared as holy and regarded as inspired by all civilized men? And how did those, our patriarchs, achieve greatness and distinction? By building their fortunes upon the shattered ruins of the possessions of others? By depriving of their well-earned and established rights those who lived around about them? By no means. Was there ever a nobler, a more beautiful, a more admirable character than that of him whom we call our father Abraham? A man who stood in the midst of his fellow-men as a prince by the grace of God himself, he would rather suffer wrong than inflict pain upon the meanest of his brethren; the most unselfish friend imaginable, who paid with benefactions and deeds of charity him who had been so ungrateful to him; who was liberal-minded enough to pray even for the most wicked and degenerate; who was justly called a friend of God, and whose highest ambition it was to make a covenant with the Heavenly Father for himself and his descendants, that as he had fulfilled his recognized mission, "Be a blessing" to thyself, to thy family and thy community, to thy people and mankind, so they should forever recognize it as their holiest duty to be a blessing to humanity, to do the noblest missionary work, which does not mean to make others *believe* as we do, but to teach them that all can be good and noble and virtuous, independent of their honest belief which is their own individual property, and thus fulfil the word of God, "In thee and thy descendants shall all the families of the earth be blessed!"

Is not this a sentiment worthy being proposed and responded to once a year? Must it not have the influence of a sacred inspiration upon our children if they learn, we have a past history, four thousand years old, upon which we can look back with pride and satisfaction, but which also entails holy duties upon us and solemn obligations, which it would be faithlessness to shirk.

The second sentiment is one which has inspired the noblest acts whereby mankind has ever been graced. It is independence and liberty to which the second cup is devoted. It is to the memory of Moses. To our eternal glory the idea of liberty and human rights, forever connected with the name of Moses, had its origin in the midst of Israel—a circumstance so much more surprising, as it is in direct conflict with the conceptions of the eastern nations, in whose midst the Jewish religion was born. For among the oriental nations of antiquity, as of our day, liberty and freedom are unknown and incomprehensible terms. There the individual has no right, everyone is a cipher and a slave, the whole people a combination of men whose life and property are owned by the one despotic ruler. So it is to-day, so it was in olden times. King Pharaoh asked Moses, "Who is God, that I should listen to his voice, I know him not," I am God myself. And how much would despots of the present time like to act in the same spirit, though they lack the boldness of announcing it in so many words! How many set up their own desires and inclinations as their highest, their only law, and deny the existence of anything ideal before which they have to bow down and to whose dictates they have to yield? Surely just is the praise which the latest historian (Fred. M. Holland), of the "rise of intellectual liberty" bestows, when he says, "History can show forth no grander figure than that of Moses before Pharoah."

And should we not point with pride at this miraculous birth of liberty and independence amidst our ancestors? When the forefathers of the most highly civilized nations were naked savages or crude barbarians, the Israelites were a law-abiding people and excelled through the consciousness of human liberty and the respect of the rights · even of the stranger who lived in their midst. And is not this second sentiment the noblest one imaginable? And is it not meet to remember it at least once every year, and thereby to teach the lesson to each and even the meanest, that he is born free, that his conscience needs to bow down before no human master, that he is at liberty to choose for himself, but that he has also to bear the moral responsibility for his actions, of which none can relieve him?

The third cup at the festive board is devoted to the memory of our suffering fathers in their long wanderings without rest and refuge amidst the hatred and prejudice of the nations so undeservedly heaped upon their innocent heads. "It is to thank God, that he has watched over us and saved us amidst so many enemies, and has preserved us amidst so many persecutions, and has given us food and raiment, and never forsaken us."

O, how pitiful is it, that this long history of suffering is not more familiar to our people who in ease and happiness are so apt to forget the sad experience of the fathers! How inspiring is a reminder of their heroic deeds and the great sacrifices they were ever ready to make for their truth and the freedom of their conscience. Would that everyone realized the truth so beautifully expressed by Zunz and translated by George Eliot, "If there are ranks in suffering, Israel takes precedence of all the nations; if the duration of sorrows and the patience with which they are borne ennoble, the Jews are among the aristocracy of every land; if a literature is called rich in the possession of a few classic tragedies, what shall we say to a national tragedy lasting for fifteen hundred years, in which the poets and the actors were also the heroes"? Who can fail to be filled with enthusiastic love for his people and his religion, if but once a year he is reminded of those heroes, and a vista is opened before his eyes of many generations of men, women and children, who were always ready rather to give up their life than their freedom of conscience, their independent thinking?

And now we have reached the fourth and noblest sentiment, the one which, natural as it may seem to us, reflects the highest credit upon our fathers, and is the most characteristic feature of our faith. It is the sure victory of liberty in the future, the ultimate conquest of the world by the truth of God, as first so confidently announced by the ancient Jewish prophets. This firm hope and unshaken confidence in the final establishment of virtue and justice kept our forefathers courageous amidst their seemingly unbearable trials and the continual wrongs they had to endure. It revived their enthusiasm, so that in spite of constant disappointments they would never grow tired to repeat every year, "Though this year we are slaves, next year we shall be free men." They were swayed by the conviction, that

"Freedom's battle, once begun,
Bequeathed by bleeding sire to son,
Though baffled oft, is ever won."

This noble sentiment has become constitutional with the Jews from long inheritance. Since the oldest times the so-called *Passover of Egypt* had always been celebrated with reference to the *Passover of the future*, the deliverance from spiritual as from bodily bondage, which was expected in the future time, and as early a prophet as Jeremiah could say, "Behold days are coming, saith the Eternal, when they shall no more say 'as the Eternal liveth who brought up the children of Israel from the land of Egypt,' but 'as the Eternal liveth who brought forth the descendants of Israel from all the countries whither I had driven them.'"

In the Jewish religion it has always been recognized that no ceremonies can retain their vitality which refer only to the past, but while refreshing the memory of the past history, they must deal with live issues, must consider the present time and continually direct our look upon ideals to be realized in the future. Our fathers in their toils and in their misery never tired to repeat this hopeful sentiment, the fourth cup is devoted to the final establishment of freedom, the victory of justice and truth; they became never weary of inculcating it into the minds of their children until at last they reached the only freedom and liberty in store for them, that of the grave, and though they were laughed and scoffed at by their adversaries, for resigning worldly happiness on account of an ideal hope, never gave up their sublime expectations.

We can celebrate our *Pesach* festival with a lighter heart than our fathers, and in the third sentiment already we are able to include the termination of the wrongs and the injustice under which we had to suffer. For before all other countries of the earth our beloved land was dedicated to freedom, was predestined by Providence for liberty, and, while lacking the attraction of romantic ruins of mediæval castles, its virgin soil has never been violated by the footstep of the tyrant who tramples human rights under foot for his own advantage and aggrandizement. Liberty was destined to rule this favored land, and from it her sway shall spread to the uttermost corners of the globe, to fulfil the ancient word, "In thee shall all generations of the earth be blessed."

But is it therefore now time to discard the fourth sentiment? True freedom is still an unrealized ideal of the future for which we have to work hard, as long as there is not a perfect mutual understanding between all classes of men and all denominations, that goodness and virtue and charity and love are not the property of one part of the community to the exclusion of all others, but are perfectly unsectarian, independent of the mere accident of the religious creed, the common good of all men, only limited by the boundaries of a common humanity. Freedom and liberty will only be won when the ideal of our old prophets is generally understood of the universal fatherhood of God and the universal brotherhood of man. In the broad light of day we must teach this essence of our faith not by words merely but by actions, not only by professing it as a creed but by deed, by working in harmony with all our fellow citizens for every good and noble aim, ever ready to make sacrifices, as taught by the examples of our fathers, never deterred from practicing love and charity in the broadest sense, even when we have to suffer from narrow-mindedness and have to face remnants of mediæval prejudice. Only then can we expect to do our share in the work of Israel to prepare a time when all men will grant to each other full and unlimited liberty.

Let us continue every year to drink our four cups to the sentiments proposed on the *Seder* night, Abraham, the founder of Israel's mission, Moses, the father of liberty and independence, our noble, suffering sires, and our hope for ever-growing freedom and enlightenment.

JUDAISM AND TEMPERANCE.

SKETCH OF A SERMON FOR PESA'H, BY DR. G. GOTTHEIL.

Text: Thou shalt surely admonish thy neighbor and bear no sin on account of him. (Leviticus xix-17.)

The chief elements of the Paschal meal (סדר) with which we open the celebration of our ancient festival are: The unleavened bread, the bitter herbs and the wine. Of these three the latter is a Pharisaic addition to what the written law prescribes. Its symbolism is uncertain. Perhaps, as the unleavened bread is called "bread of misery," the wine was added as a sign of festal joy. Jesus, in celebrating his last Passover, treated the tradition of the fathers with the same deep reverence as the revealed law; blessed both and instituted both as mementos of his life; nay, in predicting his future triumph he omitted bread and chose the wine as a pledge of hope, which he assured his disciples he will drink new in his father's kingdom. Jesus solemnly recognized Pharisaism as preordained by God for the founding of the new covenant. He laid into the foundation stone of the church a scroll on which the Scriptural and the traditional law were traced with the same characters. The Paschal wine of rabbinical invention became the sacramental element on the Catholic altar and in the Protestant Lord's Supper, which is something worth remembering when the "Pharisaic enlargements of the law" are spoken of. A new interest has been awakened by the temperance agitation. Was the wine Jesus drank fermented or not? If the former, then there can be no wrong in its use; if the latter, his authority cannot be invoked against total abstinence. In other words, the Pharisee of old must decide for the Christian of to-day, whether he may drink fermented wine or not. Their spiritual heir, the rabbi of to-day, is asked time and again to declare the law of God in this particular matter. His answer can be only one—fermented wines were never prohibited if kept from contact with leaven, which is restricted to fermented grain products only. We are sorry we cannot offer the temperance reformer the much-coveted comfort of the example of Jesus. We may render him more substantial aid.

Not as total abstainers or total prohibitionists, but as a sober people, who have been effectively taught by their religion to use every gift of God and not to abuse it. The Jew has positively no understanding for this violent remedy. The demand for total suppression is a loud protest against the culpable laxity of the law in dealing, or, rather, in failing to deal, with the most prolific source of evil in the land, but the Jew, in this respect, is a law unto himself, and does not wait for the policemen to keep him from the clutches of the unscrupulous rum-seller or the more refined tempter in artistic halls of Bacchus. Total abstinence springs from a loathing of the poisoned cup from which thousands drink destruction and death. But, as in the dread days of Egypt's judgment, the plague has not entered our homes and so we do not "fear the wine because it is red,"

The genius of our religion is anti-ascetic. It frowns upon the Nazarite as being more of a sinner than a saint, because he needs extra bridles to tame his passions. It looks upon the over-pious man, who tortures himself with long fasts, as one given to folly, and declares it more meritorious to offer to God the round sum of one hundred daily benedictions for blessings enjoyed than to smite the breast and weary the tongue with penitential lamentations. We have no cause for total abstinence among us, but we have every reason to sympathize with those who have such a cause.

It is certainly not for us to ridicule the large class of our best citizens, who see no other means of coping with the scourge; a scourge that slays its sixty thousand otherwise healthy men and women annually in this country alone and brings ruin to a hundred thousand homes, where, but for that curse, peace and happiness might reign. The prohibitionist policy is a heroic treatment of a disease that seems to yield to no more lenient handling. We think their remedy Utopian. We Jews have an excellent outlet for all too ideal schemes—we relegate them to the time of the Messiah. When the lion shall decline the lamb that browses by his side and be content with eating straw, men will probably also cease craving for stimulants and choose water rather than wine. When the last sword shall have been beaten into a ploughshare, then may men refuse to earn money by supplying a universal want. As things now are the millions invested in an industry giving bread to many honest people and the need of beverage other than water, tea or coffee make all schemes looking to total suppression hopeless, and, what is worse, drive many moderate men into the camp of the rum-sellers.

Instead of wasting time, strength, money and eloquence on a policy certainly doomed to failure and arousing violent opposition, strict legal control ought to be insisted upon, and when legalized strenuously enforced. In this scale we ought to throw the whole weight of our experience and our influence. Here is the point to join hands and hearts with those who strive to break the yoke under which our nation is groaning. Good, effective laws, carried out with a strong, impartial arm—this is what the Jews should stand for.

FREEDOM, JUSTICE AND FIDELITY.

A PASSOVER SERMON, BY REV. DR. I. M. WISE.

Text: "Exalted is Jehovah, enthroned on high; he filleth Zion with justice and righteousness. The stability of thy times, the fort of salvation is wisdom and cognition; the fear of Jehovah is its treasury." (Isaiah xxxiii, 5, 6.)

The Mosaic Law enjoins repeatedly and very solemnly the duty upon the people to remember the departure of Israel from Egypt, never to forget that they were slaves in that land, and the Almighty redeemed them with a strong hand and an outstretched arm. The revelation on Mount Sinai begins with this memorial. The Sabbath commandment refers to it. Every holy day ordained in the Law is זכר ליציאת מצרים. The Passover feast was especially instituted, "That thou mayest remember the day of thy going out of the land of Egypt all the days of thy life"; this *all the days of thy life* one of the ancient sages understood to signify, we should be reminded of that event day and night, others saw in it much more than that, they understood these words to command or prophesy that the memorial of the exodus from Egypt shall never be forgotten, not even then, when a Messiah should liberate Israel again from bondage and servitude. The importance of that event in the life and religion of Israel is evident. Why is it?

The replies to this query are numerous. The first is, that a nation was born on that memorable day; it was the natal day of the first independent nation constituted upon the principles of liberty and equality—Israel was born, the first people that started into existence with a Declaration of Independence and the proclamation of liberty and equality, and was solemnly enjoined, never to forget for a moment the principle, which is the cause of its national existence, the end and aim of its political organization, the first message to humanity it was redeemed and appointed to promulgate in words and deeds. Therefore the Passover is called in Israel's liturgy "the time of our liberation."

This is not of political importance only. It is also of the highest moral importance. Freedom is the indispensable condition of goodness, virtue, purity and holiness. The free man only can be virtuous, moral and honorable. The slave, whose doings are compulsory, coerced to do this and shun that, forced to act so and not otherwise, the person without a free will is neither virtuous nor wicked, neither moral nor immoral, neither honorable nor despicable, all his doings are indifferent as that of the animal, the tree, the fire or any other element. Take away freedom from human nature and whatever remains of it is an anomaly, some nameless thing of human form and animal indifference. "Wisdom and cognition," of which the prophet speaks as "the stability of thy times and the fort of thy salvation," are the golden fruits of the free reason, the free-willed man only, they ripen not in the dark and dismal dungeon of the enslaved soul.

Truly so, says the man of common sense, but all this is in human nature without the memorial of the exodus, which seems to be a superfluous symbol. As long as history records man struggled for liberty, and so he struggles yet. He struggled and prevailed, he struggled and failed, only to renew the combat again.

Independence, liberty and equality are the watchwords in the combat, the painful struggles of humanity in the process of history. Truly so, we might say, but it is combat and struggle and defeat all the time. Why is it thus? Simply because one portion of humanity feels and maintains that freedom is man's birthright; another, if not the most numerous, evidently the most powerful class of the human family, ever did, and does now, hold that man is a being that must be tamed, managed, oppressed, ruled, kept under the iron rod of despotism, for he is not born free and the largest portion of mankind is without capacity for freedom, reason or conscience; state and church must continually supply the rabble with these treasures. It is evidently this illogical dialectics which that perpetual combat and struggle in the process of history demonstrate; and there is none to decide which is the right, which is the wrong position; anyhow none has done so yet. There is as much theology and philosophy on the one side as on the other, as much history also for the one faction as for the other. History is a series of drawn battles between the two armies, and none has as yet spoken the last word, which is right and which is wrong.

The only decision handed down from the highest court, the court on high, in favor of freedom, liberty and equality, is the divine revelation, the manifestation of Almighty God in the exode of Israel from Egypt, the liberation from bondage. In that event Israel's Thorah narrates that God spoke in favor of freedom, the Almighty decided the vexatious question. Therefore, I think, all the miracles narrated in connection with that exode were originally intended to declare and to prove that God did so, God thus made known his will to his children that man shall be free, as the prophet verily declares, "The fear of Jehovah is its treasury"; the religious belief of Israel—this is the Yirath Jehovah—in that exode is the treasury of freedom, this is its evidence, its divine support, its eternal rock, and naught besides it. Therefore that Thorah again and anon enjoins upon us the duty not to forget, never to forget "the day of thy going out from the land of Egypt all the days of thy life."

Freedom, intellectual, moral and political, is a gift of our heavenly Father to His children to enable them to become humanly perfect and perfectly happy, to attain the ultimate good, whatever this may be. Still this much is sure, that human happiness is the golden fruit of human perfection, not the perfection of one individual or one class, but the human perfection of the human family. Freedom without equality is a false conception, as those individuals or classes that are excluded from the enjoyment of equal rights with others are as much enslaved as those deprived of the rights guaranteed to others. Therefore it is self-evident that justice is the inseparable companion of freedom, justice to all persons, things, claims, opinions, beliefs. Before we can think of love, charity, benevolence, even wisdom and cognition, any intellectual or moral exercise of freedom which we call virtue, we must necessarily be just to all. So the prophet says of God that He provides salvation for all His children. "He filleth Zion with justice and righteousness."

With us this is the ethical principle, man is a free moral agent, freedom is his birthright; this is purely subjective, the objective reverse of which is the categoric imperative, man must be just. History and philosophy, however, do not exemplify this principle. There is no wrong imaginable which at one time and place or another has not been forced upon suffering humanity as a dictum of justice sanctioned by State, Church, domineering petty tyrants or mighty potentates. Egotism forged laws, despotism enforced them, all without any appeal to justice. Revolutions, only with long intervals between, demanded justice. Compare the ancient codes of Greece and Rome, including those of Theodosius, the Goths and the Church, think of the feudal law which is still partly in force; of the despotic governments not extinguished yet; think of the oppression, persecution, torture and slaughter to which were subjected Jews, heathens, schismatics, infidels, foreigners, serfs, slaves, the vast majority of mankind; think of the wrongs and outrages perpetrated yet under our very eyes, partly even in our own country, and tell where is the principle of justice actualized in the history of mankind. The impartial and fair-minded observer can find in every chapter of history only arbitrary selfishness, reckless egotism forging laws, irresponsible and remorseless despotism enforcing them upon enslaved and persecuted masses, blind dupes of State and Church, submerged in superstition, enraged to fanaticism, dancing or groaning madly upon the graves of freedom and justice. Therefore, philosophy does not, cannot tell with any degree of certainty what justice and righteousness are, because history is its sole source, and in this neither justice nor righteousness are actualized anywhere or at any time. Therefore the history of ethics is a long chain of errors, each reasoner seeks to correct the errors of his predecessors and producing new fallacies to be corrected by his successor. The progress achieved in 2500 years in this continuous wrestling of the spirits amounts not yet to an established code of ethics, of freedom and justice.

Here again your Thorah steps in with a resolution,

decision and certitude, which apparently is not of man, and tells you what is justice objectively, what is righteousness subjectively; and all nations possess only that much of those divine treasures, as they have taken, adopted and carried into practice from that Thorah. Strike out from the codes of humanity that which is taken from Moses and the prophets, and what remains are blank leaves with some uncertainties here and there which, like Jonah's gourd, spring up over night and perish over night. Here again your Thorah comes in and enjoins upon you "Remember that thou wast a servant in the land of Egypt, and the Lord thy God redeemed thee." God himself, the ancient expounders add—God himself did it, not by an angel, not by a messenger, not by a mediator, not by a Messiah, king or priest, but He himself in his glory did it. God revealed himself in that redemption as the God of justice who sets free the oppressed and punishes the oppressor—who executes justice, evenhanded justice, He is himself the eternal justice, and has told man what is justice, and how to be or to become righteous; to "fill Zion with justice and righteousness." It is only from the exodus that we know God's justice, for there is reward on the one side and punishment on the other, and the punishment also is for the correction of the wicked, "And the Egyptians shall know that I am the Lord." It is from the Thorah only that we know what is justice objectively and righteousness subjectively among men of freedom, that seek human perfection, the fort of salvation.

Fidelity, the inviolable adherence to and unshaken reliance upon God and his laws of freedom and justice, is the third cornerstone, upon which rests the structure of the Thorah. Fidelity is the import of the covenant between God and Israel, the covenant which was made at the foot of Horeb. It is that אמונת עתיך "stability of thy times" which the prophet calls "the fort of salvation"; the treasury of which is that "Yirath Jehovah," the religion of Israel. Moses, Isaiah, Jeremiah and most of the other men and messengers of God prophesied, that this fidelity, this covenant shall remain forever inviolable; inviolable on the part of God, inviolable also on the part of Israel. On the part of God it must be inviolable, for He is the אל אמונה God of fidelity, ever true, ever faithful, immutable and unchangeable. Man's sins do not annul God's promise to Israel, the ancient expounders of the Thorah maintained, basing upon Moses (Leviticus xxvi, 44, 45) which underlies also the similar prophesies of Isaiah, Jeremiah and Ezekiel.

Wonderful is the fidelity of Israel in its steadfast adherence to the covenant. There exists no nation on earth that preserved the God or the gods, the religion, the literature, the language of their ancestors of old, none besides Israel. Most nations changed their faith several times, abandoned and forgot their gods, abandoned and condemned their ancestors in their graves, forgot their languages, aye forgot where their cradles stood and where the graves of their ancestors are. Most all nations are the children of renegades in religion, language and country. Israel alone kept its faith to its fathers and the God of its fathers, their religion, language and literature. Israel alone, dispersed among the nations these 2000 years, without a visible head, without a country, standing everywhere and constantly within reach of the enemy's deadly weapons, maintained its identity with all its peculiarities as Isaiah prophesied 2500 years ago, "And their seed will be known among the nations, their offspring among the peoples; all that see them will recognize them that they are the seed blessed of the Lord." This is unshaken fidelity, this is divine covenant, or rather the proof thereof, the testimony of living witnesses. After a hundred generations passed away the world has changed, rocks have been ground to dust, mountains leveled, seas dried up, here stands the one hundred and first generation with the same God, Bible, language, the same hopes and faith—this is fidelity, this is divine covenant and irrefutable proof. This is a special feature of Israel's character, it is the nation of fidelity, therefore it is the covenant people.

Fidelity, stern and immutable adherence to any ideal cause, is the natural consequence of wisdom and cognition, and the fear of the Lord is its treasury. Those who embrace a cause without wisdom and cognition and are not supported by a strong religious conviction, will naturally waver and change and desert their flag occasionally and repeatedly. If you find any man changing principles every now and then, contradicting himself on main principles, flying from his own center in a tangent, you will surely come to the conclusion that man did not reason correctly at the start; when he embraced that ideal cause, he lacked wisdom and cognition from the beginning, or he has not religious conviction enough to sustain him in the position taken. This was the case with the nations with their infidelity and desertions. This is the case with all wavering, changing, self-opposing individuals. The reverse thereof is also true, if one embraces an ideal cause, and adheres to it firmly under all trying circumstances, all afflictions and obstacles, that cause must be one of wisdom and true cognition, rooted in the depth of reason and the opulence of religious conviction. Israel's unshaken fidelity is a strong evidence of the truth of the cause, to which it did and does cling and will for evermore. This fidelity is the testimony that Israel is the covenant people, and the substance of this covenant is truth, freedom and justice manifested by this noble virtue of fidelity to the cause, as also to the human family, the country, the society, fidelity in all walks of life.

This fidelity is a law of God, an attribute of the eternal Deity as well as freedom and justice. Therefore again the Thorah enjoins so often upon the covenant people to remember the exodus from Egypt, as that was the ocular demonstration of God's fidelity, God's faithfulness, God as the *El Emunah*, as Moses in his last song proclaimed Him. What He had promised to the fathers, as the Thorah narrates, he fulfilled to their descendants three centuries later, as Moses tells us (Deuter. vii, 6–9). The exodus was the evidence that Jehovah is the God of freedom, justice and inviolable truthfulness, and there is none besides him. These are the three pillars of Israel's religion, not because it is so true and right in our opinion, which runs contrary to the world's opinion, actualized in the world's history, but because God manifested himself to Israel in the exodus from Egypt in his attributes of freedom, justice and fidelity, and made these high and exalted towers of strength the indestructible monuments of his covenant with Israel forever. Therefore in remembering the departure from Egypt we unfurl again the immaculate banner of Israel, the symbol of truth, which is in freedom, justice and fidelity.

THE TEN COMMANDMENTS, OR OLD PICTURES IN NEW FRAMES.

BY REV. DR. HENRY BERKOWITZ, PHILADELPHIA.

The texts which are emblazoned in most commanding letters upon the scrolls of sacred writ spell out the telling mandates of the *Asereth Hadibb'roth* עשרת הדברות. We familiarly call them the Ten Commandments, but more correctly they are ten precepts, or propositions. It is sometimes said, "Let a man keep the ten commandments and he will fulfil all the requirements of religion." This is truth, but not the whole truth. He must keep all that the commandments express, but also much more. They are the seed, not the ripened fruit, nor the full blown flower. They are the cornerstone of religion. The cornerstone but not the capstone. The foundation but not the building. These are the axioms of conduct. The axioms of mathematics are not all of mathematics. But based on these self-evident truths are all the propositions of Euclid. The architect and the engineer start with these fundamentals and with them they work out the exact and detailed calculations by which a bridge is built to sustain so many thousand tons, or a building to serve as a magazine for the storage of so many hundred weight of bales and barrels of merchandise,

So likewise the Ten Commandments do not contain the solution of all moral problems, though in primitive and rudimentary form all ethics is embodied within them. With these brief and apodictic injunctions we must begin in order to clearly form our moral judgments and to decide our course of conduct. On them we build our characters. By them we solve the complex moral problems which from day to day confront us, growing out of the involved motives and issues of life, its unceasing conflict between duty and desire. They remain still unimpeached, the invincible, inviolable and everlasting truth. It is therefore not possible to say otherwise than that they are the voice of God —the divine above man speaking through the divine within man.

Each one of the Commandments is like a masterpiece of artistic genius. In a few bold lines it tells a whole story of human life and pictures a lesson of matchless power. These pictures have withstood the wear and tear and the test and criticism of ages.

Look upon the first picture! It represents the political life of antiquity. The background shows the massive masonry of Egyptian pyramids and sphinxes, the mighty battlements of great cities and their splendid temples and palaces. Here the lines between ruler and ruled are firmly drawn. Power is absolute. The governed, exist by mere favor. Thousands in burnished armor, riding in golden chariots, or trudging heavily through the burning sands, are the slaves of war. These are fettered in the bondage of arms and doomed to cruel death. Besides these other hordes of human beings crowd the canvas. They are the common people. Of these the masses are the slaves of toil, bearing heavy burdens. Under the lash of cruel taskmasters they are driven harshly and relentlessly to their toil.

For them there is neither rest nor mercy. See how they stagger and fall in their very tracks, bleeding and helpless, yet hounded on to the last vestige of their strength until they perish like beasts in their own blood. A wall of ocean waves divides all these from a little band of freedmen, who stand forth in striking contrast to all the rest. Their burdens have fallen from their backs; the shackles are loosed from their wrists. They stand erect with the light of joy in their eyes. Gratitude is written in every lineament of their countenances, as with expectancy they look up to the sweet-visaged patriarch who stands in their midst. His long, flowing beard rests on the tables of stone which he holds to his heart—his saintly countenance is wreathed in a halo of light, his finger upraised as he speaks, indicates that his words are pronounced in the name of God, for he says: אנכי יי אלהיך אשר הוצאתיך מארץ מצרים מבית עבדים (Exodus xx. 2), "I am the Lord thy God, who brought thee out of the land of Egypt and out of the house of bondage."

Around this ancient picture there is a frame of carved workmanship. It portrays the world's efforts to enlarge and expand the sublime precept of freedom which the old picture teaches. Here we see, as upon some triumphal arch, the story of the struggles, the wars, the revolutions and reformations, by which men made way for liberty from Egypt to America. Every heroic effort is here indicated, from the brave Maccabean conflict in the second century before, to the American Revolution, eighteen centuries after the Christian era when "freedom was proclaimed throughout the world and to all inhabitants thereof." The nineteenth century abolished slavery in Hungary, Prussia, Austria, Scotland; in the British, Turkish and Spanish colonies; it emancipated sixty million serfs in Russia; it freed five million negroes in North America. In our day it manumitted the slaves in Brazil. Thus the enslavement of man by his fellow-men is now forever doomed. Man in the exercise of his high moral freedom has made himself at last co-worker with Israel's God, the God of freedom. He has expanded that beneficent providence which led our sires out of Egypt, until all men, whatever be the house of bondage in which they may still be confined, are being triumphantly led out into liberty.

See the second picture! It places before us the religious life of the ancient world. Here stand restored before our imagination the great Temples of Thebes, El Karnak and Luxor, those of Memphis and Edfu with their colonnades and their columned halls, written all over with the sculptured story of man's struggles and triumphs. Everywhere is the beetle, whose spreading wings like rays emblem the Sun God, the creative force worshiped by men. Here the priests are busy at the sacrificial tasks, and in the care of the sacred ibis and cows, of the black bull and the phœnix, of the lioness and the cat, while in the long line of solemn sphinxes the stately processions wind their way to the inner sanctuary where the mystic rites are solemnized. All the world in groves and temples prostrates itself before the brutal forces of the material nature as instinct in animal creation or emblemized in the monster forms wrought by human hands. A waste of desert land stretches beyond, and on the farther side of the picture a dramatic scene is being enacted. The band of liberated Israelites is seen dancing in glee with wild noises and mad orgies around the golden calf, when lo! overlooking the camp, appears the law-giver coming down the mountain of Revelation.

In his righteous wrath he hurls upon the rocks at his feet the tables of stone. Their shattered fragments go ringing down the mountain side carrying the thundrous echo of his words:

"Ye shall not have any God before me. Ye shall not make any graven images nor any likeness of created things to bow down and serve them, for I, God your Lord, am a jealous God visiting the iniquities of the parents upon the children to the third and fourth generations of them that hate me, and showing mercy to the thousands of them that love me and keep my commandments."

There is an ancient rabbinic legend which says that when Moses thus broke into fragments the tables of stone, the letters that had been graven upon them were not destroyed but leaped, as it were, embodied in flame from their place and burned visibly and legibly in the sight of the people. There is a profound significance in this legend. It refers to the sublime fact that there a truth was blazoned forth to the world that has continued to burn in human hearts with unabated brilliancy. That truth is this, the false gods and the false doctrines proclaimed as religion, however powerfully they may be upheld, cannot last. Under the divine light of reason which burns perpetually, their falseness will at last be exposed.

The frame of this old picture is thus illuminated with the age-long record of the struggle of the human soul against the terrors of blinding passions; against the dread of dark mystery and the fears of superstitious ignorance. These created the false gods before which men cringed in abject debasement. Here is shown the triumph of light and intellect, the conquest of hope and devout aspiration. Little by little man grows into the conscious dignity of his divine likeness and dares to stand erect. Here is chronicled the change from the old motives of fear to the new impulses of love in religion. The long night of error is past in which man pursued the will-o'-the-wisp of those false philosophies, that enticed him into fatal marshes of corruption. The day has come and in the full sunlight of reason he sees the sublime heights of idealism and hears from the summit the voice which no longer terrifies the soul by emphasizing the threat "visiting the iniquities of the parents upon the children unto the third and fourth generations," but which rightly heard, calls and calls again in sweet and solemn appeal, "showing mercy to the thousands of those that love me and keep my commandments."

The third picture is one full of horrors that the eye refuses to look upon. In quick succession we see the mad practices of ancient worship. Rivers of blood flow from the altars on which the smoking hecatombs of sacrifice are offered to appease the offended deities. Behold! children are led through the fire to Moloch. Murder is done in religion's name. Every law of decency and morality is outraged. In drunken bacchanalian rites, men, women and children wildly commingle, marching and dancing to the tune of music that intoxicates every sense and frenzies the soul. Thus did men pattern after their gods of old. Ps. cxv., 8: "Like them are those that make them." They unbridled every passion, and indulged every vice when they drew near to their gods.

Round about this picture, as if to set the frame of silence about its debasing tumults, are solemn inscriptions. Above are the words of the third commandment, "Thou shalt not take the name of God for vanity." Beneath are the ringing sentences of the prophet: Isaiah i., 13-17, "Bring no more vain oblations; incense is an abomination to me, the new moons and the Sabbaths, your appointed feasts my soul hateth; they are a trouble to me; I am weary to hear them. And when you spread forth your hands I will hide mine eyes from you; yea, when ye make many prayers I will not hear; your hands are full of blood. Wash you, make you clean, put away the evils of your doings from mine eyes; cease to do evil; learn to do well; seek justice; relieve the oppressed, judge the fatherless and plead for the widow." On either side are these master words of the sweet Psalmist, Ps. xxiv: "Who shall ascend the mount of the Lord and who shall stand in his Holy place? He that hath clean hands and a pure heart. Who hath not lifted up his soul unto vanity, nor sworn deceitfully. He shall receive the blessing from the Lord and righteousness from the God of his salvation."

The fourth picture presents the industrial life of the ancient world. Kings and princes are luxuriating in palaces for whose splendor we know no name more dazzling and brilliant than "Oriental." All other human beings are spurned as of lower caste. Of these the lowest is that of the laborer. Toil is unremunerated by wages and has no rights that are respected. War, not work, is deemed the legitimate and honored occupation of men. To labor is a dishonor and a curse. Out over the hordes of fighting and slaving masses rings the strange and wondrous charge: "Six days shalt thou labor and do all thy work, but the seventh day is a Sabbath, consecrated unto the Lord thy God."

The frame of this picture is dinged, bruised and broken in places. Its inscriptions tell of the spread of the Sabbath idea from the little land of Judea among all the civilized nations of the globe. They tell how through it labor was dignified and the laborer steadily rose until in these days as never before he is free and honored, achieving the steady triumphs of his rights. The gospel of work as a divine injunction is known and heeded in the modern world. But alas, the gospel of rest, no less divine, is much dishonored, and most, alas, in Israel. Sabbath sanctity, the choicest gem which Judaism set in the crown of religions, is bedimmed and grown lusterless. The stress of the modern life has sadly invaded the serenity and joyous dignity of our Sabbath. Greed, materialism and sophistry are doing their best to utterly destroy it. Even those who are the avowed champions of right are often indeed in reality the worst foes of the Sabbath. Insisting upon the letter of its fulfilment by blue-laws and intolerant judgments they are utterly debasing its true spirit. Hapless Jews and Baptists are indicted in our courts and fined for working on Sunday. Their plea, that they keep the Seventh Day Sabbath, proves of no avail. The old blue-laws must be enforced and the fine collected. Such instances are legion. The broad humanitarianism which cares for man and beast and which gives to the commandment its divine force is totally abrogated by this inhumanity of man. Thus is the frame marred and broken. It awaits our fashioning hand to renew and embellish; to restore and adorn it as never before.

The fifth picture is one of domestic life. It portrays in contrast two distinct and totally opposite ideals of the home and its filial and paternal relations. In the one the father is the despot who owns wife and children, who rules their destinies by his absolute will, who may take their very lives and be accountable to none.

In the other the reverent patriarch lays his hand in blessing upon the child as he ardently admonishes him in God's name: כבד את אביך ואת אמך "Honor thy father and thy mother, that thy days may be long in the land which the Lord thy God giveth thee."

No frame is more beautiful than that in which this picture is set. The domestic ideal as it has been fostered and developed in Israel yields to none other. The family is the safeguard of church and state, of society and all its institutions. No thought has been more deepened and broadened than this of home culture. To-day the world sits at the feet of its teachers to learn more eagerly than ever before, the lessons of home-making and character building. Parents are finding out everywhere that honor cannot be gained by commanding, by censuring, by whipping, scolding or even by merely loving and pampering their children. Honor must be merited to be won. It must be held by worth as well as by years of experience, by wisdom rather than by ties of blood. Only such honor given at home as it is given abroad, will endure through trial and sorrow and live through loving service for life and last eternally beyond the grave.

The fifth, sixth, seventh, eighth, ninth and tenth commandments together suggest a picture of the crudest and most primitive civilization, subject to every disorder. Life and health, home and virtue, character and possessions are not safe until the stern mandate of the everlasting ought of Duty proclaims restraint in the solemn "Thou shalt not!" About this old picture the frame is of the most substantial workmanship and finished in the most skilful and artistic manner. It shows that the obverse of each one of these commands is implied and by the modern world rigorously demanded and enforced. "Thou shalt not kill" is fundamental, but civilization adds to the negative its positive, and asks also that thou shalt sustain and support life, nurse the sick, guard the orphaned and the suffering and look after the welfare of servants and employees. The humane care of life has risen to a passion in our days. Our greatest hero is the philanthropist—he who discovers some mode of relieving pain, or who founds some hospital or institution to care for the homeless, the helpless, the dependent or delinquent, the outworn and outcast of mankind.

"Thou shalt love thy neighbor as thyself" is the supreme fulfilment of the law. Because thou art created in the divine image thou shalt not defile that image by any unchastity. This sets the law of personal purity as the supreme test of a godly character. "Thou shalt not commit adultery"; and the rabbinical dictum "Let the honor of thy neighbor be as sacred to thee as thine own," sets the sanctity of the home as the keystone of the arch of civilization.

"Thou shalt not steal" requires that thou shalt guard another's rights and property. It is still a very low scale of society to which such a command is necessary. We call it at best semi-barbaric. Yet in our very days a leading maxim of the commercial world is "Competition is the life of trade." This is positively a false doctrine. In the long run competition kills. To work against, instead of with each other is a selfish, narrow and deadening policy. Only by working together do men reach the highest possibilities in the development of their country and its resources, and of their national, state, municipal or individual powers. By holding up each others hands all progress together to the truer and larger prosperity. Co-operation is coming by slow but sure degrees, in the highest civilization, to supplant competition.

"Thou shalt not bear false witness against thy neighbor." This implies on the contrary the noblest brotherhood among men. "*Noblesse oblige*," "the strong must nobly protect the weak." To advance the highest interests of the human family, lays the charge upon each one of us not to slander and abase, but to encourage and ennoble our fellow beings.

"Thou shalt not covet," sinks the plummet to the depths of all moral philosophy, and makes the motive the last and highest guage and standard of all conduct.

These old pictures from the texts of our Thorah I give you to-day framed in the larger interpretation of the deep experience and sage reflection of ages of human history. Hang them on the walls of your memory. Look up to them day by day. Study them with the eyes of the mind and let the soul be strengthened and exalted by them.

Our sages said of Moses, he was commanded "and Moses went up to God,"—*i. e.*, he looked aloft unto the ideal. "And Moses descended to the people,"—*i. e.*, he brought the ideal down to the real needs of their daily life. Therefore, he gave them concrete laws and practical precepts for the guidance of their conduct. So let us each day look up to these old pictures in their new frames, the masterpieces of religious workmanship, thus to strengthen our wills and renew our moral force so that when we come down to the commonplace application of principle in the affairs of every day, our religion may not be a vague and distant abstraction, but a real and present power for good and for truth. In this wise we may indeed make it true to say: "Let a man keep the Ten Commandments and he will fulfil all the requirements of religion."

GENIUS IN HISTORY AND THE HISTORY OF GENIUS.

A LECTURE DELIVERED IN ST. LOUIS, BY ISAAC M. WISE.

The earth on which we live is populated this moment by nearly fifteen millions of human beings, so that our country contains but the twenty-eighth part of the grand total of the human family, and it would take twenty-eight nations in numbers equal to the American to comprise mankind. Every one of those fourteen hundred millions of human beings, infants and idiots excepted, has a will of his or her own and an amount of energy to exert it. Every man's will is, in the first place, egotistical, because it is governed by the instincts of self-preservation. At a first glance it looks as though there were as many repelling and repulsive forces in society as there are individuals. And yet we behave pretty well. Neighbors live in peace. Nations live in peace. Disputes, quarrels, fights, insurrections and wars are the exceptions, occasional disorders, skin diseases on the social organism; and peace is its natural state. The idea that life is synonymous with combat, a war of each against all, and all against each, is certainly absurd. It is not true even among cannibals, inasmuch as they do not consume one another. As a general rule every man seeks peace, and the ruffians are mere exceptions.

This certainly proves that there must be in human nature a motive power to counteract and control his egotism, and this is his moral conscience. It is by the force that moral conscience exercises upon the will, that a social organism is possible, that we live together in peace. Egotism is the animal aspect of life, and moral conscience is its human aspect. The one is the manifestation of the will under the influence of the instinct of self-preservation, the other is the manifestation of the same will under the influence of the human instinct of self-elevation. It is the laudable desire of being or becoming better than one is or was before; and better in this case means more human and less brutal. Moral conscience is the sentiment that the right and good is right and good, and ought to be done; and that the wrong and evil is wrong and evil, and ought to be shunned. This fundamental sentiment is common to all men. No sane man ever did that which he knew to be wicked for the simple purpose of wickedness, nor did he shun that which he knew to be good in order to be wicked in his own estimation. The most wicked man seeks an excuse for his wickedness and cannot help respecting goodness. Also those persons who define conscience as an acquired attribute must admit that it could not be developed in a man if it were not an innate quality or capacity of his nature. Only that which is in man can be developed and perfected, nothing can be imposed on the race to become lasting and general. Mr. Charles Darwin himself, I think, cannot deny this truism of education.

Why, then, is moral conscience so elastic and variable? Why does it change so essentially among nations and individuals, under different climates and various outer influences? Why has conscience a history, a progressive development from lower to higher states? There is certainly a considerable difference between the consciences of the Russian peasant and the British philanthropist, the subject of the King of Siam and the American citizen, Draco and George Washington, the Roman patrician lady and Mrs. Lucretia Mott; whence that difference, if all men are born equal?

This certainly proves that there must be in man's nature a motive power to control both his egotism and his conscience, to balance, equipoise and direct both of them; and this motive power is reason. Reason defines and advises, selects and rejects, recommends and reproves; reason decides for the conscience what to call right and what to call wrong. Therefore, where the reason is deficient, the conscience is misguided by its definitions and calls that right which the more intelligent man would call wrong, and so *vice versa*. The conscience of the barbarian is as keen and forcible as that of a modern philanthropist, only the intelligence of the former is too limited, and therefore his conceptions of right and wrong are narrow and incorrect. Moral conscience among the generality of men, at all times and places, stands in fair proportion to the prevailing intelligence and enlightenment. The progress of the former depends on the growth of the latter. You might call this a Jewish idea, for it is thoroughly biblical and thoroughly rabbinical; but call it anything you please, it is, nevertheless, based upon facts, and has been acknowledged as a demonstrable truth by many a reasoner besides Thomas Carlyle. Wherever reason is clogged the conscience is dim. Viciousness is the offspring of ignorance; ignorance is the only original sin and stupidity is universal depravity, I think.

But here we are once more confronted by an enigmatical problem. Why are not all nations equally intelligent? Why are not all men equally wise? Nature or nature's God has given a fair proportion of latent and potential intellect to every individual, to every nation. The objects of nature are manifold and everywhere challenge the intellect to reflection and to comparison, to reason and to judge. Wherever man has dwelt, there was his school, going with him from the cradle to the grave; why are not all nations equally wise if they are equally old? If human intelligence is the sum and substance of sensual impressions from sensuous objects, as the realists maintain, and both the senses and the natural objects have not changed within historical times, why are not all nations equally wise? It is vain to maintain that some of them possessed more freedom, better means to preserve and to promulgate experience and information, for this only pushes the question one degree back, *viz.*, why were some intelligent enough to acquire or achieve those advantages, while others were too ignorant for such achievements? It is vain to speak also of elimatical obstacles, we know that Carthage, Alexandria, Athens, Jerusalem, Babylon and Persepolis flourished under the burning heat of the tropical sun, and we are told again and anon that all wisdom anciently came from India, Ethiopia and Egypt; when we know that Denmark, Sweden and Norway have given some of the finest apostles to science and art. Evidently man's intelligence depends neither on the nature of the soil nor on the position of the sun; why, then, are not all nations equally wise? If it is all systematical, mechanical action of the natural objects upon the senses, ganglia, nerves and brain, whence this marked difference in the intelligence of nations?

This proves there is a reason of reason, a lower and a higher kind of reason, a sensuous and a supersensuous intelligence. The sensuous intelligence is within every sane man's reach, can be, was and is grasped and utilized by all nations whose individuals are not deteriorated by moral corruption. The supersensuous intelligence must be taught and promulgated, because it is not in the objects of nature; hence it must be either invented by man or revealed to man by or to particular individuals, who first and originally conceived such supersensuous truisms and promulgated them among others. *The mind which originally conceives supersensuous truisms, together with the impulse to promulgate them, is called a genius.* And so we have arrived before genius. So genius governs sensuous reason, reason governs conscience, conscience governs egotism with its passions and affections, and each of them influences the will with more or less efficacy.

The characteristics of genius are (1) the original conception of supersensuous truisms, and (2) the impulse or inner necessity, to promulgate them. This impulse is common to a large number of communicative and talkative persons. Quite a number of persons speak much and say little, write volumes without inventing or discovering anything. There are plenty of books without one original idea and volumes without a supersensuous thought. Conversations quite animated and fluent are conducted for hours, or even days and weeks, without any higher idea, so that some fine conversationalists command no more than five hundred words of their respective language. Hence the impulse and readiness to promulgate many words, however beautiful and ingenious they may sound, is no criterion of genius. And yet genius never appears without this impulse. It must communicate its visions or conceptions irrespective of any benefit that might be derived from its revelations for itself or others, irrespective also of any harm or injury which might accrue from them. It must announce its revelations in words spoken or written, in song or music, in picture or statuary, in architectural grandeur or mechanical ingenuity, in the government of a nation or propelling an association onward to higher aims, in organizing masses or commanding armies upon the field of battle. It must, and does, manifest itself according to the influence of circumstances and the opportunities offered.

This idea is most strikingly illustrated in the Bible, first by Moses at the burning bush. He had conceived the sublime idea of redeeming his people from bondage, giving them nationality, organization, liberty, law and religion, and making of them God's chosen messengers to weeping and down-trodden humanity of all ages and zones. He felt the necessity of doing all that; he knew it was his duty to do it; and yet he wavered, for the task was too great, the enterprise too gigantic, the work itself too enormous. He hid his face, for he was afraid to look the fact into the face. He struggled, he wrestled, he excused himself with this and that. But in vain; he must. God's anger was enkindled against him, which is to say, against his will he felt himself compelled to embrace the great and sublime cause. Genius must. It has no will of its own.

Elijah, in the fiery wagon drawn by steeds of fire, soaring heavenward, is the most accomplished presentation of lofty genius, throwing in the shade all Grecian conceptions of fantasy. Poor, enthusiastic, inspired Elijah, who conjured the fire from heaven down upon Mt. Carmel and inspired the tens of thousands to exclaim, "Jehovah is Elohim!" flees to the wilderness for his life;

half-starved, worn-out and disappointed, he stands upon the barren rock and complains bitterly and beseeches vehemently, Let me alone, let me perish, let me rest in peace. No! says the Almighty voice, go and anoint kings and prophets, go and work. No rest and no will of his own for genius. It must. "The wise men have no rest in either this or the next world," it is maintained in the Talmud.

The same was the case with the Prophet Jonah, who attempted to escape to Tarshish from before the Lord. He refused with all his might to be a prophet of misery and destruction. But the sea stormed under him, the very deep rebelled against him, the monsters of the bottom rose up to compel him, and he was forced to go to Nineveh and perform the task of his genius. Genius must, it has no will.

Bitterly does the hapless prophet Jeremiah bemoan his lot, the dire necessity of being the prophet of woe to his people and its beautiful capital and temple. He was insulted, smitten, incarcerated and driven to the gates of death. He cried vehemently, why must just I be the messenger of wrath, and resolved to speak no more, to speak no longer. But it burnt like fire in his bones, go he must, speak he must, genius has no will.

Thousands of illustrations might be taken from history to the same effect. Not he is the great poet who writes a poem because he likes so to do; he is, whose heart bleeds and whose eyes weep over the lines which he pens on account of that mysterious inner impulse, that irresistible necessity which governs him despotically. This is true with the composer and every other genius. Some of us may, at some time or another, have experienced that pressure, that nameless force, that indescribable yearning and longing to do, say or write this or that so and so and you certainly feel the idea, which I lack the adequate words to express. However, if it is permitted to call the prophets of Israel geniuses, we must certainly be permitted to rank them among the highest of that kind; hence their characteristics are characteristic of genius. With them, there can be no doubt, one of the characteristics is that they spoke and acted by an irresistible impulse, contrary to their own will and happiness; hence this impulse must be characteristic of genius at least in its loftiest state.

Let us pause here a moment, ladies and gentlemen. I have said that the production of genius must be either invention or revelation. If invention it be, it is of man, if revelation it be, it is of the universal and supreme reason, it is of God. What compels the genius to act, speak, write or do against his own will and happiness? It is certainly not a power within him, for he protests and struggles against it, it is not by his will, it is against his will and overrules it. It must be an impulse from without, which acts upon him and compels him to act, speak, write or do against his will and happiness. The immediate cause of that irresistible impulse is the supersensuous idea which, as we say, rises in the mind of the genius; hence the idea itself must be from without, it is not invented, it is revealed, and therefore irresistible. The individual mind, we might maintain, receives communications from the universal spirit on the strength of this impulse; but we are not done yet with our definition of genius.

The main characteristic of genius is the conception of supersensuous truisms. We say, an idea rose in my mind, or an idea struck me, I had an original idea, without labored reflection or sagacious combination, and have no name for this phenomenon in our text-books of psychology, nor are we able to account for it. Gœthe and Mozart were asked how those magnificent, grand and beautiful supersensuous truisms rose in their minds, and they could not tell. Nor could ever any man of genius tell how those sublime conceptions rose from the dark background of the unconscious to the luminous region of consciousness. They appear in the mind as complete and finished pictures, symmetrical in their proportions, finished in their delineations, harmonious in their colors or sounds, melodious and self-evident in their combinations, complete and finished as was Minerva when she leaped forth from the brain of Zeus. Genius is infinitely more than talent. Talent studies, labors and combines. So are its productions studied and labored combinations, in which the joints and crevices are visible. Genius creates inseparable and indivisible units. Talent imitates, improves and groups together well-known parts to a novel oneness, deals in sensuous ideas and conceptions, and can only imitate nature to a certain extent, as Gœthe said: "Die Kunft soll nie die Natur erreichen," "art falls short of nature." Genius imitates not and constructs not; like the silk worm, it brings forth the softest tissues from its own body. Its productions are not of the sensuous order, hence there can be no imitations; they must be, and are, free creations. Talent may be inherited, acquired and lost; and genius is a commission from on high. Mysteriously Providence appoints its messengers, and bids them descend to us mortals with the messages of love and bliss, which the Father sends to His children.

And so it is genius which brings to us the supersensuous conceptions, the beautiful and the sublime, the good and the true, the æsthetical and ethical principles and the moral laws, the government of nations and the religion of the human family. Philosophy in its originality and science in its logical systems, as well as the supersensuousness in any branch of art, are offsprings of genius, and genius is heaven-born, and genius is heaven-gifted, and genius opens the curtains of heaven, to let us humble pilgrims catch a glance of the supersensuous, the good and the true, the beautiful and the sublime. Hence it is genius which makes history, which shapes history to a regular progression from lower to higher conditions, which adjusts the follies and crimes of egotism, the fanaticism of conscience, the devices of sensuous reason, all the wickedness, all the illogical doings of man, to one grand piece of logical succession and progression, one history of mankind from Adam to our day, including all and excluding none. So we can point out the place and position of genius in history. It makes and adjusts history according to the will of Providence, out of the egotism, follies, crimes, wars, conquests, insurrections, despotisms, oppressions, persecutions, fanaticism, avarice and gross selfishness, brutal passions and horrible cruelties of sensual man, governed by sensuous reason. The overruling spirit of history is actualized in the spirit of man; the logos of history operates through the geniuses in which it becomes decision, volition and action. That is the place of genius in history.

Permit me, ladies and gentlemen, to correct what I consider a mistake made by quite a number of prominent authors; also by Edward von Hartmann. It has been advanced that history is made also by senseless and apparently aimless and groundless commotions among large masses of people, who are agitated by invisible and often insensible agencies, perform useless and destructive tasks, run wildly and violently, and know not whither or wherefore. Still such indefinable, general commotions accomplish in the end some great historical purpose. This, they say, shows a visible interference of the logos or genius of history, of active Providence, in the affairs of man, and that is one of its methods to make, shape and adjust history. As illustrations of this idea they point to the Crusades and similar events in history.

I protest loudly against this horrible idea that by the will of Providence thousands and tens of thousands must be slaughtered and trampled under the feet of unreasoning and blood-thirsty barbarians, in order to actualize a certain point in the plan of Providence. The insensible and unconscious ghost of Edward von Hartmann's philosophy, as well as the dead and cold and irrational fetish of atheism, might be expected to do that or any other illogical thing, and as Schopenhauer desires, drive at last all men to voluntary suicide. We, however, who see in nature and history infinite manifestations of God's wisdom and goodness, feel and know with every fiber of our hearts and every spark of our souls, that God is the gracious and all-just father of man; we cannot admit for a moment that he leads the human family to its proper ends by a series of horrible crimes, either by vicarious atonements or the bloody sacrifices of relentless necessity. The wickedness of man is his own, in consequence of his free will, without which he could not be man. It is neither the devil nor any other outside agency which led Guiteau to slay the President of the United States. It is neither the devil nor any other outside agency which produced anti-Semitism in Germany, which infuriated the Russians to the commission of shocking crimes on their

Hebrew neighbors. The wickedness is man's wickedness, and the crimes are his own, when his egotism overpowers his moral conscience, either because his reason is defective or because oppression has obscured his intellectual light; either because he has been demoralized by others or has demoralized himself. We think that such general eruptions and murderous commotions of senseless multitudes are quieted in proper time by the proper genius, who adjusts the dissonances and leads the infuriated mobs into the rational channel, to turn the evil to good, as was often done, and especially in the Crusades. It is again genius, God-sent genius, and not blind casualty which makes and shapes the history of man.

This leads us to the history of genius itself, which is another cry of woe, a terrible dissonance in history. If Schiller had not written his *Theilung der Erde*, in which the starvation fare of the poet is so poetically and pathetically described, we would know anyhow that the men of genius by the thousands were condemned to be the beggars of society, ill-fated and badly-paid house servants of Providence. It is natural to genius to care less than others for the wealth and luxury of this earth. He is a stranger and sojourner on earth, and can expect of it no more than the possession of a grave, a sepulcher and a monument after death. Heaven is his home, he is Heaven's messenger, and with his eyes lifted heavenward he sees not the good things of this world, which the ants and day laborers of this earth find abundantly. No man eats at two tables. Those who eat of Heaven's manna cannot at the same time look out eagerly for bread and butter. No genius can be bent upon amassing wealth; hence it occurs not seldom that an ungrateful world puts him on the poorhouse list, and furnishes the starved man with a sepulcher and an artistic monument.

No man can be called a genius if he does not conceive original and supersensuous truisms, and every father loves his children best. But this world loves and values the sensuous and sensual much more, and looks upon the man of higher ideals and higher endeavors as an impractical, visionary, and perhaps, foolish man, who is pitied or derided, or thrown among the class of "cranks." So the poor genius with a world in his heart, the harmony of the universe in his soul, is refused an humble home and a frugal meal on this earth.

No man, as a poet, an author, a philosopher, a statesman, an apostle of freedom, justice, progress and elevation, can be called a genius unless he is far in advance of his contemporaries, unless he penetrates prophetically the mists of the future, sees and proposes now that which must be done now to avoid the threatening calamities and to hasten the approach of the blessing in store. Those who merely understand how to make use of passing events, current feeling and latent desires of the masses, are mere reflectors of the age, often very useful and very successful talents, but none of them is a genius, who must be far in advance of his age by prophetical penetration and executive force. Alas! the communities cannot look so far ahead, cannot perceive objects so high, so far beyond the narrow horizon, and the genius appears to them like the man in the moon, they have no understanding, no sympathy and no bread for him, and the poor genius withers and perishes. Centuries thereafter his sepulcher is whitewashed and an artistic monument tells posterity: Here lies a starved genius. Such is the history of genius in general, its exceptions are few and far apart.

The best illustration, perhaps, for the history of genius is the Hebrew people. The most sublime and most powerful geniuses ever known in the history of man are beyond a doubt the ancestor, the legislator, the prophets and the bards of Israel, whose supersensuous treasures are still the fountain of life and salvation to the civilized world. There exist no ideas and no ideals loftier and holier, grander and more universal and supersensuous than those which spouted forth from their great souls reflecting the brilliant colors of heaven and eternity to illuminate the millions of all climes and times. "Touch not my Messiahs and maltreat not my prophets," said the sacred bard.

On the whole the ancient Hebrews treated their geniuses pretty well. Wicked and idolatrous kings persecuted and even slew prophets. The people venerated and loved the messengers of the Most High. And so the spirit of those lofty geniuses was incarnated in the body of the congregation of Israel. Gradually the whole nation became the representative reality of its sublime geniuses, genius itself in its state of actualization. Open the world's history and shudder. The blood congeals in the veins and heart of every sensible man in contemplating the series of outrages perpetrated on the genius of Israel. So genius was treated by vulgar masses. Shift the sceneries, turn the leaves in the book of history and blush, Nineteenth Century, so genius is treated now, so Israel was outraged but yesterday in Protestant Prussia first, in horror-stricken Russia now. Hide thy face, benign humanity, cover thy blushing countenance, nineteenth century, so genius is maltreated now.

It is true that Germany as a nation has redeemed its name and fame in the last public election and has in part at least avenged the wrongs committed in its midst, and blotted out the stains imposed on its national character. It is no less true that the Russians are not yet out of the Middle Ages, whose spirit of slavery, ignorance, intolerance and fanaticism has been artificially preserved by an autocratic and despotic form of government, a selfish and rude aristocracy led by heartless demagogues. It is no less true that the whole civilized world condemns the barbarous crimes committed there, and has opened its gates for the fugitives from Sodom and Gomorrah. But this only proves that genius is not so universally maltreated now in Christendom as it was in the Middle Ages, when the Arabs opened their homes to receive the outcasts of the lands of Edom. At the same time it shows that the fate of genius has improved here and there, but not everywhere.

If you ask me why the Jews are forever the target of the petulant and barbarous assassins of human happiness, I must answer with the question, why is genius, why are the representatives of genius, the target of the same assassins? The Jew is the representative of eternal and the loftiest genius, he suffers the fate of genius. Are we not a century in advance of the world in our religious conceptions, in our charitable practices and in our fraternal oneness? Is not the Russian Jew also a philosopher in comparison to the vulgar peasant and nobleman of Russia? Are we not the perpetual protestation against the world's superstitions and atheism? Are we not the loudest voice crying in the wilderness for toleration, humanity and the unity of mankind on the moral and intellectual basis? Are we not, like all genius, centuries in advance of the vulgar ideas and ideals which govern the millions? Well, then, ours is the common fate of genius, because such is human nature, with this only exception that you or he and she may go and leave us to our fate. But you do not, you would not; you know why? Because you cannot; genius must, it has no will of its own, it bears a commission from on high which compels it to go and do the will of the highest authority.

These facts of history almost compel one to believe in a future reward, in the world of spirit and eternal bliss, where all those glorious geniuses, who have brought heaven's revelations to man, find their reward in light and life, in bliss and glory eternal. But they also bestow upon us the hope of a better future for the human family on earth. For in the same ratio as culture, science and enlightenment advance among individuals, communities or nations, the higher genius is respected, protected and honored. And the more this is the case, the nearer man approaches its loftiest ideas, and its ideal of ideals, God, love, virtue, righteousness, freedom and unity. Sleep not, slumber not, worry not, gifted sons of God, chosen messengers of heaven, blessed vision of genius; announce thy glorious messages of beauty, grandeur, sublimity, truth, love or goodness to weeping humanity, distil heaven's dew upon nature's languishing offspring; bring light, more light of truth and goodness into this labyrinth of obscurity, and let him who sent you take care of your reward. The fiery chariot drawn by steeds of fire carries Elijah heavenward. Below on earth stands Elishah, whom he has taken from behind the plough and made of him a prophet; below stands posterity, and admires the genius as it soars aloft heavenward, and leaves on earth its blessings in the minds of its benefited disciples, as it soars aloft in majestic grandeur and casts its mantle upon benefited humanity.

The grave of the greatest genius, Moses, is unknown to man. Genius has no grave. The true and the good cannot be buried. A tear for the sufferings of genius on earth, and thanks to God, that genius has no grave, and the good and true, the beautiful and the sublime, live forever imperishable monuments of genius.

THE NEED OF A LIVING CREED.

BY REV. DR. K. KOHLER.

In opening our Friday evening lecture course tonight, I wish to speak of the principle upon which we stand, to unfurl the banner around which we must rally, Israel's living God, and emphasize the need of a living creed. We call creeds such beliefs as are obtained from books and recited in formulas dry as the leaves in autumn. No such creed made and shaped by men have I in mind. A creed that makes and shapes our lives, that lends meaning and purpose to our existence, is what we need. There was a time of great distress and depression in Israel, and the farmer's son Gideon had to hide his wheat crops from the rapacious Midianites when an angel of God addressed him saying: "The Lord is with thee, valiant hero." "Why, if the Lord were with us, no such calamity could have befallen us," rejoined Gideon; but the angel said: "Go thou with this thy might, and thou shalt save Israel from his foes, for the Lord *is* with thee." Here is the history of all great men given in a nut-shell. They realize the hardship and woe of the time keener than the rest, but they also feel all the stronger the impulse to act, because God is a living power in them and no mere name. It is not learning and oratory, nor philosophy and science, nor any of the arts and forms of culture that make men great and give history its powerful impetus. It is the concentrated energy of faith in one single individual that moves the thousands and leads them to victory over hostile powers, however numerous.

A single man like Noah, or Abraham, or Moses saves a world from doom. A single Luther, or Cromwell, or Mendelssohn liberates generations. And by what means? By the creed that molded their lives, by the living God within them. However small their resources, they have God on their side, and His omnipotence is theirs. Doubt had no place in hearts like Elijah's or Luther's. They stood fast like a tower, though the earth shook beneath their feet.

We theorize too much. Our age of reason has raised a generation of critics, cynics and cowards. Most of us lack the strength to do great things, to bring great sacrifices for a great cause as did the men of yore. We cannot stand the flattering smiles of fortune, nor the frowns of misfortune. Agnosticism has become the disease of the century. Arguing avails nothing. All our lecturing has failed to kindle the fire of religion, the right enthusiasm of a holy conviction in our midst. Religion comes from within, not from without.

The Bible says, Noah and Enoch walked with God. "Walk before me and be perfect," said God to Abraham. And defining religion, Micah says: "Thou hast been told what is good and what the Lord requires of thee.] Do justly, love mercy and walk humbly with thy God." / To be sure, they had neither a creed nor a Bible in the days of the patriarchs and the prophets, but they felt the pangs of conscience, they carried the law of morality in their bosom, they had rules of ethical conduct even in the days of the Flood. Still they lacked a life-force, a motive power to fashion society after moral principles. There was no fear of God, no faith in God in the multitude. The patriarchs and prophets alone walked with God, held Him before their eyes as a guide and pattern of righteousness, and followed Him, and became the world's saviors.

We need a living God. Cold abstract principles do not create characters, do not make men just and good. You must have the animating spirit of goodness in you in order to be good. Whatever virtue and manhood the atheist displays, it is the fruit of the religion of his fathers.

Neither will all philosophy, all theories on optimism and pessimism, impart to you the strength to bear up bravely under trial and grief, unless you have learned how to walk with God as with a friend, to be sustained by the realization of His love and sympathy and for His sake to suffer and to sacrifice whatsoever He demands. "Have I God with me in heaven, I need nothing on earth," says the Psalmist.

To Judah, the Saint, a Roman emperor sent a rare jewel as a gift, and in return he forwarded to him a little scroll with the "Sh'ma Israel" written on it as a charm, saying: "Mine is more valuable than yours. Your treasure I must constantly guard against robbers; mine will guard you and your treasures." Yes, whatever men prize, life or earthly goods, is not safe and needs watching. Your religion watches over you, shields your character, lifts you above trial and temptation. For your own safety's sake choose God as leader, make Him your strength and your victory!

But you do not stand alone. Religion is not, as you imagine, a mere matter of choice. Whether you recognize it or not, you are, with every blood molecule in your veins, with every cell of your brain, with every fiber of your heart, Jews. You cannot shirk a duty imposed on you by all the force of a four thousand years' history. Either good and loyal, or bad and disloyal Jews—this is the issue before the world. To be or not to be, to be either godless humanitarians, lost in a vast sea where there is no anchoring ground for the soul, or firmly planted upon the Rock of Ages and pointing to the goal whither the centuries of history are marching? This is the question for the enlightened Jews to-day.

What gave the Jew the power to resist a world in arms and become the unconquered conqueror of the centuries? Not his treasures of gold, nor his worldly wisdom, though he knew how to appreciate both. It was his faith that preserved him and kept him alive. It was his God who triumphed over all the art and philosophy of Egypt and Greece. It was the living God of Israel who vanquished all the dead gods of Pagandom and challenged the God of Christianity who died on the cross.

The secret of monotheism is that it defies the rule of arithmetic and asserts that the One is more than the many. Count all the wheels and rudders, the sails and masts, the men and goods in a ship, what are they against the one who stands at the helm and steers it towards its goal? So are the myriads of hosts of heaven and the millions of forces and forms of the universe nothing against the Unseen, yet All-seeing One who shapes and directs their course. And of what account is million-headed humanity, what are all the mechanical and dynamic powers that keep the machinery of social life going, what are the political or ethical motors of history, the ages, the nations, the races and sects, compared with the One Mind for which all minds yearn, the One Source of Love from which all hearts derive inspiration and comfort, the majestic Being who marshals them all and, wherever and whatsoever they are, His everlasting arms are beneath to carry them whither He wishes. With this God our fathers walked and braved the fire and the sword, the onslaught of time and the deluge of sin and suffering round about. This God of the Bible has become humanity's God, the luminous center of our civilization, the Tower of Christendom, the Shield of every home, the Refuge of every devout soul. And we, the first-born among God's children, dare deny Him and suffer His name to be desecrated in high and lowly places and fall into oblivion in our own homes? As was said to Jonah: "While all the rest lie on their knees in prayer and adoration before the Most High, darest thou, God's prophet, sent forth to preach His truth to the Gentiles, remain asleep in the face of the raging storm?"

No wonder that the modern Jew is despised, disliked and distrusted. The Jew without a God is a monstrosity, an object of fear. We are weak and count little in the council of nations, because we are divided, we are split into factions, without the uniting bond of a living creed. Doubt and unbelief have sapped our strength, our manhood. In quest of mammon, we have lost sight of our goal, of our God.

Let us again stand for the living creed of the Jew, for Israel's Holy God, for Israel's Bible, for Israel's Sabbath, for Israel's home sanctity, for Israel's law of justice and truth, and united we shall be invincible. Let us rally again around our synagogue, as the Christian does around his church. Let us bring the needed sacrifice for our father's faith to make it our source of strength and our purpose of life, and we shall see the world at our feet. Too long have we been trifling with the name of Jew. Let us be Jews in creed and in deed, positive and emphatic both in belief and observance, proud of our history, eager to work out our task as Jews, and, like Gideon, we may leave thousands that are timid behind, but go with the hundreds that are faithful and true and win the battle, for the God of mankind will be with us. Amen.

"WHO IS THE REAL ATHEIST?"

BY REV. DR. ADOLPH MOSES, LOUISVILLE.

Time was—and that time does not by any means belong to a remote past—when atheism was regarded as the most heinous crime of which a human being could render himself guilty. To be accused of atheism meant to be dragged before the tribunal of the state, as was done in the days of antiquity, or before the bar of an ecclesiastical court, as was the practice during the Middle Ages and for nearly two centuries after the Reformation, there to be arraigned as the worst of criminals, compared with whom even a murderer seemed to be an angel of innocence. If convicted, and an atheist was rarely acquitted, he was condemned to die a felon's death. The curses of the community followed him to the place of execution. No tombstone was allowed to mark his resting-place. One suspected of atheism was shunned like a leper, and hated as if he were a fiend incarnate. Yet how many glorious champions of truth, how many path-finders of humanity, how many saints of the earth, whose noble lives were the best indications of the belief in a God of holiness, have been persecuted with merciless fanaticism as atheists, as the worst enemies of the human race! The Greek philosopher, Anaxagoras, who taught the profoundest of all religious doctrines, that the universe was shaped into purposeful harmony by an All-wise and Almighty mind, being accused of atheism was thrown into prison, from which he secretly escaped and then fled from Athens in hot haste. Even his powerful friend Pericles could not protect him against the suspicion and the hatred of the masses. Socrates, the wisest and most pious of all Greeks, whose philosophy marks an epoch in the history of the human mind, and whose life came to be to the Hellenic world, what that of Jesus is to Christendom, was condemned by an Athenian jury as an atheist, and in his 70th year compelled to drink the cup of deadly hemlock. Giordano Bruno, on the 17th of February, 1600, was burned in Rome as an enemy of God. And yet that reputed atheist taught, that God is the unity of the universe, the universal substance, the one and the only principle, the efficient and final cause of all, the beginning, middle and end, eternal and infinite. Spinoza, whom Schleiermacher called "a God-intoxicated man," he who ascribed real existence to God alone, declaring all finite beings to be mere manifestations of the Infinite and Absolute, was not only excommunicated by his own co-religionists, but was until recent times universally regarded with horror and hatred as the worst and most dangerous of atheists. The Jews were loathed by the Pagans as a people that believed in no God. So utterly fallible and so baneful in its effects has the world's judgment in all times and among all nations proved to be, as regards atheists and atheism. As a rule the so-called atheists of one age become the venerated religious teachers and spiritual guides of after ages. Those that perished amid the execration of their generation came to live transfigured in the mind and heart of later generations as types of an ideal humanity.

The fact of the matter is, no original thinker, no genuine seeker after truth, has ever been a real atheist. The alleged atheists simply differed more or less profoundly from the theology of those who passed judgment upon them. The Greek philosophers who were indicted on a charge of atheism did not believe in the Olympian gods, holding as they did monotheistic views. The Jews were hated by the heathen world as atheists, for the reason that they denied the existence of the gods of the Gentiles. Similarly the men that were hunted down and brought to an untimely end as atheists in Christian lands, only rejected certain dogmas, held by the established churches to be essential principles of faith, without which it was believed religion would be destroyed.

Again, most scientists are reproached by over-zealous theologians with being atheists and teaching atheism. "You teach an atheistic science," they cry. "You leave God out of your astronomy, your geology, chemistry, botany, zoölogy and physiology. No mention is ever made in any of your writings of the Maker of heaven and earth." Only blundering stupidity, going hand in hand with blind intolerance, can speak thus. It is not within the province of science to teach religion or metaphysics, to prove the facts of experience by referring them to the highest and last cause, to trace all phenomena back to the ultimate ground of existence.

There is certainly no religious mathematics, there is no room for God in a treatise on geometry. The engineer who elaborated his plan for the Brooklyn bridge was not expected to start with the premise, that all the physical laws on which he based his calculations, measurements and adjustments, were perennial manifestations of an infinite, eternal and immutable power, that we worship as God.

It is the sole office of the investigator of nature to ascertain by conscientious observation and careful experiments all the knowable facts within the range of his experience, to arrange them in the order of their closer or remoter relationship, to find the bond of union which binds them altogether into a systematic whole, to discover the laws, according to which they live, move and have their being. It is the function of science to drive the notion of accident and caprice from her entire territory, to show every physical event as flowing of necessity from a preceding physical event as its cause, to demonstrate that no phenomenon in nature stands apart for itself, but forms a necessary part of the whole order of the universe, to connect by a chain of cause and effect whatever is or happens in the present with the remotest possible past of the heavens above and the earth beneath or the waters under the earth. Science is neither theistic nor atheistic. It is as little religious or irreligious as cooking, building, sewing, or ploughing. It deals only with what is within the ken of the senses, and its boldest conclusions and theories in the last resort go back to what the senses bear testimony to. Science proper has nothing to do with what is supersensual or beyond the reach of the senses. It does not meddle with questions relating to the origin of things, nor does it extend its inquiry to the ultimate ground of all being. It is exactly where science ends that philosophy begins. The subject matter of philosophy is the infinite and absolute, the eternal ground of all existence, the inscrutable power behind all phenomena, the cause of all causes, the beginning, the middle and end of all existence that which alone is, was and forever will be. The existence of the Infinite and Absolute is to all systems of philosophy the highest and most certain of all truths.

The idea of the Eternal is incomparably more incontrovertible than the several finite things which we may touch, taste or smell. The Infinite is to philosophy the only true reality, while the finite is regarded by it as enigmatic, doubtful. And shall we decry these supreme philosophical ideas as rank atheism, because the philosophers prefer to call the eternal source and cause of all existence the Infinite and Absolute, instead of calling it by the name of God? The Hebrew name Yahve, he that is, was, and will be, he that causes all being, corresponds exactly to the philosophical term of Infinite and Absolute. The philosophy of Spinoza, the best hated and calumniated of all reputed atheists, ought to be called, according to Hegel, acosmism, the doctrine of the nothingness of the world, while reality is ascribed to God or the Infinite alone. What is true of Spinoza holds good of all philosophers, from Thales down to Herbert Spencer. None of them was an atheist, popular prejudice and priestly fanaticism notwithstanding. "But have not your philosophers," some might ask, "asserted over and over again, that we cannot prove the existence of God? Has not your master Kant used the gigantic powers of his mind to demolish one after another, all the time-honored proofs of the existence of God?" It is not in wisdom that you ask thus. It is because Kant and other thinkers of equal originality stood like Moses face to face with the Eternal and Infinite, that they wished to show that all theistic arguments are either untenable or insufficient. How can we prove that which is itself the proof of everything else, upon which all other truths hang, without which all knowledge would be vanity and a striving after wind? To prove means to trace back what is uncertain and doubtful, to what is certain and beyond a doubt, to explain the unknown by referring it back to what is known, by showing it to be akin to what is recognized and understood. But this process of proving must at last reach a limit. We must finally arrive at something, a proposition or cognition, which we cannot demonstrate, because there is nothing beyond it, in which it might be included or to which it might be linked. It is the supreme truth, the most certain and immediate of all cognitions, it is the foundation upon which all other verities rest, and without the recognition of which all truth vanishes.

It can neither be proved nor does it require proof. "The idea of God or the Infinite is this most general truth, which cannot be reduced to a more general one. It is the deepest truth to which we can get. It cannot be explained, it is inexplicable, unaccountable." But what of materialism, is it not atheism? Are there not philosophers who derive all life from the lowest to the highest from matter and motion, and deny the existence of mind or anything akin to mind in the universe? My answer is, no serious thinker in our days holds such views. Materialism has been refuted and exploded as a theory of the universe. It does not account for the existence of mind in man and animals. How can mind, which is absolutely different from matter and motion, be the offspring of matter or the child of motion? We can by no effort of thought conceive how matter and motion could be changed from what they are and be transformed into consciousness. It is simply unthinkable. And if all matter is believed to have an inner side to it, to be endowed with the qualities of feeling and the dim germs of thought, then it is no longer matter, but something else, something higher. From whichever point of view we look at it, philosophical atheism turns out to be a mere fiction, a mere delusion of theological zealots. But who are the real atheists? They whose *conduct* belies their belief in the existence of God, whose *life* forms a glaring contrast to the idea of God. The belief in a God is not simply the highest and most certain of all truths, it is also the greatest and most potent moral idea. The idea of God implies the idea of divine perfection and absolute goodness. God and goodness are synonymous, interchangeable terms. If we believed that God was not goodness, we might fear Him, but we could not adore Him. A good man would appear to us more worshipful than He. Religion and philosophy agree in holding that morality is the highest manifestation of the infinite in and through the soul of man. Whatever we may think of its origin and development, as it is, it doubtless is the most glorious incarnation of the inscrutable Power, of the Universal Self. To believe in God does not mean that we simply allow that He exists, it means that we strive to walk in the luminous footsteps of His holiness, to walk in the ways of His justice, truth and mercy. Every virtuous action is a true act of worship. To curb our passions in obedience to the laws divine engraved upon the tablet of our hearts is the grandest homage paid to the idea of God. To smite and overthrow the vaulting instincts of selfishness in order to serve the common good of all, is the strongest proof that a God of goodness inspires the breast of man. He is an atheist who professes to believe in God but whose deeds put his faith to shame. He who declares that he considers the Ten Commandments a revelation of God and yet violates one and all, he is the real atheist. He who acknowledges that we should recognize no other God beside the Eternal, and yet worships his own poor self as the highest being and places his own interests and pleasures above the highest interests and aims of humanity, he is a real atheist. He who perjures himself, who swears a false oath or utters lies to obtain profit or gain favor, he does practically deny God, he demonstrates that he does not believe in Him "that will not let him go unpunished that taketh His name in vain." Whoever fails to honor his father and mother as the representatives of God on earth, whoever, in heartless selfishness, neglects his aged parents and refuses to surround their declining years with blessings and comforts, he is an atheist, though he daily bend his knee in adoration to Him and sound His praises in the midst of the assembly. He that makes of himself a slave of Mammon, who in his greed to amass wealth, lets the higher powers of his mind and heart run to waste, verily he is an atheist; he does by his conduct prove that he does not believe man to be a child and image of the Most High, destined to pattern his life upon that of divine perfection. He that defrauds his neighbors in any matter great or small, who uses false weights and false measures, is an atheist, he does not believe in a God that hates deception and injustice. He is an atheist that deprives the toiler of his wages, and takes away from the needy the fruit of his labor. That man is indeed an atheist, who robs the substance of his fellow-men by violating the laws of the land, or by bribing legislatures to enact wicked laws to favor his iniquitous schemes.

Whoever sacrifices duty and conscience to his passions, is a rank atheist. The priest at the altar is an atheist, the teacher of righteousness and faith, whose heart burns with the unholy fire of lust. Though he make many genuflections and lift his eyes in prayer to Heaven, he does deny God in his sinful soul. All those were real atheists, who persecuted their fellow-men on account of their faith, who tortured and murdered the children of God in the name of God. Torquemada and Arbenas were atheists, in spite of the fact that they scourged their bodies and sang many litanies in honor of their God. That ruler is an atheist and an enemy of God, who grinds the faces of the poor and needy, who oppresses men on account of race and religion, who deprives human beings of the right to earn a livelihood, who withholds from them the means of acquiring knowledge and leading the lives of human beings. The Czar of Russia is an atheist, although he is at the head of the National Church; his wicked counsellors deny God, because they rebel against the laws of divine justice. He is an atheist who calls darkness light and evil good, who praises the despot, that drives mothers with their babes out of their homes in mid-winter, and causes many infants to die of cold and starvation. The irreverend Dr. ...... is an atheist, though Sunday after Sunday he cuts capers in his pulpit, and calls himself the servant of God. The God of truth and justice is not in his heart, else he could not call a tyrant a benefactor of his people, who causes infinite woe and misery throughout the length and breadth of his land. All those teachers of religion are atheists, the Stoeckers and the Bohlings, who on Sundays preach from their pulpits, "Love thy enemy as thyself," but as soon as they step out of their church, preach and practice hatred and malice, spread calumnies and baneful falsehoods, and excite in the breasts of the masses vile and blood-thirsty passions.

Whoever holds that a man can be religious without trying to be absolutely just, truthful and merciful toward all men, denies and blasphemes God. Whoever treats his fellow-men with contempt, and deems them unworthy of associating with him on account of race or religion, is an atheist, because he practically denies that all men are children of one Heavenly Father, that loves them all and whose majesty resides in them all. It is on account of such practical atheism that the earth mourns and is full of desolation. It is on account of such practical atheism that the cries of the depressed and down-trodden are heard. Such atheism is the parent of infinite woe and misery. Such practical atheism has drenched the earth with the tears and the blood of the innocent. Alas, how many are entirely free from practical atheism? Ministers and laymen, men and women, Gentiles and Israelites, one way or another deny God in their conduct. Oh, let us not glory in the religious doctrines we hold, let us not boast of the principles of faith, which we profess. By our fruits alone let us prove that we believe in an all-just, all-wise and all-merciful God. Let us gird ourselves with strength and strive to establish the kingdom of God, the kingdom of righteousness and love on earth. Let us endeavor to make our lives symbols of the perfection of God.

WHAT WE HAVE TO BE THANKFUL FOR.

BY REV. DR. ADOLPH MOSES.

Pricked by the whip of anti-Semitism, the Jews have, within the last fifteen years, been dwelling with a sense of bitterness bordering on despair on the painful difficulties which beset their path and on the cruel wrongs which are being done to them in so many civilized lands. Our best men abroad as well as in our country have been busy averting the stings and arrows of outrageous prejudice to which we are everywhere exposed. Our pulpits and our press have of late years been ringing with solemn protests in the name of humanity against the superstition, the pride and fanaticism of race whose poisoned shafts are aimed at us as alleged aliens. Most sensitive and refined natures have been consuming their hearts with grief because they see the Jews' ardent love for their fatherland and their fellow-citizens despised and met with haughty disdain. The curse and shame of anti-Semitism is uppermost in the minds of the noblest sraelites. They are compelled to reckon with it for good and evil, and to grapple with it along the whole line of battle which it has opened. The warfare of ages which a quarter of a century ago was generally believed to be fast drawing to a close, and soon to terminate in permanent peace and spiritual fraternization, has been renewed on the continent of Europe with a fierceness and virulence which may well appal the stoutest hearts, and fill the most hopeful with gloomy forebodings for the future.

Yet it behooves us not to look too steadily at the dark side of the struggle, but to take into account the many bright and cheering elements in our present condition for which we ought to be thankful to the conquering spirit of humanity. Above all, we should not contemplate the old yet ever new struggle for light, for recognition and brotherhood from a purely Jewish and narrow standpoint, but from the point of view of universal progress, moral and spiritual. We should regard the ceaseless struggle we are engaged in as the most typical form which the perennial war of evil against good, of justice against injustice, of broad monotheistic humanity against narrow and race-bound paganism assumes. Let us be grateful for the blessings of liberty, religious, civil and political, which the worshipers of Jehovah in America, England, France, Holland and Italy, in Sweden and Denmark, enjoy to the fullest extent, which are guaranteed to them by the fundamental laws of Germany and Austria, although the practice in those Germanic empires is still sadly halting behind in the theory. Let us be thankful for the countless gifts of material civilization in which we are allowed to participate. Let us more especially render thanks to the genius of the nineteenth century for the invaluable boon of modern intellectual and artistic culture in which we are freely permitted to share in accordance with our capacities, aspirations and labors.

Compared with the deplorable and to all appearance hopeless condition of the Jews throughout the Christian world down to the latter part of the last century, their present situation in all civilized countries may be called a veritable paradise. Had a prophet arisen among our great grandparents and drawn a truthful picture of our life and its favorable surroundings, of our free and fruitful activities, of our achievements and our position in the world, they would have declared that so happy a change could only be brought about by the coming of the Messiah, whose superhuman power would overthrow the established order of things and substitute for it the kingdom of heaven. For an Israelite born and bred in the atmosphere of American liberty and equality, of material ease and comfort and intellectual expansiveness, it requires a strong effort of imagination to realize the state of utter wretchedness, of social degredation and mental isolation in which his forefathers were forced to live from the times of the Crusades down to the last quarter of the eighteenth century. Only an acquaintance with the poorest Russian immigrants, fresh from the land of barbarism, persecution and despostism, may give to native American Israelites a somewhat adequate idea of the lamentable state of the Jews in Christian Europe, before the liberating forces of enlightenment and tolerance had issued forth from America and France, and started on their career of world-conquest. The Jew was hated as a natural-born enemy; he was despised as a pariah and treated as an outcast. There was no species of wickedness in the whole register of vice and crime of which the Jews were not believed capable. All good Christians were convinced that the black heart of the Jews was constantly brooding over ways and means to inflict all possible harm on the body and soul of the followers of Christ. It was generally held that the Jews of every country did year by year torture and murder a number of Christian children or adults for religious purposes. The blood of the victims, it was asserted, was by secret messengers distributed among the various congregations, to be mixed with their passover bread. More innocent Jewish blood has been spilt under the impulse of this mad belief than all the blood of martyrs shed for the glory of the cross. Whole families, whole congregations were often massacred or burned alive, because a Christian child happened to be found dead. Priest and layman, nobleman and serf, alike gloated over the agonies of the tortured Jews. The shrieks of dying Israelitish mothers, fathers, and children mingled horribly with the hallelujahs and anthems chanted by fanatical monks in praise of the holy Trinity. The feast of Passover was celebrated with fear and trembling; for a furious mob might any moment burst in the doors and with murderous yells fall upon the helpless wretches and turn their songs into lamentations, their feast of joy and liberty into the gloom of a subterranean dungeon.

Let us be thankful for the progress the Christian world has made with regard to that dreadful belief, which was once held by high and low, by the learned no less than by the ignorant, which transformed human beings into demons, and changed gentle women into blood-thirsty furies. Let us be grateful to conquering reason for the victories which light and humanity have already won over darkness and blasphemous fanaticism. Only the vilest, the most benighted of men, nowadays, still hold fast to the mediæval blood-story. Only a dwindling minority of degraded wretches, of dehumanized calumniators, pretend to give credence to the disgraceful fable. True, only a few years ago enlightened Germany gave to the world the pitiful spectacle of a trial in which the old monstrous belief in ritual murders by Jews was in all seriousness upheld, both by so-called witnesses and lawyers. True, a number of secular and religious papers, both Protestant and Catholic, stoutly maintained that such murders were likely to occur even among the Jews of to-day. But the world at large cried shame on these proceedings. The conscience of the German people rose in indignation and wrath against the shameful instigators of that trial. The voice of perjured priests, miscalling themselves Christians, the voice of vicious and lying men accusing us of the most heinous and senseless of crimes, cannot prevail against the great heart of modern humanity, which repudiates with horror the falsehoods and blasphemous calumnies of those disguised worshipers of Moloch. This change of attitude of the European mind with regard to the most brutal and cruel calumny fabricated against us, is due to no isolated cause, is to be ascribed to no special line of reasoning, setting forth the baselessness of the mediæval accusation. It was rather the outcome of a general process of moral transformation and regeneration which set in with the Reformation, with the return of Christendom to the teachers, lawgivers and apostles of Israel; with the return to the living fountains of righteousness and mercy perennially welling up in the Bible. Till that age of moral awakening the European nations were Christian only in name. In their modes of feeling, habits of thought and ways of action, they were pagans like their forefathers.

The very essence of paganism, ancient and modern, consists in relentless hatred of those regarded as strangers, in sleepless suspicion of those who do not worship the same divinities. The pagans of all times and climes do not believe in the humanity of all human beings, in the attributes of goodness more or less common to all men. The very conception of humanity embracing all the families of the earth, the idea of the spiritual and ethical unity of mankind is foreign to their minds. They do not realize the supreme truth, taught by the prophets, that all men are stamped with the spiritual likeness of God, that the divinity of reason and free will resides in all souls, and makes all the children of men of one kind. The true Israelite, be he called a Jew or a Christian, has therefore the most exalted opinion of human nature. He venerates in every man, in the son of every people and race, the reflected majesty of God. He cannot bring himself to think evil of any man, until he has amplest proof that evil is habitually and wilfully done by him. He cannot even believe in the total depravity of criminals, seeing that the degradation of any soul implies the defeat and degradation of the divine in humanity. The true worshipers of Jehovah, whether they call themselves followers of Moses or of Christ, consider it rank blasphemy to regard any class of men, whatever their racial affinities, their religious beliefs and historical affiliations, as devoid of the higher qualities and ideal aspirations of humanity. If God is not in man, then He is nowhere. If His holy will, His beneficence, the attributes of His goodness, fail to manifest themselves with more or less vitalizing energy in all the families of the earth, then He is not the all-pervading, all-animating, the omnipresent and omnipotent Spirit of all mankind. If any people, race or sect is left without His grace, His love and guidance, then we believe only in a local God, the God of a people, of a race, of a church, and the Deity we worship is not different from the local and tribal gods adored by the pagans of antiquity. To assume that the Jews, though living for thousands of years under discipline and laws of righteousness, though in closest touch with the spiritual presence and inspiring example of God's saints and martyrs, are yet a materialistic, ignoble people; to say that their clannish heart beats with sympathy only for those of their own race, but is indifferent to the welfare of all other men, is tantamount to believing that divine government is a sad failure, that the plans of Providence with the people selected to work out the elevation and salvation of mankind, have shockingly miscarried, that the educational power of infinite wisdom has suffered disastrous defeat just where it strove to achieve its greatest moral victory. If it were true, what mediæval times asserted, and is being re-echoed by our modern calumniators, if the fear of God and the love of mankind were absent from the heart of the Jews, if ours were not the ways of righteousness, then the belief in a universal Power and Wisdom unfolding Himself in the soul of man would be a fiction, and the hope in final victory of good over evil would be a vain dream!

In fact, the mediæval conception of God and divine government was thoroughly heathenish; and the anti-Semitic idea of Judaism and the Jews is the most emphatic and disgraceful expression of the pagan theory of the world and of man. Jehovism came into the world as the deep-going reaction and solemn protest of the soul of mankind against the pagan idea, which separates man from the fellowship of man, which dooms whole sects, whole peoples and races to moral inferiority by an alleged ordinance of nature or the curse of angry and partial divinity. It is the historic mission of the champions of ethical monotheism or Jehovism, to fight in the thick of heaven's battle, for the belief in the spiritual unity of all the families of the earth, for the belief in the godlike nature of all the children of God, for faith in the goodness and in the irrepressible progress of the race towards justice, love and truth. We who have for ages been smitten with the scorpion whips of contempt, we are called to preach with tongues of angels reverence for the soul of the least of men. We who have through the long and dreary night tasted all the bitterness, all the misery caused by unjust suspicion and calumnious misrepresentations, are commissioned by the genius of mankind to teach and practice truth unswerving, justice in words and deeds, love and charity towards all men. We Israelites have suffered, and in many countries still suffer grievously, but ours has been a noble suffering, consecrated as it is to the greatest of all causes, to the unity of God and the unity of mankind, to faith in a God of infinite love and faith in the indestructible moral dignity of man. We have not fought, we have not suffered and bled in vain. The cause of God, the cause of a just and loving humanity, for which we have for a thousand years stood forth in the terrible storm of obloquy, of malignant prejudices, of the world's hatred and contempt, has at last become victorious, and its healing and redeeming light has risen upon mankind like the sun in his glory. Let us render thanks to God that we have lived to see the dawn of the Lord and of humanity. We have lived to reap in the form of the world's respect, confidence and love the first-fruits of the victory of Jehovism over paganism, of the spirit of justice and mercy over the cruel spirit of separation and distrustful hostility.

Let the blackbirds of the primæval night still croak their hoarse and hideous notes of distrust, of calumny, and hatred against us. The best part of the world, the noblest men and women of our time, the standard-bearers of the light, justice and progress of the age, do trust us, honor and love us as brothers, and call us fellow-champions in the holy war of good against evil. They acknowledge the grievous wrong the past has done to our character and name, they acknowledge that we are like them servants of humanity, that we have by our self-sacrifice helped to preserve to the world its spiritual treasures and are contributing our share toward redeeming the world from the evils of heathenish ideas and practices. Our fate, our honor, our happiness are bound up with the moral progress of mankind. We are the witnesses of the growing spirit of divine love and justice in man. The measure of esteem in which we are held, the measure of love accorded to us, is the measure of a nation's moral worth, is the sure indication of a people's rise or fall in the scale of humanity. The Israelites of every country are the infallible thermometers of that country's civilization. Let a people begin to degenerate morally, and the first symptoms of that degeneracy will show themselves in prejudice and ill-will against the Jews. Let the humanitarian forces of liberty, justice and equity stir a nation's breast with might, and among the first results of a quickened higher life there will manifest itself an eager desire to deal with the Jews in a spirit of righteousness, to accord to them equal rights, to regard them as brothers and fellow-patriots. Whatever precious gains the adherents of Jehovism have made within the last hundred years are due to the moral progress of the world, to the growing powers of humanity. The tree of higher humanity is our tree of life. On its fruits we depend for maintenance and sustenance. The more numerous and the more perfect the fruits of wisdom, of godliness, of justice and love, which the tree of humanity ripens, the safer, the richer and happier becomes the life of us

Yahvists, the more vigorous and fruitful is our own spiritual and moral vitality. Wherever and whenever the tree of humanity, planted by the hand of Jehovah's seers and messengers by the living waters of righteousness, happens to be smitten with barrenness, a blight at once falls upon us, we are the first to suffer from the effects of the spiritual famine in the land. We are the historical representatives and standard-bearers of the church of Jehovism, have been providentially appointed to be among the chief guardians and cultivators of the tree of humanity.

This is our mission and our glory. We ought to be thankful for being charged with such a high and universal mission. We may well be proud of the fact, that by spiritual succession and by the inexorable necessity of our situation, we are compelled to be champions of moral, social, intellectual and economical emancipation and advancement. The Israelite is bound to belong to the army of progress, for the hosts of retrogression are his personal and relentless foes. Woe to him, if in supine indifference to the general good, he allows the reactionary forces, which never sleep nor slumber, to make headway and gain the upper hand. Before he is aware of it, while he deems himself as secure as any part of the people, the ungodly pagan powers rush at him with demon fury and try to trample him under foot. Whether they know it or not, whether they will it or not, the members of the church of Jehovah are the banner-bearers of progressive humanity. Around them rages the battle of paganism against Jehovism, of race against humanity, of oppression against freedom, of narrow selfishness against all-embracing love. Let the banner-bearers fight with indomitable courage, let them expose their breast to the poisoned arrows of hate and prejudice. For they are fighting the battle of God, the battle of mankind for spiritual freedom, for right and equity. It is a high privilege to know ourselves and our interest is to be identical with the godward advancement of mankind, with the highest and holiest interests of the human race.

By a decree of the genius of history we are forced to stand as knights of the spirit around the fiery chariot of progress. We advance when it advances; we halt when it halts; we retrograde when it goes backward. We will not, we dare not, we cannot abandon the post of honor and danger assigned to us by our religion. We occupy the most exposed, the most difficult, but almost the most honorable position in the spiritual battles of humanity. For Jehovism is the church militant of humanity, fighting with the invincible arms of justice, mercy and truth. It is waging perennial war against the spirit of hate and injustice, against the wicked powers attempting to separate man from his brother man according to race, nationality and creed. Jehovism is nothing but the eternal battle of the powers of light against the powers of darkness, the battle of peace and righteousness against the demons of inhumanity. It is not by the accident of our birth, but by spiritual succession and free choice that we are life-long devoted champions of the church universal of Jehovism. It is not by virtue of our blood, which heaven knows has flowed together from all possible sources, but by the indissoluble bonds of sacred memories, by the identity of beliefs, principles and ideals, that we are the inheritors of the burdens and duties, of the struggles, sorrows, joys and glories of the missionary people of moral monotheism.

JUDAISM AND THE CONGRESS OF LIBERAL RELIGIOUS SOCIETIES.

HELD AT SINAI TEMPLE, CHICAGO, JUNE 4, 1895.

AN ADDRESS BY RABBI JOSEPH STOLZ.

The American Congress of Liberal Religions is but another denomination added to the one hundred and fifty that already grace and disgrace our country – is the charge repeatedly made by those whose love for this child cradled a year ago in Sinai Temple is like the love of the spurious mother in Solomon's famous judgment—so great that ere yet the infant was out of its swaddling clothes they would have it cut in twain that "it be neither mine nor thine."

I stand here to-night, on behalf of the oldest of the historical religions here represented, to pronounce a vigorous and emphatic protest against this charge, and to give public testimony that I am here as a Jew and that I not only have no thought of affiliating with a new denomination but that I never feel myself so much a Jew, never am so proud of being a Jew and never so determined to remain a Jew, as when I contemplate the aims and workings of this American Congress of Liberal Religions, a Messiah of the Jews. I do not come here in search of a freer platform— in my pulpit I have all the liberty of thought and freedom of expression I crave for.

I do not come here to be delivered from the thraldom of sectarianism, and emancipated from the slavery of creed. We have no sects. Liberal or orthodox, we are all Jews. We unite in good works and neither hate each other, oppose each other, nor condemn each other to the Sheol whose temperature, if this has been a sample the last few days, is so uncongenial, at least to Chicagoans. The Jew has no hard and fixed creed to which he must swear allegiance. Within and without the synagogue he is granted the utmost freedom of thought. He is responsible for his views to no synod and no general assembly. He knows no heresy trials. The excommunication of Spinoza was un-Jewish. It was the act of Spanish Jews who sought refuge in Amsterdam from the terrors of the Inquisition, and then adopted the very methods of the Catholic Inquisition when they got the power in their hands—as it so often happens that the persecuted turn persecutors.

I do not come here to learn that righteousness and duty are more important than rituals, ceremonies, symbols and metaphysical formulæ. With the flame of God in their souls and the fire of eloquence on their lips, our prophets again and anon proclaimed this truth and the whole of Jewish literature teems with it.

Nor have I come here to learn of universal religion. The vision of one God, one humanity and one religion has always inspired the Jews. Even in the days of darkest persecution they fed on this dream. They read it in their Bible, they put it in their daily prayers, they taught it in their schools; upon the doorway of their synagogues they carved the inscription, "My house shall be a house of prayer for all nations."

The truth of the matter is you are receiving such a hospitable reception in this temple, so many Jewish congregations have affiliated with you, nearly every rabbi in this country has transmitted to you a message of sympathy, and the Central Conference of American Rabbis has sent hither its delegates—not because they would cease to be Jews, but because they are Jews, not because they crave for a new denomination, but because they would co-operate with all those whose aim it is to direct and utilize the liberal thought of our country.

Ours is the age of free thought. It asserts itself in literature, art, music, philosophy and politics no less than in religion. Men will not in our day and in our country be trammeled by tradition, and there is everywhere a strong undercurrent of liberalism. In the large cities it is in the air, and even in the smallest villages, far away from the centers of thought and the highways of civilization, you will find men and women with a mighty consciousness that they have outgrown the old thought. This liberalism generally seeks one of three channels: either it loses itself in mysticism, as is evidenced by the many new mystical sects of our day, like Christian Science, Occultism, Theosophy, Spiritualism; or, through a misunderstanding of what the real nature of religion is, it deserts the churches altogether and robs them of some of the best minds and hearts of the community; or it degenerates into rank materialism, secularism or agnosticism.

Now then comes this Congress, not to bury any existing denomination, or in any wise to limit its particular sphere of activity, but, backed by the authority of Unitarians, Universalists, Independents, Ethical Culturists, Jews and all other liberal bodies, to speak for all of them with a voice so strong, a conviction so deep and an enthusiasm so intense that together they will exert an influence and make an impression beyond the power of any one of them individually.

This Congress is the prophet of our day crying into the wilderness that religion is not based upon superstition nor built upon selfishness, that it is not the product of priestcraft nor the fruit of mental servility, but is a part of man as much as conscience, reason, will and love are, and will exist as long as man will exist. Let all the Bibles in the world be destroyed and all the churches be demolished and all the priesthoods be secularized, as long as human beings are left, there will be religion; and new houses of worship will be erected, new Bibles will be written and new men will arise to be the religious guides and teachers.

This Congress is the prophet of our age proclaiming to them who have been enticed away by the wonderful achievements of science that religion and science are not in conflict. God's handwriting in nature cannot contradict God's handwriting on the human soul; and the truth is that science requires religion for its completion just as much as religion ever requires science.

This Congress is the prophet announcing to those who interpret liberalism to mean negation and who revel in their skepticism or materialism, what a terrible thing life would be if religion were not the dominant power in the community; if men all believed that the universe was the result of chance and all things were not working together toward a reasonable, loving and just end; if men all thought that the moral law was not something immutable, eternal, divine; and if men all acted as if the individual perished and the race did not endure and our conduct was determined for us by the unthinking forces round about, and whatever we might do had no influence upon the remoter destinies of mankind, because we were only some carbon, oxygen, hydrogen and nitrogen sojourning here three score years and ten, a tiny, impotent speck on this immense universe, a passing shadow here, food for the worms when we pass away.

This Congress is the prophet to emphasize the fact that, because there must be diversity in religion and we cannot all have the same history, bear the same label, use the same forms, worship on the same day, utter the same prayers and have the same ideas, for that reason we must not idolize our own particular forms and fail to find a virtue in any others; we must not look for the truth only in our own little church and have nothing but hatred in our hearts for all other churches; we must not be so jealous of our own little history that we cannot rejoice when some other denomination realizes the very ideals we cherish; we must not be so fearful of the fate of our little denomination that we pull down the blinds and fasten the shutters and bolt the doors and build a high wall around ourselves lest some light come in and a heretic go out; we must not be so blind in the worship of our creed that we cannot see the universal truths underlying all religion and cannot work shoulder to shoulder and heart to heart and soul to soul for their wider acceptance and truer realization in life.

This Congress is to give our convictions the strength of numbers and the force of united effort. By standing alone we have been dissipating our energy and depriving every community of our full and just contribution to its better thought and higher life. By being unorganized we have not mustered anything like our best forces against the fanaticism and intolerance or against the infidelity and materialism of the land. The liberals need organization and they need the enthusiasm which can make a sacrifice.

It is just eight hundred years since Pope Urban II. preached the first crusade at Cleremont, France. His passionate words aroused the enthusiasm of the crowd; with unanimity they declared themselves ready to make the sacrifice; the contagion spread; all classes of society,—nobles, priests, citizens, peasants and kings,— all were animated with the same idea and abandoned themselves to the same impulse. It was the first time that the countries of Europe—France, Germany, Italy, Spain and England—acted together in a common cause. It was the first time that any one of these nations found all its inhabitants united in one common purpose. That is the result of a great idea taken up with enthusiasm.

Of course, the time was just ripe for those crusades. But I believe the time is just as ripe for this Congress; and if this week we were to take up this cause in Chicago with the same enthusiasm and sincerity and self-sacrifice as did those men at Cleremont who with unanimity exclaimed, "God willeth it, God willeth it,"— a triumph would be ours in this land that would open the eyes of the most sanguine prophets and priests of the movement.

REFORM JUDAISM AND LIBERAL CHRISTIANITY.

BY RABBI MOSES J. GRIES, ERIE, PA.

A little more than one year ago, the Parliament of Religions convened in the city of Chicago. To thoughtful students of the history of the race, the day marks the beginning of a new epoch. The Parliament was not a church council. It was dominated by no ecclesiastical ruler. It promulgated no new decrees. It was a human fellowship meeting. It was dominated by the rule of love. It proclaimed to all mankind, the ringing message that love of God does not mean the hate of man.

I know not whether it was accident or design, but Judaism held the first of the Religious Congresses; and the Parliament began its sessions on the evening of the Jewish New Year, and at the Mid-Winter Fair, the lesser Parliament began on the Jewish Passover and the first Congress of Liberal Religious Societies met in a Jewish temple. To you, these things may mean nothing. To me, a representative of Judaism, they mean much. These things can be symbolical. Jewish tradition has it that the world was created on the New Year's Day. To me, it seems as though in the year 5654, according to the Bible chronology (1893 of our common era), there was a new creation. The old mankind, full of hate and standing apart, perished and the new creation was begun. We have a Jewish legend, that in the beginning God created but one man. Man, *one*, neither Jew nor Gentile nor heathen—but simply man, child of God. And Scripture tells us God formed man out of the dust of the earth. How beautiful is the thought of our legend, that from every land, from countries far and near, from this side and the other side of the great waters came the birds of heaven, bearing each in its bill a grain of dust, and a man was made, in the beginning, universal, formed out of the dust of *all* the earth.

In the beginning was God and the first of our race was the child of God, and so are we all the children of God, one family, one human brotherhood. Let that Parliament, which gathered its representatives from all the earth, on the traditional Creation-eve proclaim to you, as it does to me, the formation of the one man, child of a Common Father, member of the universal human brotherhood!

And the historic Jewish Passover is the feast of Liberty. Then was Israel redeemed from the bondage of Egypt! It was the first emancipation-proclamation, declaring one man shall not be master and his brother slave! Equal are men in the sight of God! Man shall not hate, persecute, oppress his brother, with rigorous burdens upon the flesh nor open the spirit. No creature of God was blessed with life, to be shackled and enslaved. Every man shall be free. Every man ought to be equal,—free and equal in life's opportunities. Let the mid-winter Parliament, convening on the eve of the Festival of Liberty, proclaim to you as it does to me, freedom unto all God's creatures, because they are the creatures of God, a human fellowship of love, and not of hate, of upliftment and not oppression of the fallen, of redemption and not of punishment of the outcast—a united human fellowship for helpful human service, and that Jewish Congress first of all congresses and that meeting of Liberal Christian Societies in a Jewish temple are not without deeper meaning. Then and thereby, in the sight of all mankind, did old and hoary-headed Judaism give testimony that though the burden of centuries rested upon its shoulders, it was not bowed with the weight of age but that erect it stood among the nations, strong with the vigor and burning with the fire of perpetual youth. Judaism, old, yet eternally young, a living force among the living! In the beginning was it a religion to shape the life of a nation—a faith to be lived. In the end, it is still a religion of life unto the living. Its emphasis is not upon belief. Right living is the essential. Let the Liberal Religious Congress, finding birth in a Jewish temple, proclaim to you, as it does to me, that Judaism, inheritor of the Law, bearer of the prophetic message, lives and will live.

Friends, I am here to bring you greeting. The old mother of religions salutes you! Flesh of her flesh, spirit of her spirit, though not altogether thought of her thought, I come speaking peace and good will. I will not magnify disagreements. With joyful heart do I emphasize agreements. Your pastor has asked me to speak my thoughts freely and I hesitate not, assured that I am a friend among friends, a man among men, all of us seeking the light and the truth and the way.

I have little sympathy with that prevalent indifference, Jewish and Christian, which makes light of all disagreements, which masking itself under the cloak of liberalism is false liberalism, laxity, license in religious faith and practice, truer child of thoughtless convienence than of thinking conviction. I do not feel inclined, for the sake of the pleasure it may give the unthinking to slur over, to conceal disagreements. Between Judaism and Christianity there are fundamental differences. Reform Judaism and Liberal Christianity have but drawn near, one to the other, but the chasm is unbridged.

What does Judaism, what does Christianity teach regarding man and his life on earth? Christianity declares "man born in sin, a creature fallen from grace. He needs salvation! He cannot redeem himself! A mediator stands between him and his God. There is but one path of salvation." "He that believeth shall be saved, but he that believeth not shall be damned." (Luke xvi, 16.) Judaism declares "man a God-creature, fashioned in the image divine and sent upon earth to accomplish a divine purpose. He is a child of God, destined to live a god-like life. He is not a perfect nor a sinless creature. But salvation reaches him by no process of faith nor by the help of a mediator. He must save himself." Man does not lie prostrate in the dust, cringing, fearing, trembling before his God, He stands erect and turns his face to see his Maker. The Christian prays, Lead me not into temptation, and the Jew, were he to write the Lord's Prayer as his fathers had the thought, would ask for strength to meet temptation and conquer it. Temptation comes to all, the weak fall and are swept away, the strong standing upon the rock of righteousness cannot be moved. Christianity offers salvation unto all men. In this it is universal, but it insists upon the one path and thereby it makes itself less than universal. It still clings to the last remnant of its creed. "Believe in a fallen world and Jesus as the Redeemer." I like your name

Universalism—it is not narrow. It seems broad—all-mankind-inclusive. But I would welcome the fact more than the name—a universalism in truth, with no barrier to the gate of Heaven, with more than one path leading to salvation's portals, a universalism also on earth, on this side of the grave, in life, and not only after death, above. Judaism in its doctrines of salvation approaches a true universalism. All may enter into the covenant of God—redemption is unto all the righteous, Jew and non-Jew, believing and unbelieving. In the prayer in memory of the dead, a prayer of sanctification unto God, expression of mourning hearts trusting in God, prayed daily in synagogues and temples, we reverently ask "may the Lord of heaven and earth grant eternal peace and a full participation in the bliss of eternal life, grace and mercy to Israel, to all the righteous and to all who departed this life by the will of God." Faith does not save. Conduct and character make for salvation. As spoke the Psalmist. "This is the gate of the Lord, the righteous enter into it."

I know that Judaism is supposed to be narrow, provincial, tribal, national, racial and I know also that Judaism in its essential teachings is truly universal. Many were the laws made for Palestine, for the Israelitish nation for worship while the temple stood in its glory. They were, but they are not! The temple is in ruins, the nation has ceased to be. Palestine is under the rule of the Moslem. Though some Jewish hearts may mourn for Jewish greatness and sorrow, not to have seen the glory of God's house and cherish a longing for national power and dominion, we, I speak not for myself alone, but for the million Jews dwelling in lands of freedom, seek and desire not a restoration of the kingdom, nor a re-building of the temple. We rejoice that we are here; Israel's face is turned to the west and not to the east. God's blessing is upon all the earth. This is His holy land; the God of Israel has sent His people unto all lands and unto all nations. His people chosen not for blessings but for service, that in them all families of the earth shall be blest. Our fathers have obeyed the Scriptural command. Get thee out of thy country, out of thy birthplace and out of thy father's house. (Gen. xii, 1.) The national, the provincial, the temporal are behind us. Laws and customs and institutions of the old time may still appear in our midst. But gradually the body of our religion is conforming itself to its spirit. Our teachings and our thoughts are universal. Their expression soon will be.

Judaism is misunderstood and misjudged. It has been long in the world, but is little known of men. How many are there who esteem it an antiquated faith, an outworn religion, a curious relic strangely preserved, a religion in the midst of life, but dead! It is thought that the Jew completed life's task eighteen hundred years ago. Israel lived only to produce a Redeemer; Judaism to give birth to Christianity! It is taken for granted that Christianity is something higher than Judaism ever was or is. Christianity regards the Jew as a living testimony to the events of eighteen centuries ago. It awaits his acceptance of the Savior whom the fathers rejected. There are those who make bold to send us missionaries to convert us to the true faith and they wonder why we Jews do not lay aside the old distinction and become Christians. A few Jews may become Christians for revenue only, and a few may wear the Christian cloak to win worldly privilege and honor; but Jews and Judaism cannot and will not cease to be until the religions of mankind are representative of the broadest in thought and the highest in life, until they become all-mankind-inclusive! Let the denominational name stand, it *must* stand until there can be a fellowship true enough to ask surrender of no truth.

Ought not Judaism to yield? Its adherents are but few in number. Ought they not to surrender? Abraham was one God-believer in a heathen world. To-day "God is One and His name One" in all civilized lands. Palestine and Greece were small countries. To-day, Greece and Judea are little more than provinces, but by the might of mighty spirit, they rule all mankind in culture and in conduct. Judaism hopes not for a physical triumph and seeks it not. The Jew dreams not of dominion world-embracing. The seed of Abraham, the descendants of Judah are not to conquer; but we have trust that truth will conquer the truth of the patriarch, of the lawgiver and the prophets.

The prophets proclaimed one God over all—a Divine Unity making necessary a human unity. Reform Judaism lives in the spirit of the prophetic teachings. It overleaps and breaks through and is destroying all the barriers which past generations in self-defense erected to divide man from man. The separating walls are down, can we not clasp hands? "Have we not one Father?" (Mal. ii, 10.) Are we not God-children? Why stand we apart?

When freedom and justice shall be, when tyranny and oppression are no more, when love shall bind where hate now severs, when men will know themselves God-children, all, then, Jew and Christian, need be no more. We, Liberal Christianity and Reform Judaism, are preparing the way. We have overleaped and broken through and destroyed behind us, the narrow walls that hemmed us in. We are the leaders. We may stand far in advance but all the world follow behind.

Our religion is not a new creation nor a new discovery, and certainly not one of the modern improvements. We have but returned to the teachings of our first great masters—you to the man of Nazareth, we to our rabbins and prophets and law-givers. The orthodox may declare us of the unfaithful. "You are not true Christians, we are not true Jews." The law-giver and the prophets, the Nazarene and the Apostles would not be faithful to the religions they founded, as some judge the truly faithful. Orthodoxy has divided mankind and liberalism is seeking to unite. We have suffered and suffer now from too much denominationalism, wasteful individualism of effort, from senseless disunion of forces. Selfish individual effort is the doctrine of a past age. Co-operation we need and want. If fundamental difference compels us to live apart, it is well. The few fighting for principle and conviction to guard the truth, are heroic. But we have been too fearful for the truth. Felix Adler has well said it: "Truth can take care of itself." Our duty is to man. We were men before we were Jews or Christians or Mohammedans or Buddhists. God-children were we in the beginning. Let us be God-children now! Let us do worthy service unto God.

Let there be a union of all Liberals! not one creed—not one church doctrine! One theology, one philosophy, one religion will not and cannot be; but there can be one work to do—one service to fulfil! Let liberalism stand united in the city and state and nation, united everywhere, as the enemy of bigoted intolerance, as the champion and defender of the liberties of man, civil and religious. Let liberalism everywhere be a force strong by union, making for human upliftment. Let it sound the call to a higher life and a broader human fellowship. Then are you true Christians! Then are we true Jews! Then are Jews and Christians true men!

JEWISH THEOLOGY.

BY REV. DR. JOSEPH SILVERMAN, OF TEMPLE EMANU-EL,
NEW YORK.

The world is in dread of theology. To most men the sole functions of theology seem to be the enslavement of the mind and the oppression of those who refuse to submit to such mental thralldom. Theology seems to be master and persecutor, tyrant and executioner. Theology separates men into religious sects and engenders personal strife and animosity. Though we live in a more liberal age, we cannot forget the bitterness of ancient theological disputations and the dire persecutions and inquisitions to which they gave rise. Even at this day argumentation regarding ecclesiastical questions is not free from turbulence of spirit and personalities, and lacks that calmness and equanimity which should be diffused about converse and discussion in polite society. Even at this day theology is so deeply rooted that it can, with difficulty only, be amended, that it cannot be dislodged.

Though theology has appeared to most people as an ogre, they still cling to it. Despite its forbidding countenance, they still warm to it. Its very repulsiveness seems to have an attraction. Its dreaded aspect, its severity is due to its intrinsic worth and to the necessity of guarding it. Theology must exist.

Its existence is not only imperative, it is inevitable. Theology has its *raison d'etre* even as much as religion; it is the very basis of the latter. No theology: no religion.

Theology is not artificial, was not made and imposed altogether upon an unsuspecting world by priest or prophet. It has its natural beginning even as have chemistry, botany, etc. These sciences exist because there are facts in nature, the knowledge regarding which has been classified and systematized. There exists theology, because there is one Great Fact in the universe regarding which we have systematized our knowledge. There is theology because there is God Theology has therefore a natural beginning, since it is the mind's conception of God. And as the mind is not stationary, so theology must change. It is an evolution.

The evil of which men complain, the ogre part of theology, lies not in the thing itself, but in the men who have misunderstood, misrepresented and deformed it. They were so thoroughly convinced of the value of theology, and of its necessity, that they gave to it a fixed form and opposed every change. They overlooked the facts or did not know, that by giving theology any particular and fixed form they in reality deformed it. Theology, being a product of the mind, must grow with it or else its form will not correspond to its parent. We are familiar with the dwarfish appearance of many a child whose growth has been stunted, while its parent developed physically and mentally. There are also social dwarfs, governmental deformities, religious and theological pigmies wherever society, government or church has not kept pace with the mental growth of the age.

Every fixed creed of to-day will be a dwarf to-morrow. Every synodical edict of yesterday is to-day a deformity. Over night the mind that gave it birth has stridden far ahead. No wonder, then, that the creeds that were formulated centuries ago, and to which nothing has been added or taken away, seem like dreaded apparitions of the night, like demons of another world, like ghosts of some dead inquisitors. They are the theological scarecrows that frighten our young men away from the religious seminaries and alienate our thoughtful men and women from the churches, and torment the days and nights of conscientious ministers. Not theology, but its fixed forms, created the estrangement between itself and advanced minds. The ironclad creeds forcibly separated men into sects, and like vexed boundary lines became the cause of war and of bitter cruel persecution.

In Judaism there is no room for persecution, partly because it is a religion that preaches and practices love of fellow-men, but especially because it has nothing by which to excuse persecution, nothing that is so fixed that it can form the basis for heresy trial, excommunication or anathema. A Jew is born, not made; that is, he is born, not in a physical but in a spiritual sense. He is born with a mind that can appreciate the existence of God, with a soul that realizes itself to be a part of the Universal Soul, with a spirituality that is an image of the Deity. The more this mind grows, the more is the conception of God elaborated. A Jew is not made in the sense in which I have seen converts made, that is by studying a creed by heart, reciting it before witnesses and being sprinkled with water which has been blessed with some incantations. A Jew is born spiritually and reborn each day as long as mental development is possible.

Creed has never been obligatory in Judaism. Our theology is a philosophy of the universe, of human and divine life which must be understood and known. Merely to assent to certain doctrines does not, in a strict sense, constitute a Jew. We have in reality no catechism except for convenience. Every man must make his own system of theology out of the knowledge which he has. Religion must come from within, and not from without. Blind faith is mere superstition. To say, I believe in God, Providence, reward and punishment, in immortality because my father, teacher, priest or prophet has believed in the same doctrines, is not religion. Such a faith does not constitute belief in God, but in another's report about God. To believe in God one must know God, must have comprehended Him by His manifestations in the universe. That is the first desideratum of Jewish theology—knowing God. Theology means knowledge of God. The Scriptures tell us: "Thou shalt *know* this day and consider it in thine heart, that the Lord, He is God." The Psalmist says: "The beginning of knowledge is the reverence or fear of God." In the book of Isaiah (xliii, 10) we read: "Ye are my witnesses and my servants whom I have chosen, saith the Lord, in order that ye may know and believe me and understand that I am He—before me there was no God formed and after me there will be none." In fact, man is not commanded, in the Bible, to believe. He is only enjoined to study, understand and know. The so-called ten commandments are not altogether commandments, but rather ten principles, ten words as the Scriptures call them. They do not command belief in God, but merely declare that there is God, the same God that brought Israel out of the land of Egypt and the house of bondage.

Jewish theology, being dependent on knowledge and being as progressive as the mind, cannot be cast into fixed moulds. Many have tried to formulate a Jewish creed, and failed. Even the notable efforts of Maimonides gave no universal satisfaction. His thirteen articles of faith have for us merely a historical value showing one particular stage in the development of Jewish theology. It is of constant interest to know that his articles of creed specified belief in God as Creator, His unity, spirituality, eternity, the worship of Him alone, the authenticity of prophecy,—the distinction of Moses from the other prophets, the law of Mosaic origin, the immutability of the law, God's omniscience, reward and punishment, the Messiah—resurrection and future life. Some Jewish philosophers increased the number of these articles, while others reduced them to as low a number as three. But there was never agreement as to whether these three doctrines were revelation, reward and punishment or creation, omniscience and Providence or God, revelation and immortality. Some deny reward, others revelation, and still others the immutability of God's law. There is no agreement as to a fixed creed in Judaism.

All are agreed, however, that the principle "There is God" is the foundation of Jewish theology. God can not be defined in set terms and phrases. The Bible merely postulates Him, accepts Him, as an axiom. The Bible merely states "In the beginning God created heaven and earth." "The heavens declare the glory of God and the expanse tells of the works of His hands." There is no attempt in the Bible to demonstrate the existence of God—and no expectancy is expressed that man will ever reach a perfect knowledge of Him. The Scripture is quite plain in regard to man's inability to fathom God, in saying that God declares to Moses, "Thou canst see me from behind,"—that is, know Him by His manifestations—"for no man can see my face and live."

It is this very feature of Jewish theology which requires a study of God in His works and manifestations as a condition for knowing God that makes our theology distinctively Jewish. It can never be narrow and never lead to bigotry and intolerance. It is the natural enemy of ignorance and the friend of all learning. It courts wisdom and welcomes every science, philosophy and criticism. It grows as the mind expands. Just as in climbing a mountain our horizon widens in proportion as our plane of vision becomes higher, so the older we grow and the wiser we become the truer and grander becomes our conception of Deity. Every new fact of history, every new experience in life, every new revelation in the world of matter by the means of science opens up new views of God and greater glories of His infinite wisdom, love, power and justice. The more we know of God, the more we realize the incapability of the human mind to comprehend Him and the insufficiency of human language to define or describe Him. "The heaven and earth cannot contain Thee, how much less this house which I have built," says the sage in the Bible. How much less can the finite thoughts of man and his feeble tongue, interpret Deity. We have a God whom no particular name is able to connote. Whether you call Him, God, Lord, King, Creator, Love, Wisdom, Truth, Freedom, Justice, the Infinite and the Eternal, the One, spiritual, omniscient and most holy, or all of these names together, you cannot fully express our conception of Him. The finite cannot wholly grasp the infinite, the imperfect can only approximately reach the perfect. It is vain to attempt to imagine God or fully represent Him in highest diction of prose or poetry. "Who is like unto the Lord our God that hath His seat on high, that humbleth himself to behold the things that are in heaven and in the earth." (Ps. cxiii.) "I dwell in the high and holy place (says God) with Him also that is of a contrite and humble spirit (Is. lvii). Not in the wind was the Lord, neither in the earthquake, nor in the fire, but in the still small voice (compare I Kings xix, 11-13). No human reason or expression can reach infinite heights and depths as does God.

Jewish theology is unique in this supremely lofty conception that surpasses expression. It is an effort of the mind to fathom the mystery of this universe— of man and of his relation thereto. Here is this mysterious, intricate universe, this daily panorama of natural phenomena, in the heavens, on the earth, in the seas, and in the depths of the earth—all created and governed; though seemingly independent, yet showing harmony, design and purpose. Here is man just as wonderful and intricate, and as inexplicable. Jewish theology says there is unity in creation, and unity in man and that there is an intimate relation between man and all creation which science itself can prove. Whatever exists must have had a cause. There must have been a first cause. Whatever exists in the effect must have in some form or mode existed in the cause. The unity in all creation and in man and between the two—a unity which is manifested by design, harmony and purpose—must be the result of One supreme Creator. God is the creative unifying spirit in man and all the universe. Whatever we comprehend in man as spirituality must be the image of God. This spirituality manifested in thought, will, freedom, love, mercy, justice, must exist in infinite quality and degree in God. This Deity means life, power, intellect, freedom, love, mercy, justice, etc., infinite and eternal. Life eternal means immortality, divine love, mercy and justice, means reward and punishment; divine wisdom means revelation and inspiration. God as unity is the great bond of force that unifies creation and the bond of love that unites mankind.

"This Jewish idea of God eclipses any and every conception of Deity that has ever been advanced." Science may speak of the Unknown and Unknowable, Judaism believes in a God who has revealed something of Himself and is constantly unfolding more of His nature. It is our duty to read the revelations of God in the stars and rocks, in the earth and in the sea. We can know much of God by his manifestations—by studying His laws in the world of matter and of man, as well as in the spiritual world. We can know God through our own soul, through our own likeness with Him in spirit, through our conscience and our consciousness. Modern science with its doctrines of the conservation of energy and the correlation of forces, comes very close to the unity of God, of man and of creation. This unity in terms of science means the one final element and force that will be found to underlie the universe. In æsthetics this unity is translated into blending of colors, in music, into harmony of sound, in architecture, into symmetry. In chemistry it means affinity; in ethics, the universal brotherhood; in religion, the common fatherhood of God; in statesmanship, the universal republic.

In comparison to this Jewish theology, the doctrines about God that other systems have taught are vastly inferior. Zoroastrianism teaches a Ditheism, or belief in two coequal gods: Ormuzd, the good, and Ahiram, the

JEWISH THEOLOGY. 267

evil, who are involved in a constant conflict. Brahminism maintains that there is but one reality, the Spirit, absorption into which is the highest good. This system tended towards pantheism and led to an ascetic life. Buddhism is a reaction against this extreme and one-sided spiritualism, and became equally as extreme and one-sided an advocate of naturalism. It lost sight of the Creator in its regard for the tendency of events and the invariable laws that controlled them. Confucianism reverses the past, teaches a prudential morality, i. e., obedience to the proprieties and conventionalities of the times. It is eminently practical, but imperfect because of its atheism. The religion of the ancient Greeks consisted mainly in the deification of human nature; the creation of gods out of the human qualities. These gods were supposed to inhabit Mt. Olympus, revel in feasting, and, in the intervals between their feasts, to rule the world. The religion of Rome was similar to that of Greece, with the difference that the mythology of Greece was poetical and romantic, while that of Rome was prosaic and more identified with the ordinary affairs of life. Thus, for instance, the Romans had a god who was charged with the care of bakers' ovens, and another who looked after the welfare of Roman coin. In the religion of the ancient Egyptians God appears in every phenomenon of nature. He is not, as in Brahminism, a unit, but divided and parcelled out in every planet, animal and form of nature. While the Brahm represented the spirit world, the God of the Egyptian was the material world worshiped under the form of a polytheistic idolatry. Mohammedanism teaches the worship of one God as the supreme will, but surrenders man to an irrevocable fate to which he must submit.

All these various theological systems emphasize only

one or the other side of the great questions before man. They all recognize the divine element and find it either wholly spirit as the Hindoo, or wholly matter as the Egyptian, or wholly natural law as the Buddhist—or they deify man as the Greeks and Romans, or lose sight of man as the Mohammedans, or else involve us in an endless struggle as the Zoroastrian, making religion a battle instead of rest and peace,—or lead us into atheism as did Confucius. Christianity tried to remedy these defects by a medium partly God and partly man to represent what each of the religions had or omitted.

As the theology of the so-called polytheistic, pantheistic or heathen religions is inadequate, so also is Christianity. We have no room in our theology for a medium between God and man. The relations between God and man are direct, and cannot, by proxy, be turned over to another. Man is responsible to God alone and God can only act upon him directly. The efficacy of prayer depends upon this direct communication with God. As our relation to the universe is direct so must also be our relation to God. This is another aspect of God's unity, omnipotence, omniscience and immutability which has never been fully understood by the heathen or Christian world. Any medium between God and man must necessarily, by so much, weaken God's influence and curtail His omniscience and omnipotence. God has sent no special vicar to earth, commissioned no church to enslave the world, and does not divide his powers of the dispensation of justice with any mortal. God is all-powerful and self-sufficient. Unitarians who have rejected the divinity of Jesus arrive at a monotheistic conception indirectly, through a *negation* of the Trinity. Judaism is based on an *affirmation* of the unity of God. Judaism is the first and only truly monotheistic religion, minus every taint of polytheism and heathenism. To surrender one tithe of it would be untrue to a noble ancestry that fought and bled for the truth, would be unfaithful to the covenant of our fathers who, at Sinai, pledged for us that we will hear and do, *i. e.*, that we will become the banner bearers of the One God, a kingdom of priests to teach and convert the world. Is our mission ended? Is the world converted? As long as there is a heathen altar on the face of the earth, as long as men bow down to idols, as long as children are thrown into the Ganges and men hurl themselves under the Juggernaut, as long as men worship gods of stone, wood, silver or gold, as long as the church and state are not everywhere separated, as long as men seek to impose their particular theologies on the world, by sword, fire or ballot box—so long must we remain Jews, a living protest against superstition and error, and a witness that God is our Lord, that God is one.

JUDAISM AND UNITARIANISM.

BY REV. MAURICE H. HARRIS A.M., PH.D., RABBI TEMPLE
ISRAEL OF HARLEM, N. Y.

Christianity, having wandered off into paganism in its early stages, has in its latest phase—Unitarianism, returned so closely to its first parent—Judaism, that some people have asked whether there be any substantial difference between them, and whether amalgamation might not be possible. Should any Unitarian, or for that matter a member of any religion, desire to affiliate with Judaism because of identity of belief, the fold of our faith is always open. We do not seek converts but we do not reject them when they come to us with honest conviction. We do not seek them, because one of the doctrines of our faith is that salvation is not confined to its members. Furthermore, since Judaism has been a common fount whence many religions have drunk and from whose literature they continue to draw both doctrinal and ethical teaching, even he who continues as Christian or Mohammedan, remains necessarily largely Jewish.

That any Jews should become Unitarians, because of the similarity of belief would be equivalent to asking the ocean to flow back into its tributaries, and reminds us strongly of the old lady who complained of a Shakespearean play, that it was full of quotations. We have never deviated from our strict monotheism, to use the Greek term, or from our strict unitarianism, to use the Latin term, when once we had attained it, and if after all this lapse of centuries the most intellectual and cultivated Christians, of whom the Unitarians are mainly composed, are coming to our way of belief at last, it only strengthens our confidence in our grand old religion, that has withstood the ravages of time and of man, and encourages our determination to remain true to it.

I say this even accepting for a moment the hypothesis that the faiths are in dogma identical. But are they? The difference between Judaism in its most radical form and Unitarianism according to its latest acceptation are still decisive. But let us first see briefly what Unitarianism is.

There have always been some individuals even in the earliest stages of Christianity, who could not accept the logic of the Trinity nor believe in the divinity of Jesus. At times there were sufficient of these dissenters to form distinct schools or parties differentiated according to the modified form in which they accepted these doctrines. By about the middle of the 16th century we find them grown numerous enough to become a church in Poland and also in Transylvania, where they exist still. While persecution kept the movement from swelling to the importance of a denomination in England till as late as the last century, England and the English speaking countries have since become its stronghold.

Till recent years the ties that bound it to orthodox Christianity were many and close. At times it was hard to see where Presbyterianism left off and Unitarianism began, while both the Baptists and the Quakers have Unitarian wings. The conservative Unitarians accept the miracles performed by Jesus of Nazareth, and although they reject his divinity they believe he was divinely sent, entrusted with a mission from God to man, some even still maintaining that he was pre-existent and superangelic. They reject the doctrines of vicarious atonement, original sin and everlasting punishment, but the ceremonies of the Lord's Supper and Baptism are retained.

The advance Unitarians accept the modern rational view of the Bible, and that modern scientific thought, that *Weltanschauung*, that has been given to the world chiefly by the great thinkers of Germany, though the progressive ideas of all nationalities have contributed a share. But even with these, the character of Jesus of Nazareth is so sublimated above all humanity, that his adoration, if not divine worship, is at least semi-divine worship. But Unitarianism has a still more radical wing that declines to put its signature to any creed but which stands on an ethical and non-theological basis. It will not even necessarily accept the cardinal doctrine implied in the name, the doctrine of one God, so that some of its teachers are pantheistic and some agnostic. Its *modus vivendi* is simply free inquiry, in fact, this extreme wing is little more than a free religious society, in which the life of Jesus of Nazareth is made the ideal example. For this reason, it has been called by its more strictly Christian critics —"A System of Pale Negations."

Such, briefly stated, is Unitarianism in its different phases. Whatever further shades of difference specific congregations might assume would simply arise from the personality of the individual minister. As one of the exponents in a recent utterance declares, "In Unitarian congregations exist every shade of belief, from those who are not sure whether they believe anything, to almost the border line of orthodoxy."

From this cursory outline a resemblance will be seen between the advance Unitarians and the reform Jews:—both accept the higher criticisms of the Bible, both heartily endorse the well-established conclusions of modern science, both take the same point of view on the great things of life and the world, and both are, of course, anti-trinitarian. There are yet fundamental distinctions between them, what are they? Religion is more than a matter of creed or philosophy. What makes the high-church Episcopalian and the radical Unitarian really at one, in spite of the different way in which each interprets the common faith that they both accept? What constitutes the bond of union between an orthodox Moorish Jew and an advance American Reformer, in spite of the wide divergence of their respective views of Judaism?

The answer is involved in the complex character of religion. Those who think all religion can be summed up in a dogmatic creed are as wide of the truth as those who think it is all contained in a moral code. Belief and conduct are provinces of religion but do not include its whole territory. "Believe and you shall be saved" is the cry of the orthodox Christian. "I am just to my neighbor—that's my religion," says the modern rationalist. Another conscientiously fulfils the ceremonial and ritual observances and calls himself a religious man. And while we realize the insufficiency of the last more fully than of the two preceding, a sober second thought is seeing a relative value in the forms of religion, that a little while ago it was considered liberal to despise. Professor Toy declares: "There is no instance on record of a wide popular acceptance of a religious system, whose essence was merely a principle of inward life; there is no reason to suppose that a reformer who should confine himself to this subjective ethical religious sphere would be successful unless his work were supplemented."

A religion is a system by which one regulates his life in all its various phases. For this reason it becomes bound up with social institutions. In Judaism, for instance, not only birth, marriage and death had their religious sanctification, not only the week, the year, the spring, the harvest, the autumn were ushered in by Sabbath, New Year, Passover, Pentecost and Tabernacles—but even the daily meal, the morning rising and the night retiring recalled the relation of man to his God in prayer and praise, and fed the fires of faith and spiritual life. In this way the beliefs and morals of religion taking tangible form in appropriate and beautiful symbols clustered in inseparable associations around the home as well as the synagogue and hallowed by some suggestive observance every circumstance of life, dedicating as it were every act to God. Gradually some of these religious forms fall away when they cease to interpret the inner life or to suggest the highest religious ideals, gradually the faith takes to itself new symbols that better express the needs of the generation and stir its emotional depths. But a symbol of some sort is necessary to meet all grades of intelligence, to appeal to sensation as well as to thought and to clothe humanity's profoundest conceptions with a drapery of helpful association. We cannot deliberately create the form any more than the doctrine. They grow as we ourselves. A distinct mode of religious life develops special characteristics and brings out what we call individuality. The nature of Judaism has tended to sanctify family life and strengthen family ties. Another trait it has engendered in its followers to a remarkable degree is optimism, for which Schopenhauer never forgave them. Mohammedanism, Buddhism, Christianity, Judaism, all have their symbols, their ceremonies, their religious organization. They are not of to-day nor of yesterday. They began in the dim past, they are engrained in the very being of their adherents, part not only of their inheritance but of themselves. They are bound up too, with belief and moral practice all grown into one comprehensive whole and known as religion.

Whether Catholic or Unitarian the cross is the symbol of the whole of Christianity. It has taken various forms: it has entered their poetry and their hymnal; it has become a metaphor for sacrifice and suffering, and in this way is made to do service in ethical instruction, and whether they believe that on that cross Jesus suffered for the sins of mankind in their place as vicarious atonement, or simply "lived and died to save men from their sins," which is a distinction the Unitarians make, in a little statement of principles drawn up by their association—it will be seen here how the symbol persists after the belief has changed, and how it becomes modified to meet the changed belief.

The fast on the Day of Atonement, and the day itself may mean the same to the orthodox as to the reform Jews. To the latter, the observance of the day, the abstaining from food, and the faithful reading of its services may in themselves have a certain atoning power, although it is distinctly stated in the central climax of the service that the repentance and righteousness must accompany the fasting and prayer to win God's grace. To the reformer, the day may be rather an inspiration to better life than its absolutely necessary forerunner. But to both it is the great day of Israel's religious reunion, when the associations of childhood are recalled and the higher prompting of the soul awakened.

Dr. Bellows, a well-known Unitarian minister of this city, who has since passed away, voiced the conviction of his sect when he pointed out the necessity of retaining the ceremony known as the "Lord's Supper." To Unitarians it does not mean what the Sacrament means to the orthodox Protestant and their acceptation of it is, of course, still more widely divergent from the Catholic view of it, which under the name of "transubstantiation" maintains that the bread and wine partaken at this religious ceremony become the flesh and blood of their Savior. Yet both extreme wings of Christianity observe the same ceremony, and in spite of the wide divergence of belief between them, are linked by it.

There are some modern Jews who do not accept Israel's departure from Egypt, in quite the way in which it is given in the Bible, while nevertheless admitting the general fact. But the Passover celebrates the great event that marks the birth of the Jewish nation for conservative and radical alike. They recognize it as their starting-point in history. And knowing how closely religion for the whole world is bound up with Israel's marvelous history, it becomes to them also the memorial of the birth of religion in general. In the first and fourth commandments and throughout all the liturgy, it is blended with the belief in God and the institution of the Sabbath. It is therefore annually commemorated as the feast of moral and physical freedom. It is made also the Spring Festival in a natural as well as in a human sense; the Festival of Joy and awakening after Egypt's long winter of discontent. Each of its varied significations then tells a chapter in their history, brings forward an article of their belief and impresses a great moral principle.

This brings us to another all-important feature of every religion which must never be left out of count— the historical. That the history of a religion is part of a religion is truer of Judaism than of any other. Our history has been called "Sacred History" not by ourselves, but by the Gentiles, and the land which formed its setting, they call the "Holy Land."

What a sublime series of pictures it calls up. Moses and Samuel and the prophets; Sinai, Canaan, Jerusalem; the wanderings, the captivity, the dispersion; the poets, the scientists, the philosophers; the law, the Talmud, the liturgy, the Maccabees, the rabbis, the martyrs. All these are our inheritance, and the sad is as precious as the joyful. Each represents a stone in the structure of our faith and all were needed to make the glorious whole. Each of these leading names and incidents are interwoven in our ritual, our festivals and our observances. The growth of our conception of God makes our monotheism all the more intense. How each great soul added something to that great belief; how it broadened and deepened and grew in spiritual force and moral sublimity, as each successive prophet-hero breathed his inspiration into it. How at length the vital God-idea so filled the horizon of our ancestors that they could give themselves thoroughly to nothing else. So letting conquest and art and many other civilizing forces sink into subordination, they felt impelled in spite of themselves to make religion their mission, for it had taken possession of them. In spite of themselves, I say, urged by a persistent prompting within, they must protest against the worship of idols, the worship of matter, the worship of men, *Sch'ma Yisrael* became henceforth their watch-cry, in the synagogue certainly, but if necessary, also in the Roman amphitheater, at the stake, on the torture-rack, in the dungeons of the Inquisition, in York castle, in the ghetto, in the pale of settlement—everywhere. The epithet applied to Spinoza should rather be ascribed to the race—"God-intoxicated"—Hear, O Israel, God is one, there is but one God; He is one, because He is all. And thou shalt love the Eternal thy God with all thy heart and with all thy soul and with all thy might.

Unitarianism has also a history behind it. Up till comparatively recently, its history has been the history of Christianity. The Apostles and the Church Fathers are its progenitors. The Holy Roman Empire and the Reformation are great landmarks in its past. The Arian movement, the Socinian movement, the Church synods, Calvinism, Puritanism and perhaps Universalism indicate so many steps in its growth. Unitarianism has been a development out of Trinitarianism. Some Unitarians claim that this is not the case, that the earliest Christians were unitarian, believing in but one God and accepting Jesus only as their Messiah. But it must not be forgotten that so long as that was their belief, they were still Jews, a sect within the fold, observing all the ceremonial law, even anxious to wear the Tephillin (phylacteries), and there are many special injunctions in the Mishna applying only to these Jewish Christians.* Not till the

---

* Little that we know of Jesus, no impartial critic believes for a moment that he intended or desired to found a new religion distinct from Judaism, any more than Amos, Micah or Isaiah, and we may add than any reformer who pleads for the spirit as against the letter of religion. He not only lived a Jew, he died a Jew, never for a moment supposing that years after his name would be used for the institution of a different faith.

temple was destroyed, not till Jesus was raised to a divinity and the logos through Greek mysticism was transformed into the Holy Spirit—the third person of the Trinity—does this Jewish sect that had so far only believed that the Nazarene was Israel's expected Messiah, part company from the parent faith and become a new religion—Christianity.

With the growth of enlightenment, with the spread of scientific truth this doctrine of the Trinity has been found more difficult of acceptance by thinking men and women. Milton, Locke and Newton never could believe it. Gradually the Holy Spirit was rarified into an influence, gradually the "Son of God" was explained away in a figure of speech, gradually the divine man became the man almost divine. In the next stage he was a man only but with a miraculous birth, able to perform miracles and resurrected from the grave. Later still, he is depicted as differing from other men only in being better than they, including in himself all human virtue, and free from all human sin. The later developments have only tended to make him more natural, but still the ideal of humanity—the noblest man that ever lived, whose example is all-sufficient for moral training and human advancement.

This gradual decline of the belief in his divinity and the consequent falling away of the doctrines that grew out of it, is the history of the development of Unitarianism. But why is Jesus still given a unique place in their belief and ritual, such as they have, and in their teachings generally? Why out of the few meager facts of doubtful authenticity of but two years of his life,* as found in the New Testament, is a fanciful

---

*It is even maintained by some that the events in the

and ideal character still created, probably as untrue to history as the divine idea? Why out of the teachings ascribed to him, which are not original and personal—but largely the teachings of his school, the Jewish Essenes, a fact which is being demonstrated with growing clearness from recent discoveries—have they thought fit to clothe him with every noble quality known to human experience?

Because the glamor of the old belief is on them still. Because the influence of Christianity of which they are a part will abide with them and ever give color to their teachings. They will never be able to look on the character of Jesus in the cold light of history. They will never confess to any failings of his; he will never be to them a normal man. While Socrates may be as noble or nobler, while Moses may even excel him in meekness and self-renunciation, while the martyrdom of Akiba is just as thrilling, and the teachings of the prophets as sublime, while their own heroes, Paul, Huss, Luther and Father Damien may have been just as great, as far as we can compare human characters at all from our occasional glimpses and rough approximations—they will

---

Gospels cover but six months of his life. The silence of contemporary history about him is more than strange, it is significant. Philo-Judeus, sometimes called "the elder brother of Jesus," because of the similarity of their teachings, does not mention him personally though he survived him. The father of Josephus, from whom the historian obtained so many of his details, though he was a contemporary of Pontius Pilate and lived in the heart of these scenes, has nothing to state about him. At this late day it is needless to say that the one isolated paragraph about him in Josephus, is a forgery. Finally Menelaus of Damascus and Justus of Samaria, contemporary writers, also refrain from mentioning him.

never be able to bring themselves to acknowledge it, even though in their exaggerated estimate, they may do injustice to many of the world's heroes. The divine man in some sense, he will always be to them, for this is their inheritance from Christianity that has become part of their very being. He is still the Master, with a capital M. Even with those Unitarians, who doubt God, who are agnostic—the worship of Jesus abides. Here we see that force of sentimental association and historic background in religious life. It is true a bold statement was made by a Unitarian. "We must get outside of Christianity in order to teach the truth which Jesus did not teach, and to practice the good he did not enjoin." But it is immediately met by the disappointing but not unexpected reply: "Christianity has no outside; the spirit of Jesus is the spirit of free progress, in that name we can go on toward perfection for ever."

Reform Judaism and Unitarianism are distinct religions—because of these historic and sympathetic divergences which react both on doctrine and on practice. For that matter, Mohammedanism is a Unitarianism too; and Mohammed was very surprised and disappointed that the Jews would not accept it, since it was so largely Jewish. We appeal to the testimony of history whether Judaism was justified in not permitting itself to be absorbed by its second daughter. Israel's intense monotheism could never compromise with hero-worship—whether of Jesus or Mahomet. While the fact that Jesus is really God for half the world, is in itself sufficient to exclude him from the synagogue. Even Moses, whom he is made to supplant, is treated as but one in the line of great men that remind Hebrews they can make their lives sublime. While Judaism, like Unitarianism, has always evaded the limitations of a creed* giving the mind full breadth of thought, the doctrine of the One God has always been regarded as a *sine qua non* of Judaism, so that an agnostic wing of our faith would be impossible.

Although Unitarianism then is a distinct faith from Judaism, and can teach it nothing, and indeed has no new truth to teach the world at large, being in itself but an eclectic gathering of modern teachings and beliefs, still it can, and through the spread of its literature, it is rendering a beneficent service to orthodox Christianity by holding up to it a more rational and liberal ideal—a service it would be less likely to effect did it cut itself adrift from the old moorings and start as a new religion. In the same way reform Judaism is rendering a similar service to orthodox Judaism, in loyally standing under the banner of the old faith and in regarding all its modern departures as unbroken and organic developments from our ancient creed.

But partly for the reason that it lacks the organization and symbolic ceremonial of a church, partly because of the uncertainty of its belief, partly, perhaps, because of its very vague requirements of its members, and because it seems to represent nothing positive and to teach nothing that was not already taught before it came—it has not grown in public confidence and hence in numbers, to anything like the extent of other denominations. It is an indication of some fatal weakness when a faith appeals to a cultured few, who least need its discipline, and does not reach the masses. But even among the cultured, it is a significant fact

---

*So many have repeated Mendelsohn's statement, that Judaism has no dogmas, that it has become a dogma itself—the dogma of dogmalessness.

that two of its greatest representatives in America, Emerson and Frothingham, left the Unitarian Church. Why? Because it either meant too much or too little. If too much—they could not pledge themselves to the acceptance of any beliefs of which they had a lingering doubt; if too little—there was no object in placing themselves under that particular banner. That is where too broad a platform may defeat itself. If I am to be so untrammeled that I can believe or disbelieve anything I please, apart from the implied desire to further the general human good, which is the back bone of every true and genuine religion, a distinctive name seems unnecessary.

A religion is helpful in the sense in which religion should be helpful, to the extent that it stands for something distinct and positive.

While then we feel the value for the cause of truth of stating minutely the difference between Judaism and Unitarianism, where the latter seems to fall short for us, we are glad to recognize an intellectual kinship growing out of similarities that also exist between them. And so we will go on our different ways, with kindly thoughts for each other and with occasional friendly interchange of views. We feel nothing but admiration for the boldness and sincerity of the Unitarians and for their manifest honesty of purpose, even while we sadly realize the insufficiency of their creed. As a further cause for good feeling between us, I am glad to speak here of our grateful indebtedness to Mr. Fox, of London, who, in the early part of the century worked hard both in and out of Parliament for the removal of Jewish disabilities. He uttered some strong words in our behalf and in condemnation of our enemies. Let me close with a word of thankful acknowledgment of what we all owe to the fine thoughts of those great Unitarians—Channing, Martineau and Parker. May many souls for many years to come draw inspiration from their living words.

CONGRATULATORY ADDRESS.

DELIVERED AT THE DEDICATION OF THE TEMPLE OF THE
NORTH CHICAGO HEBREW CONGREGATION,
BY RABBI JOSEPH STOLZ.

On behalf of the sister congregations of this city I beg to extend cordial congratulations to this North Chicago Hebrew Congregation, its rabbi, its officers and directors, its members and pewholders and all who with money, goodwill and loving labor contributed towards the erection of this inviting religious home. Owing to the sectional divisions of our wide-spreading city, the rapid change in the character of our streets and the great Chicago fire, you have had extraordinary difficulties to contend with; but nothing daunted, you have, in a period of financial depression, by dint of courage and faith in the future, succeeded in erecting on this beautiful street this attractive house dedicated to the worship of God and the eternal spirit of Judaism. It has cost you many sacrifices; but that which is not worth a sacrifice is not worth having; that for which men will not make a sacrifice cannot stand or prosper. Judaism survived because there were those who made unparalleled sacrifices for it; let the men and women of Israel cease to forget themselves and Judaism will cease to be, no matter how much it may deserve to live. That is the law of the universe. The strength of the Catholic Church lies not in its hierarchy and not in its wealth or political power; it lies in the abounding sacrifices which they are capable of making for their church who swear allegiance to the Roman Pontificate. The remarkable growth of the Salvation Army under our very eyes is not due to its teachings or its methods; but in spite of these it has taken root and grown to such vast proportions because self-sacrifice is the sunshine and fine rain that makes any institution grow strong.

You have reason this day to feel a just pride in your achievement. May this temple ever be an inspiration in your prosperity, a consolation in your sorrow; may it give hope to your youth and support to your old age; may it cast light upon your darkness and through its association with the deepest experiences of your soul and the richest events of your life become dear to you as a home.

But upon the completion of this the sixth Reform Temple in this city, there is cause for rejoicing far beyond these confines. It is a triumph of Reform Judaism as it has found expression in America that we are celebrating to-day. The principles underlying reform Judaism were first enunciated and expounded in Germany. It was the Jews whose cradle rested on German soil that carried those principles to this country; but it was in America and not in Germany that those principles were most unequivocally expressed and most consistently carried out. Practically and officially German Judaism to-day is orthodox. The German synagogue is pre-eminently oriental, though the German Jew is thoroughly occidental in his life, thought and activity. It was in this youthful land—and especially in this youthful west where the conservative spirit is not yet strong and the thought of the people does not yet run in fixed grooves and along certain well-defined channels,—that within the synagogue as well as without, in practice as well as theory, Reform Judaism has found the most consistent interpretation. Of course, the results have not been all that was anticipated. We can indeed point to magnificent temples, to the finest charities in the world, to a better appreciation and a sincerer recognition of the Jew, to a freer and a more cordial relationship between Jew and non-Jew, to a free pulpit and an outspoken declaration to the world of the claims and rights of Judaism, to a greater consistency between the synagogue and life, to a better understanding of our religion and a greater willingness to be Jews. If we have not accomplished all that enthusiasts expected, that is not the fault of reform principles. Orthodoxy has fared much worse; and if, with the life and with the trend of thought of our country, our synagogues had remained officially orthodox, there would have been a greater desertion and a worse apostasy in our land than ever was known in Berlin five decades ago.

Reform Judaism has been suffering from a peculiar concatenation of circumstances. The transition from the conservative life and thought of a German village to the progressive life and thought of an American city was too sudden and too insufficiently prepared for not to leave its evil effects.

The general life of these three decades has not been favorable to religion. The spirit of the age, the whole force and pressure of the time, is not idealistic. Ours is an era of material progress, of useful inventions, of great practical ambitions and achievements. We have annihilated space and time and made force and matter our docile servants ; and these accomplishments have reacted upon our own spirits. They have imbued us with mechanical modes of thought and material standards of deeds and have almost produced a spiritual paralysis. Literature and art are degenerate. Business is selfish. Patriotism since the war has become sordidly selfish. Social life is selfish. Wealth is the standard of good society. An idealist is considered a crank. Men barter the glories of the universe for the few trinkets they call riches. The main study of the average man of the street is bread and butter; and if no winged creatures are hatched from such a chrysalis and the study of the Thorah has become almost a lost art, and the Jewish father's highest ambition no longer is that his gifted son shall be a rabbi in Israel,—the fault lies principally with the materialistic trend of the times and not with reform principles.

The thought of the period, too, has been anti-religious. Never before has religion been put to the severe strain of the last quarter of a century. Every belief was undermined. One thing was declared unscientific and another unhistorical. Religion as it was systematized in the creed, religion as it was described in the Bible, religion as it was practiced in ceremonies, religion itself was questioned. The Bible was questioned, revelation was questioned, immortality was questioned, the very existence of God was questioned, and this not by a few scattered skeptics but by the masses. The result was that religion being such an uncertainty the people were not inclined to give the church their hearty support; they would not pray if there was no being to hear prayer; they would not send their children to Sunday-school if what had been taught them they might later have to unlearn. Religion, in short, was thought to be good enough for superstitious women and fearful old people, but nothing for strong, thinking, active, free-minded men and women.

The tide is fortunately now turning. The night is already far spent and the dawn is at hand. Balfour's "Foundations of Belief" is a mile-post pointing towards the opposite pole. Yet, that despite these overtowering obstacles you have enthusiastically put up this grand temple is a triumph for our American interpretation of Judaism, and from the Atlantic to the Pacific all who are in spiritual bond with you send you a message of congratulation that your measure of life and of truth has been vast enough to make this sacrifice. A larger circle than is bounded by the two oceans rejoices with you to-day,—all Israel. It is not the walls of this building, however beautiful their design and charming their decoration, it is the spirit for which this building stands that has gathered us together.

What a miracle that without a single bond of union and despite all persecutions "ye are standing to-day all of you in the presence of the Eternal your God!" But even a greater miracle is it that after 3,500 years there should be anyone possessed of the thought of rearing a temple to the glory of Judaism. Discredited are the systems of Socrates, Plato and Aristotle; Dun Scotus and Albertus Magnus; Maimonides, Albo and Ibn Gabirol; Descartes, Leibnitz and Spinoza; Kant, Hegel and Fichte; even Herbert Spencer's system is already discredited, yea, during his own lifetime has he partially retracted his own agnosticism. The word "agnosticism" is just twenty-five years old; to-day it is acknowledged to stand for an "utterly baseless dogma." The philosophy of one age is rejected the next. The science of to-day is antiquated to-morrow. Not only is the science of the Greeks ludicrous and that of the Middle Ages puerile, but Weissman refutes Darwin and Romanes goes back on himself. The religion of Greece furnishes our children their fairy tales; the religion of Egypt and Assyria is the archæological pastime of the chosen few at the universities; and yet those old patriarchs who wore turban and tallith, who carried their burdens on the backs of asses, who conveyed news by heralds, who spent weeks in traveling from Dan to Beer-Sheba, who fought with sling-shots, who ploughed the ground with a stick and threshed their wheat with a flail, who conducted their business by barter and paid their wages every night and sent to Tyre for mechanics, who depended upon witnesses to announce the appearance of the new moon and who preserved their literature by word of mouth—interpreted the religious yearnings of the soul and the summons to duty so correctly that we, with our Republican institutions, our schools and libraries, our telegraphs and telephones, our railroads and electric lights, our gatling guns and men-of-war, our printing-presses and threshing machines, can still say to them אלהי אלהיך עמי עמך "your religion is our religion!"

Not Homer or Horace, not Shakespeare or Burns, not Gœthe or Schiller, not Moliere or Lamartine, not Dante or Petrarch, or any other author is read in his own country or cherished by his own countrymen as is to-day the literature of those Bedouins that 2,500 years ago and more trod the plains of the Jordan and climbed the hills of Lebanon. That, too, sounds miraculous. But greater still is the miracle that the most advanced religious thought of to-day is the thought and inspiration of old Israel. The essence of Judaism is taking possession of the best spirits of the world. The modern passion for social justice is Biblical. Prof. Felix Adler confessed that his movement was nothing more than the movement of the prophets. The Congress of Liberal Religions, if rightly understood, is but a fulfilment of the prayer every orthodox Jew has been repeating thrice daily for a thousand years. Oh, if we only had faith in ourselves, the enthusiastic appreciation of our heritage, a consciousness of the spiritual wealth of our symbols, of the strong foundation of our history, of the sanity of our "Weltanschauung," we would not to-day be lagging behind, we would be in the vanguard; we would not be the caboose with the green flag hanging out warning others to keep away, we would be the engine equipped with the spiritual force to lead and guide others to the coveted goal. The thought of the world is with us now as it has never been before. Prophetical are the cry for ethics and the clamor for social regeneration now in the air; prophetical is the liberalism that despises creed and looks beyond the ceremonial and the temporary to the righteous and the lasting; and if we but devoted ourselves to our religion with the intensity of passion with which we throw our souls into our business and professions, if we were but ready to make for the congregation the sacrifice we make for our clubs and our charities, Israel would to-day be the engine, and to Judaism there would flock converts even more than 1900 years ago flocked to Israel in Palestine and Asia Minor and way down in Rome.

FAITH WITH REASON.

BY RABBI JOSEPH KRAUSKOPF, D.D., PHILADELPHIA.

Man is not worse than he has been, nor as bad. If we know more of evils done than our ancestors knew, it is because we have better means for knowing. A single electric wire stretching across our continent, a single cable spanning the ocean, will communicate, in one day, more news of crimes committed than could, in a year, all the carts and ships, all the riders and runners, a century or two ago.

Yes, man is better than he has been, but truth also bids me to add, that he is not as good as he ought to be. That with all the progress he has made in the arts and sciences and liberties, with all the knowledge he has acquired of the curse and consequence of evil, with all the teaching that is being done on the benefits of right-living, the press must still dish up for us, at every morning and evening meal, such a revolting mass of crime, is a matter of serious concern.

I am even of the opinion that it is a severer judgment on mankind of to-day to say, that it is not as good as it ought to be, than that it is not as bad as it was. The past had a better palliative for having been as bad as it was, than has the present for not being better than it is. And the moralist has better grounds for complaint. When a farmer spends much labor and means upon the cultivation of a field, and finds that the yield from it is but slightly better than it was before he spent a wealth of work and money upon it, he feels more discouraged than he was at first. When a teacher expends much thought and patience and time upon the education of a pupil, and notes but very slight improvements, he feels disheartened over the poor result.

Farmers or teachers of such experiences generally throw up their work, and direct their attention to things that promise more satisfactory returns. The wiser among them, however, persevere till they have studied out the disturbing cause, and, remedying it, obtain at last the desired result.

This latter course must be that of our teachers of morality, if they would overcome the frightful amount of evil, which festers uncontrolled on the very surface of society, and which, penetrating its every artery and channel, poisons the whole system, down to its very life-giving, life-quickening centers.

As one of these teachers, I have for some time past studied the question of modern evils, and traced the disturbing causes that prevent morality's fullest growth and fruition. I have pondered on the unprecedented means at man's command for knowing the difference between right and wrong. Never before have schools been so abundant and so well equipped. Never since the ken of man have the printing-houses and bookstores sent into the homes of the people, from the highest to the lowest, from the most learned to the most simple, such vast supplies of books, magazines and papers of such an elevated moral tone, as now. Never since society exists, has man had as clear a grasp of the unity of human kind, and of the obligation each individual member of it owes to himself, to his family, to his descendents, to his fellow-men, to his government, to humanity, as at present. Not even in the much-sung golden ages of the past has man had so inspiring a view of the grandeur of the universe, and of the marvelousness of the laws and forces and intelligences that pervade it, as he has now.

And yet, unless my researches greatly deceive me, never before has man drawn, proportionally, as little for his stock of morality from the sources at hand as in this present era. Morally he is still diseased. He has risen from his sick-bed, only to hobble about, woefully plastered and bandaged, on crutches, with little hope of a speedy cure. I cannot ascribe ignorance as cause of his painfully slow recovery,—he knows more than ever before. I cannot attribute it to a greater sway of the lower passions,—he is further removed from the beast than ever before. I cannot assign as cause of it greater temptations to wrong-doing on account of greater poverty,—he is wealthier than ever before. I cannot account for it on the ground of greater restraint from right-doing.—he is freer than ever before. I can ascribe his slow recovery to one cause only: to lesser faith in God, to a lesser belief that life is of Divine origin and has a Divine destiny, and that in the unfolding process of man's spiritual life, every wrong will count, and every stain will taint.

Had the rational faith of former times allied itself with our modern superior reason, it would long since have turned this vale of misery into a Paradise. Peace would have spread its golden pinions unto the ends of the earth. Swords would have been beaten into plowshares, and spears into pruning-hooks. Standing armies would have been scattered as husbandmen over the face of the earth. Wastes would have been turned into garden spots, and wildernesses into fertile fields. We would not have had the pampered rich to breed discontent, nor the starving poor to be tempted into crime. We would not have heard the weeping of the overworked, nor the lamentations of the underpaid. Arsenals would have been turned into churches, and penitentiaries into schoolhouses, and barracks into workshops. The love of God and man would have filled the earth, even as the waters fill the sea.

But it is a different picture that surrounds us now. It is a picture of carnage on battlefield and in workshop. It is a picture of outrage in palace and in hovel. It is a picture of thievery in council-chamber and on the public highway. It is a picture of clubbing policemen, of law-defying lynchers, of murdering rioters. Nation stands in arms against nation. Class stands with drawn sword against class. Employers and employees have their hands on each other's throats. Warship after warship, costing millions of dollars, is built to rot in the water, while for the eradication of the slums, in which thousands of innocent human beings are rotting away, and which menace and attack the health and lives of countless thousands of others, there is not a penny to be had. Fraud sits at the side of the magistrate, infidelity at the side of the oath-administering court-official, deception sits between friend and friend, between brother and brother, between husband and wife. Children with inbred disease point their finger of scorn at their parents. Hardy sons of toil, with starving wives and children at their heels, go from door to door in search of labor, only to be turned away, to have the dog set on them, till they finally land in a convict's cell, or die a suicide's death. Women of fashion and luxury read of their sisters' wants and miseries, near their very doors, and yet continue undisturbed their revels of extravagance. Men are so absorbed in their devotion to the God of Mammon as to have no eye, no ear for suffering humanity. A feverish thirst for money, power, fame, rank has so violently seized upon the masses, that, in their frenzied hurry to gratify it, honor, principle, integrity are trampled down as if they were so many weeds.

The close student of human nature has little difficulty to trace the secret spring, which, through a thousand different fissures, makes its way, with ever-increasing force, to our life-centers, and there forms the noisome pools of our modern evils. Its name is *Irreligion*. Morality has lost its divine authority, duty its sanctity, sorrow and sacrifice their hope. People have thrust aside their God. To be sure, there are abundant churches, and frequent services, and large congregations. But many more attend to satisfy social requirements than real religious cravings. Often, when I see them gathered for worship, and observe their attitudes and attentions, I feel like putting the question to them which the queen put to Hamlet:

> "Alas! How is it with you
> That you do bend your eye on vacancy,
> And with the incorporeal air do hold discourse?"

Hamlet, at least, saw a ghost; they see nothing of a supernatural kind. The brilliant light that science has suddenly turned upon them has dazzled and dazed them. The more the large end of the telescope has revealed of the marvelous handiwork of God, the more contracted has become the small end's view of God Himself. The All-seeing Eye, of which the Psalmist sang that it "slumbereth not, nor sleepeth," is closed. The twinkling stars no longer breathe a message of a yonder sphere. The sprouting buds of the early spring no longer kindle a hope of another sprouting in another world. The ray of divinity in the infant's eye is no longer the fading hue of a celestial light that has preceded. The hallow light that shines upon the dying patriarch's brow, no longer suggests that sunset here may mean sunrise elsewhere. Great, gloomy gates have been reared at the grave, and on them have been written the soul-deadening words: "So far, and no farther! All there is of life is this side the grave. Beyond it there is nothing. Life is a bubble, puffed by the lips of chance into space, where it dances and glitters its brief moment, and then bursts into nothingness. Wise are they, who crowd into that brief moment the most of happiness." And eagerly men accept this teaching. Happiness is their goal. If truth and right and honor and justice stand in the way of its attainment, why should these not be cast aside, when there is no God to see it, no God to render account to?

It is the custom of many preachers, when they reach this point in their lamentations, to inflict a severe tongue-lashing on modern unbelievers, to whose doors they lay much of the responsibility for our modern evils. Ground for vexation to a godly man, I admit there is enough. But abuse is not the wisest method to rid society of godlessness. You can as little scold people into faith, as you can scold people into love. Unbelievers resent abuse. They may listen to reason. My dealings with some of them have assured me, that most of them are more willing to have faith with reason than preachers are willing or capable of giving to them. I have enjoyed the confidences of some of these decried unbelievers. I have heard them envy people of strong faith. I have heard them say: "Oh, if you could give me that trusting faith of some of the believers I know, that uplifting, strengthening, comforting belief in God, that abides the same in sunshine and in storm, in life and death, that sees Divine Love in the most cruel blow, and Divine Purpose in the most apparent accident, that sees the eye of God upon them in the light and in the darkness, and feels the guiding hand of God upon them in their every perplexity, and hears the approving or rebuking voice of God within their hearts, when they have done right or wrong; that faith, that bears the tortures of the sick-bed without a murmur, that exclaims with Job: 'Though He slay me, yet will I trust in Him'; that faith that looks down into the grave without a shudder, and up into heaven without a doubt; give me that faith, make it tangible, reasonable, demonstrable to me, and you will make of me the happiest of mortals."

How wrong in preachers to censure men possessed of such yearnings after reasonable faith! Probably they have never been rent or torn by the piercing thorn of doubt or unbelief. Probably they have never sent forth from their sleepless pillow a despairing cry for the light and for the truth. I have felt that thorn, and I have cried that cry of despair. I have wrestled, like Jacob of old, through a long dark night, until at last the light dawned, until at last the cheering rays of the morning-star burst through the mists and clouds, wafting the divine message: "Thou hast wrestled, and thou hast conquered. Thy mind shall have peace!"

It was a comforting message, but it was not sent until I had become clearly conscious of the limitations of human knowledge, of the duality of human nature. My faith secured a firm anchorage only after I had fully grasped the truth, that knowledge is of two kinds, the demonstrable and the undemonstrable, that which can be measured and weighed, tested and dissected, and that which can only be felt, divined, that which wells up within us as inspiration, as prophetic instinct, as intuition, that which is a brain acquirement, and that which is an original soul-endowment.

Man is a dual being. Part of him is material; the other and best part is spiritual. The one part is governed by the mind, the other by the soul. The one employs reason as a means of acquiring truth, the other exercises primary intuitive discernment. The reason compasses the realm of matter; intuitive discernment enters the sphere of the spirit. The one deals with the visible and the tangible, the other with that which eludes the grasp of the physical senses. The one arrives at its conclusions only after patient tests and experiments; the other reaches them by a single bound. The one studies the universe, observes therein design, harmony, law, intelligence, forethought, adaptation of means to ends, and postulates that some power different from any that are known, must have called it forth, and must hold sway over it; the other affirms, without the aid of telescope or microscope, or scalpel or re-agents, that such a power exists, that it is a living, conscious being, which has created the universe, and rules it as well as the destiny of all that live and move therein. The one observes that life is not of human make, and that it is under a law of constant evolutionary progression, and, applying its canons of reasoning, concludes that man's present imperfections foreshadow still higher development. The other asserts, at once and strongly, that life is a gift of God, and returns to God, to take up a higher form of existence, in another sphere. The one is perplexed by the mysteries that abound, by the happenings that are strange and unaccountable; the other declares them, without hesitation, to be the ways of Providence, to be the will and working of God, subserving divine ends.

We somewhat understand how the mind obtains its knowledge, but how and when and where the soul acquires its endowments no man can tell. The soul seems to enter upon its existence dowered with these intuitions by its Divine Parent, even as the body enters life pregnated with hereditary characteristics of its human parents. It is an original endowment; and a universal one as well. The whole human family has an abiding faith in a Supreme Being governing the universe, and guiding the destiny of man, in the divine origin of life, and in its continuance after death. It is the greatest mystery and miracle of man's psychic state. The mind cannot grasp it, much less prove it, and still less deny it.

When we consider the feebleness of the human mind to grasp the origin and nature of things, the littleness of its knowledge, we begin to recognize a divine aid and purpose in the vast and bold sweep the soul takes of the realm barred to our physical senses. God endowed the soul with faith to help the mind across the encircling ocean of mystery, which impotent reason cannot bridge. Five thousand years, at least, has the mind been at work, and in that vast stretch of time it has scarcely learned the A. B. C. of the most necessary knowledge. In that time it has scarcely learned to reason correctly, or to trust reliably to the testimony of its own senses. It has scarcely gotten beyond the elements of science. Its knowledge of the laws of life and health is still fragmentary. Of this earth, over which it has roamed for tens of centuries, it has only a very rudimentary knowledge, and this earth is but a tiniest speck in the countless systems of worlds, that spin with inconceivable speed in the infinitude of space. What progress could reason have made without the aid of faith! There is not a thing it undertakes to comprehend but that faith must yoke itself with it to help it out. One half of knowledge is faith; the other half is based upon it. Verily, God has given us faith to supplement the limitations of knowledge! To it, much more than to reason are we indebted for the advance of human kind. Man's faith is mankind's salvation.

It must however be distinctly understood that the word *Faith*, as here used, does not stand for unreasoning credulity, for blind belief in the *dicta* of men, it stands solely for the acceptance of the intuitive discernments of our own souls; not for what we are told by the mouth of others, but for what is revealed to us by our own intuitions.

Faith supplies the deficiencies of the senses. It is the complement of reason. Reason is verified observation; Faith is spiritualized intuition. Reason is the testimony of the mind; Faith is the witness of the soul. Reason is like the plodding of the talent; Faith is like the inspiration of the genius. Reason is the accumulation of the knowledge of the past; Faith is the prophecy of the knowledge of the future. Reason illumines the realm about us; Faith flashes its search-light beyond the unlit gates. Reason is like the glow worm's cold and fitful light; Faith is like the hearthstone's warm and cheering fire. Reason grasps the form; Faith clasps the spirit. Reason discovers the handiwork; Faith discerns the Master behind it. Reason calculates and computes the forces and energies of things; Faith discloses the spring that moves them. Reason starts with facts and ends in belief; Faith commences with belief, and, as Whittier so beautifully expresses it,

> "The steps of Faith
> Fall on the seeming void, and find
> The rock beneath."

"What of those who have not faith?" you ask. I am not so sure that they have it not. I believe that faith throbs in every breast. In some it is a glimmering spark; in others it is a blazing flame. In some it slumbers; in others it is actively awake. Where there is a mind to reason, there is a soul to spiritualize. It can never be so attenuated but that a thread will not remain. And as long as a thread remains there is hope. I have read, that, when the first cable of the suspension-bridge, that now spans the Niagara, was about to be laid, a thin thread was attached to a kite and both sent, on a favoring wind, to the other side of the river. By means of that thread, a heavier string was pulled across, and by it a heavier one still, and then a rope, and then a tow, and then the cable, and the other parts of that mighty bridge, that enables the people to pass in safety, from one side to the other, over the roaring cataract beneath. Let but those, who doubt or disbelieve, fasten the tiny thread of faith that lingers in them still, to the spiritual side of life, and gradually it will become stronger and stronger until it will grow into a mighty bridge, that will carry them safely, over the seething and hissing abyss of doubts and perplexities, unto the yonder peaceful shore.

Oh, ye of little faith, why will you not turn the tiny thread of belief within you into a mighty cable, so that it may anchor you safely in that spiritual sea, where unbeliefs cease from troubling, and where infidelities are at rest? Do you not see, how, for the want of it, you are drifting compass-less, sail-less, rudder-less, on the turbulent waters, with a thousand gales of sin and vice and crime tearing and splitting you asunder? Do you not see how, for the want of it, society is deprived of the blessed fruitage of the best achievements of the modern mind? Have you not the proofs of the past that the ages of great faith were the ages of great achievements? What would the reformers and emancipators, the heroes and the martyrs, the discoverers and the inventors of the past have done, without a mighty living faith to steel their arms, to light their ways, to cheer their hearts, to buoy up their spirits in stress and storm? And with our mental superiority over the past, what might not our achievements be, were our faith correspondingly superior to the faith of the past, or even equal to it?

Individually, too, greater faith would mean greater happiness. The divinity within us would cast a hallowed circle of divineness about us, into which sin could not set its foot, without the mind launching its eternal curse upon it. Duty would acquire the force of divine commands. Morality would stand for injunctions divinely graven on the tablets of our hearts. God would be seen and felt in the tranquil dome above and on the troubled earth beneath; in the thunder's mighty roar, and in the mother's peaceful lullaby; in the sun's dazzling fire and in the spring-flower's innocent blush, in the sigh of the oppressed, and in the groan of the oppressor; in the heroism of the martyr, and in the cowardice of the traitor; in the boldness of the reformer, and in the modesty of the maiden; in the ecstasy of the inspired, and in the shame of the offender. Sorrow would mean to us that the hand of God is but tightening the strings, that they might give forth sweeter music by and by. Death would mean to us only the end of dying here, and the commencement of living yonder, the finish of our material preparation and the beginning of our spiritual development. It would enable us to lay our dear ones into the grave with a resignation as complete as that of that mother, who, over the coffin of the last of all her seven children dead, calmly said: "Here lies my seventh and last child. Here, too, lies the will of God. His will be done. He knows best." It will enable us, in hours of extreme danger and alarm, when our every effort has failed, to commit our trust in Him who guides our destiny, feeling that all is not lost, as long as there is a God above us,—as that captain's little daughter felt, when awakened in her cabin, in the dead of night, by a terrific storm, and when told that her father commanded the ship, calmly she replied: "Father is on the bridge, I am safe." And even if the waters swallow us, it will enable us to say with the poet:

"If my bark sink, 'tis to another sea."

Faith will not clear all our difficulties, nor answer all our questions. But it will clear enough, and say enough, to keep our hearts pure, our hands clean, our eyes upon our goal, and our feet upon the path leading thither. It will not shed full radiance here below, but, once within its sanctuary, through its divinely illumined windows it will admit sufficient light from without to make the daylight sweeter, and in the night it will flash out sufficient light from within to make the darkness brighter.

Though reason has not yet opened our physical eyes to enable us to see what our soul divines, let us thank God for our intuitional discernment that helps us to construct a bark strong enough to sail in safety across life's seas. What better shipbuilders than the Herreshoffs, the makers of the victorious *Defender?* What waters have not carried their boats? What country has not felt itself honored in conferring medals and prizes upon them? The head of the firm is totally blind, and has been so for forty years. And yet, though blind, he is and has been the first and final authority of every ship built by that firm. A tiny model is made of the boat about to be built, and submitted to him. He retires into seclusion, and by his marvelously developed sense of touch, obtains a complete mental picture of the ship, and passes judgment upon it. In forty years, his judgment has never failed him, though arrived at in the darkness of physical blindness.

Faith is the elder Herreshoff's marvelous sense of touch. It enables us to see what eyes cannot see, and to pass judgments that do not, will not fail. Though arrived at in the darkness of physical blindness it enables us to construct a ship, which, if we equip it with reason, and steer it aright, will enable us to win the race over evil, and land us safely on the yonder shore.

THE HOPE OF IMMORTALITY.

BY RABBI RUDOLPH GROSSMAN, D.D., NEW YORK.

To the bedside of a dying man let me bid your attendance. The old patriarch Jacob, who in life had vanquished many a bitter opponent, has at last succumbed to his most formidable foe, death. Children and children's children are gathered about the hallowed couch. A peace as of heaven fills the chamber in which death kisses the lips of life. Forgotten is the animosity between Joseph and his brethren, and the heart of brother is knit to the heart of brother, as the last farewell of the cherished father falls on their ears. Calmly, fearlessly, without sorrow, the old patriarch awaits the inevitable end. Words of counsel and of blessing flow from his blanched lips. Before his fading sight there arises the vision of the future. With a prophet's eye, he describes the coming career of each of his sons, when suddenly his strength fails him; his voice seems to grow almost inaudible; death stands impatient at his side; his moments are numbered, and gathering together all his feeble strength, the expiring patriarch bursts out in that one cry, that voices his faith that death is not the end, that passing hence means living yonder, לישועתך קויתי ה' "In Thy salvation do I trust, O God."

From that distant day to this, wherever a sigh has been heaved, wherever a tear has been shed as the last scene of life has touched the heart with its awful solemnity, the one hope that has buoyed up the drooping spirit and deprived the fatal cup that every mortal must drain of its poison, has been the faith that found expression in the words of Jacob, "In Thy salvation do I trust, O God."

It is with considerable hesitancy that I venture to speak on this question of immortality that has so long and so deeply touched the heart of man. Baffled by the grandeur of the theme, I feel my utter helplessness in dealing with a subject that so far transcends human knowledge. And yet, whether we will or not, the question confronts us on every side, and the feeling heart insists upon an answer: must we abandon this great hope of mankind, this tower of strength in the hour of trial, this fountain of inspiration in the midst of life's conflicts?

The very first fact that strikes our attention as we look out over the world's history, is the absolute universality of the belief in immortality. You may find nations so rude, that they live houseless, in dark caverns of the earth, you may find tribes so savage, that they have neither raiment, weapon or fire, but nowhere will you find a nation without a belief in immortal life. It is the common creed of the human race. It is written in the nature of man, and written so large that the rudest nations have not failed to find and to know it. It thrilled the heart of the ignorant savage as he beheld his tribesman lying cold and silent at his feet, struck by the flinty arrow. It awakened a response in the soul of the Egyptian forty centuries ago. It gave new hope to the Buddhist as he bewailed the misery of life. It lived in the mind of the Chaldee and the Persian. It attended the footsteps of the Greek and the Roman. From the lips of all the human race, whether standing in the lowlands of barbarism or on the summit of civilization, whether gathered in heathen shrine, or synagogue or cathedral or mosque, the one cry has ever resounded, "In Thy salvation do I trust, O God," whether the God invoked be Jehovah or Jupiter or Osiris or the lowest idol or fetish.

Whence originated this universal belief? Not in revelation or reason, not from argument or observation. The human race did not sit down and think it out; did not wait till logic or metaphysics would prove it; did not delay its belief till a divine revelation came to confirm it. It is an instinct inborn in man. It awoke in the heart as awoke the belief in God, the love of man, the sentiment of justice, by the spontaneous action of the spirit within. Immortality is the writing of God on the soul of man; it is a desire that is part of his nature, deep as the foundation of his being. Shall we believe that this universal desire, constitutionally and ineradicably planted in all men, has no corresponding gratification, is but a cheating delusion? Shall we not rather regard it as the silent prophecy of endless life? What is thus in man is writ there by God, who writes no lies. Strange, indeed, were it that universal man had conceived the thought, the expectation of a life beyond the grave, if the grave ends all. Look throughout all the domain of nature, and for every want you will find ample provision; for every instinct there is some reality corresponding thereto. The plant seeks moisture, and behold, moisture is. The blade of grass yearns for sunlight and air, and air and sunshine exist. The wants of every fish that swims, of every bird that flies, of every beast that roams, find ample provision in nature. And for man's material needs there is sufficient supply. He is hungry, and the earth teems with abundance. He is thirsty, and a spring bubbles at his feet. He yearns for love, and love answers his desire. Everywhere the natural desire in plant or animal or man may somewhere find its natural gratification. Shall, in the higher realms of man, in the domain of the mind, the heart, the soul, the universal law break, and there be no provision for his most essential, most ardent longing? As well say that the stars and planets spin and shine, drawn onward by attraction and light, but that there is no central orb about which they revolve and which is the source of their light and attraction, as to declare that there is this burning hunger for immortality in man, but there is for him no such experience as an immortal life.

But hold! cries the materialist and skeptic of our day. The night of blind belief is ended; the day of clear reason has come. A time there was when authority was all-powerful; to-day, thought is the only court of authority. What I cannot understand, I will not believe. Only that which my mind can compass will I accept; all else is fiction, dream, imagination. This modern cry, "Explain all, or we will not believe," may sound scientific, but it is related to true science as the smoking street lantern is to the sun. Explain all! What science explains all in the department with which it deals? Does Darwin leave no mysteries unsolved? Can we account for every fact in our daily experience, the truth of which none would presume to question? Can we explain the wondrous force in the plant that drives leaves and blossoms to their fruition? Can even the most profound student lay his finger on that mysterious something we call life, and explain thought, will, feeling? One-half of knowledge is based on faith, and every science is pillared on unsolvable mystery. And you—you would presume to deny, to repudiate the belief in immortality—a belief that has been the shrine before which all religions bow in common—a belief that has been the staff and support of all peoples, ages and climes—because your reason cannot grasp it? What avails the flat denial of unripe minds over against the firm belief of profound thinkers like a Mendelssohn, a Lessing or an Emerson, who clung to immortality? The very first requirement in a consideration of a theme so perplexing, so mysterious as this, is modesty, humility, the recognition of the frailty and the impotence of human reason over against the marvels of the Infinite.

It is reported that when a certain well-known atheist and skeptic, whose best powers have been devoted to demolishing the bulwarks of religion and to scoffing at God, stood before the open grave into which was to be deposited all that was mortal of a brother dearer to him than all else, it is reported that, in the anguish of his soul, he cried aloud, "My God, this is not the end." Strange irony this! Bitter inconsistency! It was the cry of his heart, mightier than the frail voice of his mind, yearning for immortality. It was sentiment, more powerful than thought, that had burst the bars of reason, and insisted on a life larger than this little span of years. Who is there who has shrouded in darkness and silence one beloved, who has not shrunk back in horror from the awful thought of annihilation, and every chord of whose heart has not thrilled with the conviction: No, no, a thousand times no, life is not to end in "a Stygian cave forlorn, where brooding darkness spreads its sable wings"; life is more than pain and pleasure, alternating as the rise and fall of the waves on an agitated ocean; life is more than a fleeting shadow ending in the darkness of the tomb? Who is there who has stood before the grave, looking his last on the marble face of a dear one, to whom hope has not whispered its blessed message, to whom love has not spoken in accents sublime: "Nay, nay, this is not all, the soul is more than dust, it is a breath from the heights, it is a spark of the celestial fire, 'in Thy salvation do I trust, O God.'"

But can we say no more for this grand belief than that affection sustains it, and that hope yearns for it? Will it not bear being looked at in the dryest and sharpest light of logic? Truth never flinches before reason. There are arguments that are fair, logical and just, which must satisfy the mind and afford a basis for the sentiment that disposes the heart in its favor.

The first of these is drawn from the world of matter around about us. One of the laws that science has most positively established is, that in the material world nothing is ever destroyed. There is no such thing as annihilation. Things are changed, transformations abound, but essence does not cease to be, even when nature has manipulated it in all her laboratories for a billion years. Take a quantity of matter, divide and subdivide it in ten thousand ways by mechanical violence, by chemical solvents, still does it exist as the same quantity of matter, with unchanged qualities as to its essence, and will exist even unto the end of time. Shall matter live and spirit perish? Shall the lower outlast the higher? Shall the frame survive, the husk continue, and the soul, thought, affection, will, be crushed, annihilated?

But look further, and other proofs for immortality

come crowding to our minds. Here on earth, every plant and flower in its place and time matures. The acorn ripens every year. The rose reaches in every season its complete maturity. All earthly things reach their highest development, all attain that for which the Creator destined them. Man alone never reaches his complete maturity. Even in the best and highest, all their qualities are not fully grown. Man is never complete in the qualities of a man. What human soul does not feel the full force of the poet's words:

"'Tis life whereof our nerves are scant,
Oh life, not death, for which we pant,
More life and fuller than we want."

Often are we like plants that live in an inhospitable clime, bearing leaves and blossoms, but no fruit. We are cut off, just when we grow strong enough to do something. We are driven by a universal truth-hunger, which no earthly acquisition can satisfy. We have wings that are eager for flight to the very summit, eyes that long for fuller vision; but fell circumstances, adverse conditions, restrain our flight and darkness and misery blind our eyes. Through ages and millenniums myriads and myriads have lived in hunger of mind, and heart and soul, and have died questioning and unsatisfied. Shall we believe that this fervent yearning that thrills our very soul for life, for light, for truth, is all a hollow mockery, a chimera that lures us to deception? Shall man have no superiority over the brute save the mocking knowledge that the deepening shadows are to end in night, and the brilliant hopes to culminate in annihilation? Are we to regard the Creator's work, to use the words of John Fiske, "as like that of children why build houses out of bricks, merely for the pleasure of knocking them down?"

I need no better proof that I am more than cold clay, than the voice of my own heart that whispers to me the assurance, not in vain "Do I trust in Thy salvation, O God." I believe in the existence of a God. I believe that there is divine justice in the world. Justice cannot be without immortality. Every star whispers the message of divine love. Every flower speaks of infinite goodness. The whole creation thrills with the one refrain, God is just. Shall that love, that justice, that is, the universal pæan of praise to the Creator, bursting from the lips of all His handiwork, be denied to man alone? As surely as the rising walls of yonder building suggest the finished structure, so surely do the wrongs and the sufferings of earth, undeserved, point to another life where what is incomplete here will be completed, and what is dark here will be illumined.

Shall we believe that they who have gone out of life in childhood, in manhood, before the natural measure of their days was full, have been forever hurled into the darkness of oblivion, no morning to follow the long night? Shall we believe that the great, the wise, the generous, gifted with the noblest talents, aglow with sublimest aspirations, who have been summoned hence long before their qualities could even in a measure be unfolded, have utterly perished, their early demise being no prophecy of yet another spring and summer and harvests, too? Shall we believe that the millions made wretched by adverse circumstances, or dying the death of martyrs for truth, or living in want and anguish, enduring the pangs of persecution, have suffered with no divine voice to whisper to them the assurance, "fear not in your trial, lose not courage; battle on, there is a celestial love above you?" "What a piece of work is man. How noble in reason. How infinite in faculties. In form and movement, how express and admirable. In action how like an angel. In apprehension how like a God." Has the Creator fashioned so masterly a work as man, that only like a piece of worthless clay he might be demolished? To believe this, it is not profane to say it, were to believe that God is a cruel tyrant, and not a God of Justice. To believe this were to believe that virtue is a deception, and truth a lie, and self-sacrifice a mockery, if all they lead to is darkness and annihilation. To believe this were to affix the seal of approval to the words of a Robespierre, who in his dying moment is reported to have exclaimed, "let the candle be snuffed. Let life, the great cheat, be ended." Without immortality, life is indeed a delusion, and not to be is happiness. Without immortality, the world is a moral chaos, and man a blind machine. Without immortality, injustice sways the scepter and falsehood sits on the throne. With immortality, the tomb is the gateway to a nobler realm and death the messenger from celestial heights. With immortality, earth is the pathway to a brighter sunshine and man the child of Him whose days are without end.

I confess that, in the discussion of this theme, I have been led by the promptings of my heart. I put forth no claims to any rigorous demonstration. I have uttered an aspiration, nothing more. But who will say that an aspiration is at times not worth as much as an argument, if not more? Who will say that the promptings of our hearts are not as valuable and as true as the voices of our reason? You who have never suffered, no tear has furrowed your cheeks, no thorn has lacerated your flesh, to you, too, will come the night of crisis. Then, and then surely, you will realize how weak, how impotent, how helpless a thing is human reason. Then, and then surely, you will feel the full force of the words, "In Thy salvation do I trust, O God."

I know full well that nothing that I can say can make real and tangible for you this belief in immortality. I see full well the clouds of mystery that surround it. But I appeal to your sentiments, to your desire for happiness, cling to this child-like trust. The hope of the poor, the hope of the desolate, the hope of refinement, the hope of everything that is noblest in civilization, rests on the belief in immortality.

It may be that it is only a dream, only a vision of our own hearts, but even so, let us dream on. There is happiness, there is comfort, there is inspiration in that dream. Even a vision, if it bring hope and peace, is better than reality that only wounds and pains.

> "Learners are we all at school,
> Eager youth and weary age,
> Governed by the self-same rule,
> Poring o'er the self-same page.
> Life the lesson that we learn,
> As the days and years go by.
> Wondrous are the leaves we turn
> On the earth and in the sky.
> Oft our eyes with tears are dimmed,
> As we seek in vain to tell
> What may mean some harder word
> Than our wisdom yet can spell;
> But we read enough to trust
> That our grand hopes are not lies,
> That our hearts are more than dust,
> That our home is in the skies."

THE LAW.

BY RABBI LOUIS GROSSMANN, D.D., DETROIT.

I am often asked: Why does law figure so much in your religion? There is your Biblical law, your Talmudic law, your Rabbinical law, and you, reformers and orthodox both, seem to agree in respecting the principle of religious law (as Jews have done throughout the history of Judaism), and you differ only in the question how much of it is expedient and of what kind it should be under modern conditions. I confess that I am embarrassed by the question; as I feel embarrassed every time I am asked a sweeping question like that. For generalities are not easily made plain, and it is not easy to bring down to the level of the average person that which has been in the mind of prophets and statesmen. People take it for granted that religion is a simple and plain matter, or, at least, that it ought to be simple and plain; and, to be sure, this is true enough, but in theology simplicity and plainness are rare virtues, and it is quite to the point to say that, outside of philosophers and ignoramuses, no one else ever got much out of abstractions. We take an interest in religion not because we have a fancy for it, but because we feel that it is a serious matter. We wish to be told about it, because we wish to bring it home to ourselves. Inquirers, however, often have more curiosity than earnestness, and while it is true that many ask in good faith, it is the experience of Jewish rabbis that their congregants are frequently after scoring a point. The laity of all denominations are dominated more or less by a certain spirit of opposition, by what I might call an anti-clerical mood, which endures, though the reformatory times it came out of are almost entirely over. So a good deal of skepticism is afloat among the people as a sort of undefined protest against something, though few know now what that intolerable something really is. I do not wish to say that the question what point there is to law in Judaism is one of this kind, for it is too leading a question; but it is apparent that those who put this question lack that sympathy which he who endeavors to respond feels that he has a fair right to expect. Without the assurance that the answer will receive a due measure to tolerate hearing, not even the soberest inquiry can be satisfied.

You will remember that Simon the Just used to say: "Upon three things the world stands, upon law, upon worship and upon charity. I prefer to give it this form: Upon Thorah, upon worship and upon the mutual recompense of kindness; but we will not go into that now. It will be sufficient to notice that he puts law first. Of course, it is not clear on the surface of his maxim what he meant by law; still I think it is safe to suppose that he meant by it neither regulations nor statutes, but that peculiarly Jewish sense of law, which identifies it with religion. He could not have meant priestly law, for he saw to what unworthy things it had led in his own day, and being quoted at the head of one of the most important tractates of the Talmud, in a compilation of ethical sayings, it is likely that he was known not to have referred to conventional and casuistical jurisprudence. He laid down what he had found to be absolutely necessary if the Jews were to continue in the world. Simon the Just was as much a statesman as he was a high-priest, and we have a hint that he was equally wise and able in that pretty legend which tells us how he went forth to meet Alexander the Great and brought the conqueror to worship where he had come to scoff. In this day the tide of a new culture was pouring over Jerusalem and Israel, and what he says has not only the force but also the suggestiveness of a statesman.

I wish that you would see now, in the light of the celebrated saying of Simon the Just, how little the world understands the real point in Judaism. There is a good deal of gossip about our "legalism," or at least of the legalism of Moses and of the Talmud, and church people do not tire to bring out the awfulness of it. If we should ask in all candor, what is the offense in this charge of "legalism," we should not be enlightened. There are words which float about in the cheap rumor of partisans, and they seem conveniently to carry the intended stigma, and one of these incriminating words, in the conventional language of sectarianism, is "legalism." It is sufficient to fix that name upon Mosaism, if what you are after is to scandalize it. But after people have had the unchallenged pleasure for a long time I think we may be allowed to ask: What, after all, is this sin of legalism?" Judaism is not the only religion that has been legalistic, and when two or three religions do the same thing, it is fair to try to understand the common trait. As far as I can see every denomination has had a legalistic period, and Catholicism itself is that to-day still! There may be a difference between the Jewish phase of it; it is entirely home-grown, and the others may not be such growths out of their own roots; but that ought to tell in favor of Judaism. Christian law is christian, Roman, pagan, primitive and derivative; but the Jewish dispensation is all of one piece and native. And I am inclined to believe that the church was rather much in the business of law-making and that it has not even the merit of originality in the business. It was only a century or so after the close of the Talmud that Rome went into the "legalistic" enterprise; the rabbis were simply some time ahead of the church fathers, and Christianity seems to have profited very little from the forbidding example of rabbinical casuistry. It is gratuitous, it seems to me, for modern Christians to denounce without, what is equally blameable within.

But there seems to be an impression that the Judaism of to-day is still within the vise of this "legalism," while Christianity, at least the Protestant portion of it, is not, and the assertion is made that Judaism is committed to it for all time to come. I am ready to concede neither that Protestantism is entirely free from every ambition to rule and that there are no Protestant dilletants who try their hand at government out of all sorts of religious motives, nor am I willing to acknowledge that modern Judaism is legalistic as Mosaism is or as Talmudism is, and that nineteen centuries count for nothing or that, if Judaism is to be committed to an unbendable policy, all coming centuries are to count for nothing. If people would know what history Judaism has had, a history of ideas, not a history of mere politics, if people would know that at the same time when the Jews stepped out into the European countries, Rome began to forge chains upon believers, and that while there was the awful interval of the Middle Ages, Judaism unfolded into a bountiful life, a life fertile in the best things of culture as of faith, I doubt whether they would be so positive either to prophesy for Judaism an unpromising future or to summarily dismiss it as "legalistic"! The centuries between the council of Nice and Martin Luther are among the Jews the reverse of what they were among Christians. On the one side we have literature, art, science, philosophy, morality; on the other side we have illiteracy, superstition and the lowest ebb in culture. Judaism had undergone a great renaissance long before the Reformation came upon Europe. It would be a misunderstanding of the facts, if we should say that modern Judaism is radically different from ancient Judaism, but the one is different from the other by reason of an eventful interval. Jews have not altered much in matters of temperament; students of ethnology may be puzzled by this fact, but it is nevertheless a fact. Our temperament to-day is pretty much the same those Israelites had whose whims and passions tried even a Moses and whose virtues and peacefulness enthused a Bileam, so that he blessed when he had come to curse. Though our ancestry up to the very threshold of our day have had experiences, which went to the roots of their being, they have transmitted an unaltered semitic mood and mind so that we are as typical to-day of Israel and we are as alternately loved and hated as they themselves were. We have withstood every kind of attack, the open, the insidious, the attack of the learned, the clumsy attack of the mob, attacks theological, attacks that disenfranchised us, attacks that were meant to demoralize us, preconcerted and guerilla warfare, every conceivable kind. We are the marvel of history, but also its embarrassment. We came out of the ordeal unscathed, but also undejected, spiritually unimpoverished, morally unreduced. We have our good humor, as if it all had not been; perhaps you can detect some pathos in it, but will you wonder?

So long as there is one skeptic, one pessimist in the world, we are safe to say that Christianity has failed; despair, suicide, the church is responsible for. Instead of putting the stigma upon the unfortunate, it would be wiser and better if the sect could see that, if they had been efficient in what they do for the community, the nation, the world, these things could not be. The modern world is as yet impotent to dispense equal justice or equal confidence; and the modern world is largely Christian. The best proof that religion is of avail is obvious when it can preserve the good nature and the moral health of its professors, and it is unworthy if it fails to achieve that. The ghetto was happy and pure despite the persecutions. That narrow street was never too narrow for fun and never too dark for morality. The Jew of the Middle Ages loved life as much as the Jew of Palestine. The Jew does not know despair and suicide is practically unknown. There is no race on the face of the globe with as sad a history that has been as uniformly contented. In this the distinction between Jew and Gentile is absolute. But it is not a difference that comes from a variance in theology. All the theologies in the world, and the most correct form of them, do not go deep enough into human nature. It is not theology that makes a good temperament. The world is learning this at great cost.

Now, I may say that Judaism is more than a certain kind of theology. We may have had to speak of the unity of God and of other doctrines as peculiarly Jewish, but we did it merely because we had to make clear why we could not be Christians, not because these doctrines made up all there is to our religion; nor have we ever had that way of thinking which will exact of each man a personal profession of belief. We have never been fond of the formal things of religion, or at least, we have never been disposed to make much out of them. It was Christianity which brought the question of personal salvation into relief; this de-Judaized it and made it unsocial and engendered a kind of pious selfishness.

Seeing that the theology of the church was disintegrating society, the state rushed to the rescue and sought to recoup by law what religion had lost, and ever since then we have an aversion to law, and we have a resentment against it as if it were a restriction in what we feel could safely be left with us. It is at the door of the church we must lay the blame of modern unrest. Law is not a burden, it is a liberation. This is the Jewish view. It brings you and me to understand one the other, to respect one the other, to help one the other, and holds us in mutual regard despite whims and passions. Law is a sacrament. The fanatics who were ingenious, indeed, to devise ways of persecution by which to harrass the Jews, did not dream that the very cruelties they contrived, touched not even the threshold of the "Jewish heresy." Nothing was more apt to perpetuate Judaism than to throw the Jews together closely and compactly, and to multiply points of contact between them. Association intensified the feeling of the common sorrow and chastened it through the pathetic communion.

The world stands through law, but not through statutes. The 20th century may get to understand the point of this old word; the 19th did not. If there is anything which Judaism has reiterated more than anything else it is that truth. But the religions of Europe have made of it either philosophy or police. The Bible is more than philosophy and it is more than police. The Talmud is less than a philosophy, that is, it is no catechism, but it does not enjoin precept upon precept in any such way as a modern legislature passes a bill, and then, having found that the enacted statute does not operate well, passes another bill to nullify it. The manifold prescriptions of the Talmud are not the law, but "a fence around the law," the orderly guardians of a conscience, which is set on preserving its peace and serenity—the means to a consummate end.

To the Jew the Bible is more than a catechism. Nothing is more curious to him than the cheap talk he hears: "Believe this, the Bible says so. Disbelieve this, for the Bible does not say so," but similarly nothing is farther from the truth, so far as Israel understands it, than the opposite extreme which would reduce the Bible to being a mere literary classic. There is something in the Pentateuch which will always be forceful and more than mere literature. Judaism is greater than its sacred books. Judaism has been translated into Christianity and Mohammedanism, not because these in the west and those in the east could not get elsewhere the verifiable truths of religion, but because the Jewish mould of them was available for and helpful to the respective needs of the tribes of Arabia and communities of Europe. "Thorah" is not law, complete, fixed, stereotyped, but law in the make, as it were, an organizing function, a social factor, an agent for order. Abstractions are useless for the business of life

Let me illustrate it. You stand before the Alps, close up before one of its steep mountains—you will never take in the grandeur and the majesty and the pride of them. You have no perspective. Over your head are clouds, you see nothing more. I supply the parallel. You face the profound problems of life and fate, face to face with God. Unless you are a Moses, you cannot encompass them. The awe of it will apall you. Theology or philosophy either unman or transfigure. Let me take the other side of the figure. Go down into the valley, far down into it, till you see the rising mountains and the sun descending between them. You see glories of light and shade, and you bless the great God who made them. So Judaism, far from being oracular, beholds the life that is its moving scene and sees God in the heart of it.

If people would only understand that religion is not arranged for us but by us, they would understand that when they call a certain religion a religion of law, they imply practically that that religion is forever what it was at first. But an adaptive legislation is a free legislation and a progressive legislation, and that it is so is proved in ample ways by the history of Judaism, which is practically a series of displaced legislations. Leviticus is followed by Deuteronomy, Deuteronomy is followed by Ezekiel, Ezekiel by Esra, Esra by the Mishna, the Mishna is followed by the Rabbanim and these by Reform. And these several efforts to organize a people came from its throbbing pulses.

In fact, we are rather glad to see that the sense of adaptation prevails, for while we feel there is something in all of this which they share, we know that that which is not common to them all, is incidental to each, not essential.

But there is great power in law. It is the church

which has made the distinctions between civil and religious law. In reality, they are identical. There is a point of view by which all laws of the state are really religious laws, and there is a side to the teachings of the religions which makes them obligatory. But Jews have never differentiated the two aspects. You may say this was the theocratic way; but naming it so does not clear up the matter. We have too long already winced under the stigma of that name: It is the priesthood and its arrogance that are to be blamed for it. Nothing can be said against the feeling and the conviction which makes public obligation equally religious with private duties. Politics has tried hard to rouse every man to do his share of the common cause; but politics is always national, and what is national is always partisan; so that politics from the very character it has, is utterly powerless to do much for the larger love and larger justice. In other words, it has been impotent to do much for religion. Here and there church and state have been allies; but this implies surely that the church had reduced itself to the limits of the state and that the state never aimed at more than a truce among its subjects and a truce with its neighbors. Christianity has achieved little more than this provincialism. It is only when the spirit of culture transcended the artificial barriers of countries and the tide of commerce broke through the dams, that, upon the dawn of international politics, there came also the denationalization of the church, though this is scarcely yet a *fait accompli*. The separation of church from state would have been impossible, had not the business of the world demanded a new jurisprudence. The several states were ready enough to meet the new conditions, but they had first to enancipate themselves from the thraldom of religion, which was incapable to meet exigencies in any adequate degree and was unsuited to the commercial spirit which arose. The church has no special function of its own, and it never had any capacity for the business and its statecraft has always been pitiable. Christianity could not serve in the crisis of the 19th century and therefore, having no potency, it was uncrowned. The numerous sects it broke up into are witnesses of its inefficiency to organize mankind.

This reproach can never be given to Judaism. It is true Judaism had to deal with only a small contingent, but it may be no less difficult to recruit the few into an orderly group and to give these permanence; the problem is different in degree; but not in kind. The spirit of Judaism was a powerful force in saving the remnant of Israel. Under what various circumstances this small body subsisted, what terrible vicissitudes it had to reckon with, what crucial tests of its morals it has had to endure, and how grandly it has passed out of them! Let anyone cite a parallel instance of the vitality of a race, of the vivility of a race, of the morality of a race under similar disasters, under similar hardships, under equal temptations when it could have exchanged everything that is hard and painful at the cheap price of a pretended conversion. When was the price of hypocrisy greater than when Christians tempted Jews to desert; when was the premium on a lie greater than that offered by the proselyting church to poor, oppressed, degraded and disgraced Jews, who might have bought immunity and peace so easily, if they had wished?

It was their sense of right which gave them strength. The church could not make that spurious; the state could not wipe it out of their hearts,

They saw it desecrated under the holy name of religion. They spurned the church for doing so, and all the fascination of the world could not reconcile them to it. The state trampled all their privileges under its mighty heel, but it has no resentment. Not even centuries of wrong could unman Jews. Contrast with this the French revolution, the provocation for which was, taking it all in all, no greater than the accumulated wrong of ages which the Jews had suffered. See how virulent the uprising then; or rather what a weak hold centuries of church discipline had upon its children. If the revolution is a protest against political wrong, it is no less a telling witness of the failure of religion as conceived by the western world that is of a religion of opinion and of personal beatitude.

The history of the Jews is a pathetic experiment before the eyes of the world of the saving doctrine that politics is not statesmanship and churches are not religion. For that handful of people has been more successful than the wealthiest and busiest nations of the world; successful I say, but by saying that I run the risk of being misunderstood, for I do not mean the successful in the market, but successful in that larger sense in which those will conceive it who know that a nation may be prosperous and still be wanting every feature which in the march of culture is the final and only honorable achievement. Jews have today as keen a sense of right as they ever have had; their original doctrine of justice is still respectable and classical. The prophets have not in vain become the teachers of the world. The Jews have, if anything, intensified their virtues, their love of study, their fondness for all that uplifts the mind of men; they are morally purer, by common acknowledgment, than many a nation that has been more fortunately placed.

They are intellectually sound and vigorous and religiously they are still a model of fidelity. We are as callous to the wiles of missionaries, as we were when the Dominican friars forced their sermons on us in the synagogue of Rome, and even the iron hand of the czar is impotent to bring the Jews to the baptismal font. What a wonderful organizing power must that be which leads a whole community to mourn for a proselyte as over the dead, to-day in the open day of the 19th century, and what must that "legalistic" religion be which attains to so transfiguring!

LIFE.

BY RABBI SAMUEL GREENFIELD, PITTSBURG, PA.

What is life? asks the scientist. Mark his answer. It is the existence of a protoplasm, a living germ which has in some unaccountable way passed over from inorganic to organic bodies. Evolution would teach the progressive advance of objects until man appears upon the stage, man endowed with both reason and consciousness. In other words, men like Huxley would give us a physical basis for life. Can he prove how the non-living become alive, how the stone passes into the flower, or the worm, or the bird, or the least of all man? Life is a vital principal which moves, animates, actuates living things. But that is no definition, it is merely a term that is fuller and more expanded. Experiments have been made in the laboratory, by chemical means, after every possible means of analysis had been exhausted, in order to produce something living, moving. By the process of very high temperature, spontaneous generation has also proven a signal failure. The theory referred to is that under certain given circumstances, and this was supposed to consist mainly of a high degree of heat, life can be generated. If this could be done, evolution would receive additional support in its evidence. Man has thus far not been able to produce life where there was none before. He has failed in every attempt to prove that living beings graduated from non-living, by any process whatsoever. The scientific theories of life do not and cannot conform with actual facts. The case has been made out on insufficient evidence and life remains as much of a mystery and with as clouded an origin as ever before. This offers a stumbling block to evolution which it cannot overleap by any rapid strides or careful study, inasmuch as its object is to trace back existing objects as far as possible, but it must stop at the point which would be of great interest, the passage between the cliffs, with a chasm which cannot be bridged by the human intellect, however great. So at the outset, in asking what life is from a scientific and physical standpoint, we are compelled to admit the insufficiency of any theory that has for its object the establishment upon a basis of matter, this non-material force. We must, until other proof is given us to decide the question positively, believe in Biogenesis, or assuming that life is caused by previous life, thus tracing man to his original creation.

In the Talmud is recorded the fact that for two and one half years was a discussion carried on by the two opposing schools of Shammai and Hillel, the one maintaining that it was better for man that he had never been born, the other that it was better that he was created. Finally it was decided by both, that it would have been better had he not been created at all; but now that he has been brought into the world, let him engage in good deeds and noble work.

A disputation such as this did not arise from the mere desire to indulge in argument. Pessimists of to-day represent the thought which is traceable throughout the history of man, that life is a burden, that it presents a smiling aspect for the ignorant only, that it is full of the deepening darkness of pain, replete

with torture, anguish and sorrow. To these there are
no flowers on earth, no goodness in nature, no redeeming feature in all this world for man. Life is but the
entrance into a room where fly about the evils set
loose by the mischief-making Pandora. From the
cradle to the grave do dread diseases gnaw at the
body, rendering it weak and helpless and powerless.
Hurricanes enter upon the scene of human activity
and blight the growth of prosperity; a pestilence inoc-
ulates the very air necessary for breathing; storms
ravage human habitation on land, and wreck vessels
at sea; earthquakes and natural convulsions storm and
rend the land and countless human beings are en-
gulfed in the awful yawning gapes of earth; a severe
north wind attacks frail man and he shivers and becomes cold to find his resting-place finally under the
cold ground. No less are the calamities that enter his
hearth and home. Perhaps at the very opening of his
life, the universal apparition of death intrudes upon
his meditations and changes joy into sorrow, merry
laughter into bitter tears. For lo! the bright star of
home, she who nursed and watched and tended, towards whom his affections clung like the young tendril
to the mother plant, whose heart was open to his
own, whose thoughts were for him and his better-
ment, who kissed away every childish vexation and
youthful disappointment and manly discouragement,
whose love centered about him and his growth, she
whose radiance lit up, moonlike, the gloomy earth and
firmament of his experience, with the motherly counsel, the advice of a friend and well-wisher; or may-
hap, some violent calamity has seized at the outset,
the sustaining rock of family life, the father and husband whose one, whose only solicitude was to shield
his beloved ones from hurt or harm, to protect them

against the assailing blasts of misfortune, who, like the sun, gracious and benign, cast the glow of cheerful manhood upon those he protected and covered from the enslaving toils of disasters. Thus doth many a weeping heart bewail life and its adversities, pining for death as a release from a chain which galls and embitters. Gloomy are the forebodings of such an one. For misery has branded him a victim of fate with its many minions of destruction. From the cradle to the grave is his path beset by monsters and demons, in forms of hideous sprites whom he at last despairs of conquering and finally asks, "Wherefore do I live, what is life but a series of heart-rending tortures?"

"Is then life worth the living?" asks the anxious soul and troubled. Deep buried in the bosom lies the question. Tumult of thoughts surge in upon him with the momentous interrogation. The answer to it is the decision arrived at by the two contending schools in the Talmud. To the young is there not opened up a vista of bright prospects? Does it not hold forth cheerful views of the content of life? Is not the future a golden goblet from which might be drunk the most intoxicating pleasures? Duties urgent and pleasant require fulfilment. Life questions form a series of accomplishments which might or might not be realized. Here stands man with a purpose, both egotistic and altruistic. He is confronted with a host of what-must-be-done. A multitude of oughts are before him. An unbroken array of must-bes request a conquest.

He stands not alone. His duties involve others. Every man lives more or less for other people. No man is perfectly selfish. No man has his own well-being at heart. He is surrounded by companions, friends and relatives. His action and their actions form his world. His circle is bounded more or less by limitations that cannot be overcome. His existence with and among others necessitates work on his part. These assume the form of duties, the obligations that demand imperative recognition and immediate satisfaction. According to the greatness of the individuals is the respective work of each marked out for him. The meanest and humblest comes in contact with other people, therefore, he has his function as one of the many. His duty then consists of bringing as much happiness as possible into the world. Happiness, the sum of human achievement, the totality of his efforts, he obtains when not pursuing entirely selfish aims. What makes the father happy? His performance of duties involving his family. And because he contributes to their happiness, he increases his own, and is satisfied that he is working out his destiny. What causes the patriot to die happily at the cannon's mouth? He knows he has done that which contributed to the general welfare and at the same time his duty was discharged when the last breath issued from his body. In that word is comprised the whole lifetime of man. In duty lies the fulfilment of his hopes.

In thus creating a center for the magnetic current of happiness, each man feels that he is living a life both useful and bestowing happiness. It is in the power of every person of however little strength or energy to cause sunshine to emerge from every dark and cranny nook. A social creature such as man is cannot be conceived as living unless he live under social conditions. All men form a unit, not one. All men compose mankind, not one. All humanity works for an end, not one man, except as individual of the community. Behold the life of a great reformer, of a noble philanthropist, does he work for himself? Does the poet exercise his muse and imagination for himself? If so, his work becomes annihilated by time. Does the philosopher reason merely for himself? Does the prophet announce truths and denounce kings for his own amusement? The common end of all is to elevate mankind, to spread happiness everywhere. Each man's life is worth the living in that he does that for which he is eminently fitted. Hero, soldier, martyr, as well as the toiler in the field and the machinist, finds life where work is given him to do, to enrich the race in its treasures of spiritual possessions.

Ask then him whose duty is being executed in the interest of them whom he loves, with whom he sympathizes, whose fate is irrevocably woven into his, whose misfortune is his bane, and he will tell you that life is worth living for that which we do for others, and in their happiness is ours also involved.

In what direction lies the aim of life? What object shall we pursue in order best to attain that for which all are striving? Is it wealth, the aftermath of the struggle for existence? Our best experience shows us that this is but a transitory object, a mere chimera which, like the will-o'-the-wisp, lures on the victim to final ruin and destruction. Admitting the necessity of it, its usefulness and the desirability of its possession we cannot, nevertheless, make it the sole and important object of life, however much the tendency of the day may speak in its behalf. Is it pleasure, pure and simple? Conceding that to be one of the mainsprings of conduct, we must yet deny to it the prerogative of being the goal of man's higher desires. It has its time and place, but the very fact that it caters more to the satisfaction of the body, excludes it from the choice of man's aim in life. For we cannot believe that the satisfaction of bodily desires is all that we should live for. Granted the existence of a dual nature in the composition of man, body and soul, or matter and mind, we are necessarily compelled to conclude that the latter is the more lasting, less evanescent, more permanent, less destructible.

The main pursuit of the mind and soul is truth. It scans the heavens for it, it searches the earth and penetrates the depths of sea and land. Man suffers pain, endures privation, exhausts physical vitality, courts poverty and invites a martyr's fate and all for truth. He seeks knowledge at the risk of non-indulgence in pleasure, rejects wealth in the interest of higher gains, by which mankind profits immeasurably. The true alchemist is not he who wishes to compound gold for its own sake, but because of the truth that discovery unfolds for the race. Lives are thus spent in toiling constantly and incessantly for the good and welfare of the spiritual nature. Sorrow and pain leave the indelible traces of a hunt pursued ever since the first student entered the universe, but yet man exhibits his resolute purpose and steady aim for higher things, thus putting to shame the material in quest of gold or pleasure simply.

The true object of life is then the perfection of the mind and soul to the utmost capacity, the cultivation of a character true and sterling, the reaching upward for the happiness to be gained in this wise. With each making the effort, the whole race is benefited, for a higher individual raises the standard of the lower aggregate. In the study of man, there have been found laws as inviolable as those which govern the physical world. Where else was demonstrated that there exist the abstract good and bad? How account for the supremacy of love, for the immutable conviction of freedom? Where else find the yearnings for a comprehension of a first cause and of an Infinite existence? The physical becomes removed from the psychical in man by just that distance which spans the points of the finite and infinite, of the changeable and unchangeable, of the temporary and the eternal. Progress without end, advance without pause, effort without remission, marks the propelling power in man, that power never ceasing in action, but continually impelling to fresh endeavor.

To us is it given to fashion and frame our lives, and mark this is most important to those who admit man's freedom to do and act. We can so shape our lives by good and noble deeds that we need have no cause to regret having been created, or we can so mar the beauteous harmony by improper and unworthy conduct as to cry out in despair, as of old did Job, "wherefore was I born." But like Job, who became a poet and philosopher when adversity overtook him, and loss of property weighed him down, and loss of family depressed him, we must also say: "Shall we receive only the good from his hands?"

Calamity and diversity are the salt which purifies and cleans, for it is not until we are so afflicted that we comprehend the mutability of earthly conditions, and with wings shorn of earthly thoughts, rise to a better comprehension and conception of life's ordainer and of life's mission which depends neither upon local nor transitory power.

Within the variegated cameo lies the compass of human life, the hue of green tokening the child, that of red, rosy youth and the heavenly blue, the old man. Though changed the years and different the colors, behold the same individuality passing through all.

Each a beautiful type of divine handiwork, each with peculiarities. Innocent childhood, gay youth and serene old age! From the breast of all issue love, wisdom, gladness, and finally death closes the kindling eye, stops the beating heart and the living witnesses of a life well spent, surrounding the couch of the beloved kindly aged one, testify to the affection of kin and family. Yet say the old rabbis, "no man dieth with half his wishes fulfilled." Restless yearning to toil, a spirit of unrest for labor, to achieve, to surmount, to accomplish, leaves ambition but barely satisfied. So doth man come and go, the child prophesying the youth, the bud of manhood remains but a few years, ere the calm and peaceful age seizes upon him and his struggle and worry and torment end with the final hope for a future, with the acknowledgment of a God supreme. With a breath he expires and his soul is launched upon the sea for a voyage into realms unknown, into regions unexplored. Thus ends a life of trial, of vicissitude, encouraged and spurred on to everlasting efforts.

THE WEAKNESSES OF BIBLE HEROES.

BY RABBI EDWARD N. CALISCH, RICHMOND, VA.

"There is no man who may not sin."—I Kings viii, 46.
"For though the righteous fall seven times, he will rise up again."—Proverbs xxiv, 16.

Certain theologies base upon the event of man's first disobedience the doctrine of total depravity. It is maintained that man is inherently corrupt and vile, that he is conceived in sin and born in iniquity, that his existence is evil and his life is wickedness, and that he is savable only by vicarious atonement and the sacrifice of a pure and perfect savior.

It is hardly my intention to criticise or point out defects in others. I have mentioned this doctrine of total depravity, only that I might emphasize, by contrast, the differing and nobler conception of our teaching. To teach the total depravity of the human being is to stultify the sacred writings, which declare that "man is made in the image of God." (Genesis i, 27.) This creation in the image of God means in the God-like capacities with which the soul of man is endowed, the powers of will, reason, conscience, the impulse to strive for that degree of perfection which is by man attainable, the power to achieve a high and glorious destiny.

The rabbis of old said that Adam, when he was created, was so large that, as he stood with his feet upon the earth his head towered into heaven. This quaint rabbinical conceit means only that man, though bound to earth by the limitations of his mortal frame, has yet the power to reach heavenly heights in moral aspiration and spirtual flight.

It is precisely this doctrine which I desire to teach to-day. Man stands with his feet on earth, but with his head in heaven. The claims of his earthly frame are constantly tending to pull him down, and does he often yield, yet though he should stoop so low as to lie prone on the earth, even then can he, and he himself, without external or adventitious aid, raise himself upright again.

The wise Solomon knew full well this truth, and in the two verses that have been taken for our text he states it plainly. When in that magnificent prayer of dedication, with which he opened the portals of the glorious house of God, he prayed for the pardon of the people when they should sin, he recognized how persistent and powerful was the earthly weakness of the human race, and he says "for there is no man who may not sin." (I Kings viii, 46.) But he knew as well that the recuperative power lay, too, within the man himself, and he tells us that "though the righteous may fall seven times, yet will he rise again." (Proverbs xxiv, 16.)

This truth is likewise evidenced in the lives of almost all the famous figures and heroes in the Scriptures.

The heroes of the Bible were heroes in moral conflict. Yet we find that they all had their weaknesses. Noah, though called a just and righteous man, and one who walked with God (Genesis ii, 9), was guilty of sod-den-witted drunkenness. Abraham, the patriarch and founder of our faith, the man of perfect obedience, of generous and unquestioning hospitality, of justice, mercy and philanthropy, was twice guilty of cowardice and the accomplice of a heinous crime. The deceptions and the strategies of Jacob cannot be glossed over. Moses, Aaron, and Miriam, all three suffered the wrath of God because of their disobedience. The weakness of the mighty Samson made him the plaything of Delilah. Saul felt, even in his lifetime, the results of his errors. David is, perhaps, the best illustration of the truth which we teach. He was a man who sunk to the lowest depths and rose to the highest heights. The whole gamut of human weakness and human strength was run by him. He played on every key in the great organ of the human heart, from the lowest bass of passion to the highest and shrillest note of spiritual frenzy. He fell, fell often and deeply, but each time he rose again. Though Solomon walked in all the ways of wisdom and laid down many a noble precept of life, yet was not himself free from sin.

To those who oppose, these sins and weaknesses of the Bible heroes have been made the object of much scorn, ridicule and contumelious attack. They will pick out the flaws and weaknesses of each one, and, dwelling upon it and it alone, cry out, "Are these the men you hold up as models? A Noah, guilty of drunkenness, an Abraham, of cowardly desertion, a Jacob, of falsehood, a David, of murder, a Solomon, of a hundred vices?"

But to the one who reads rightly, these weaknesses of the Bible heroes are their strength. The Bible, above all things, is for human guidance, human help and assistance. Its lessons are the lessons of human life, and its heroes, therefore, are human. The presence of the faults and the follies of its great men is doubly creditable to the writers of the Scriptures. It shows the absolute fidelity and accuracy with which they chronicled events. Naught was set down in malice, naught glossed over, naught extenuated. When a sin was committed it was not hidden or condoned. Often its punishment was given by its side. Noah is rebuked by the conduct of his sons. Jacob feels the humiliation of his acts, when twenty years later he meets Esau again. Miriam was struck with leprosy; the great law-giver and leader was not permitted to cross the Jordan. The intrepid Nathan stood before the monarch, who had sinned, and flung the reproach into his face.

By these very things does the Bible press home to us the lesson of our human and our God-like being. These men were heroes and leaders. They sinned, yes, and by the very reason that they rose superior to their sins are they strong, do they appeal to us, are they kin to us. They stumbled and fell, therein were they men, not gods. They rose again, therein were they heroes. The true strength lies not in never having fallen, but in rising after one has given way. "Though a righteous man fall seven times, yet will he rise again." Had the heroes of the Bible been flawless, stainless, immaculate, perfect, they would not appeal to us as they do. That they were weak, we know them to be our brothers, fighting the same battles of lust, passion, temptation and allurement,—that they conquered their weaknesses and rose to the sublime heights of moral truth, aye, to the very summit and acme of spiritual life and conception, teaches us that we too have these God-like possibilities within us, we too can and will climb the Moriah of obedience, the Sinai of steadfast loyalty, the Nebo of sublime resignation, and by our moral strength defeat and destroy the weaknesses of our mortal garment.

For this reason, too, let us be wary in stern judgment. The human being is compassed by too many limitations to be perfect. Perfection is only of God. Indefectibility can only be of that omniscient One whose power permeates the worlds, whose mercy is as fathomless as His wisdom. Striving to be, if to an infinitesimal degree, like Him, in purity of thought and deed, let us, like Him, also remember the weakness of man, and be generous in thought, kindly in speech, slow in condemnation, but swift to approve where approval may be had. As the best tempered metal is flexible, so the true story of human endeavor is not that of rigid and inflexible indefectibility, but in the recuperative power of the soul, that saves and raises us, though we have fallen seven times.

This, personally; communally let us take home the same lesson of modesty of bearing and absence of assumption, for we have need of it. We have fallen into the habit of considering ourselves, the Jews, as almost morally unassailable. We deem our history the most glorious, our mission the most sublime, our faith supreme among the annals of men. Of ourselves we have a hardly less exalted opinion. And when some time-server, some seeker after our suffrages, or our patronage, or our influence, or charities, comes to us, and often by our own invitation, and pours the honey of fulsome flattery before us, tells us "the Israelites are among the best and most highly respected of our citizens; you never meet a Jewish beggar, and you never see a Jewish drunkard, or convict, or burglar," then we gulp that honey down, and pat ourselves on our vain and foolish backs, and tell ourselves we are not only the chosen people, but we are the perfect people, we are the leaven and salt of every community, flawless, stainless and sinless.

There can be no greater weakness than that which denies all weakness. With the first part, the abstract, I will agree, our history, our mission, and our faith are sublime and supreme. But Judaism and the Jews, while they should be in perfect unanimity, are often widely diverse. The faith is better than its followers. It is folly for us to consider ourselves flawless. We know our weaknesses. We cannot hide them by, ostrich-like, hiding our heads in the sand-heaps of self-interested flattery. "There is no man who may not sin," and no people, for a people is but a number of men. We know our faults and our sins as a people, our cruel coldness to our faith, our heartless indifference to its needs, our deafness to its calls, our shamefacedness in acknowledgment of it, our avoidance of its duties and obligations, our selfish, cruelly selfish, disregard of all that crosses our convenience or our pleasures.

There is greater crime in knowing and continuing these faults than in the faults themselves. You have fallen. Raise yourselves up. The heroes of the Bible have shown the pathway. Be ye heroes, not in never having fallen, but fallen, in raising yourselves up, for the righteous man is not he who has never fallen, but he who has risen up, though fallen seven times. Amen.

MANHOOD.

SERMON BY REV. DR. E. SCHREIBER, TOLEDO, O.

Text: והאיש משה "And the man Moses."

Poets, thinkers, philosophers and orators since time immemorial have been singing the praises of *Man*. " What a piece of work is man! How noble in reason, how infinite in faculty! In action how like an angel, in apprehension how like a God!" These words of Shakespeare re-echo the Biblical passage " Let us form man in our image."

When Mark Antony sums up his eulogy on Cæsar in the words "This was a man," he only imitates the Bible which knows no greater title of distinction than that of "man." "And the *man* Moses," "Elijah the *man* of God," "Mordecai the *man*, the Jew," are some instances.

The history of *man*, not of the Hebrew occupies the first chapter of the Bible. *Man*, independent of race, nationality, creed or previous condition, is the message of Judaism. The Midrash embellishes the story of man's creation by adding that the dust of which Adam was formed, was taken from various parts of the globe, thus conveying the lesson of the equal origin of all men. The prophet Micah, in summing up the essence of *Ethical Monotheism* or of the *Religion of* the *Prophets*, lays stress on the passage : " He (God) hath told thee, oh *Man!* what he requireth of thee. Nothing but to do justice, to love kindness and to walk humbly." (Micah vi, 8.)

But who is a man? Not he who because God made him passes for a man. Saadiah says this passage "in our image" means that man is the king of creation. He shall rule, govern; "Thou, oh God, hast placed everything beneath his feet," sings the Psalmist (Ps. viii, 8).

Indeed man includes all life before him. His achievements are wonderful. He levels mountains and raises valleys. With lightning's speed he almost annihilates time and space. By bonds of iron and steel, by the interests of commerce and industry he renders the wide world one. By his intellect and moral energy he traces the path of nature, makes seemingly hostile forces and elements his allies, binds them to his chariot and behold! like swift steeds, they carry him whithersoever it pleases him and on, on, they draw his car of progress. Like God Himself man "makes the winds his messengers, the burning flames his servants"; he is, as our sages put it, "God's partner in the work of creation."

But does material success constitute all the elements of manhood and God-likeness? No. Manhood means the reverse of selfishness. Man must not only conquer nature but subdue his passions. Selfishness is the privilege of the lower animals and of the savage who comes nearest to them. *Man's* duty is to work, like God, for others; to be his brother's keeper.

Moses is called "the man" because he was in the highest degree unselfish. Although reared in luxury, bred under the enervating influences of an Egyptian court—although honored, distinguished, great, he "went out to see his brethren, the *slaves*." This meant more in Egypt with her system of castes, so well symbolized by the pyramid, than it would mean among us. He entered their workshops to see for himself how they were treated. He saw a grave injustice done to an Israelite. "He looked around" and suggestively the Midrash adds "in order to see whether among the thousands of fellow laborers one man could be found who would not quietly look on while another was struck, perhaps killed." But there was not one אין איש.

Did Moses selfishly calculate the possible evil consequences for himself which might result from this interference? No; emulating God who "cannot bear the sight of wrong" he made the cause of weak suffering innocence his own, and killed the Egyptian. "He was a man" who dared to protest against tyranny, to defend the oppressed and to maintain the principles of justice even in Egypt where "calves were kissed and men were slaughtered"; even in Egypt, the "house of slaves."

This unselfishness forced Moses to leave his splendor, his power, his home and, as a poor fugitive, to eke out a frugal existence. Again his unselfishness prompted him to take up the cause of the wronged shepherdesses in Midian against their persecutors and to choose a calling which in Egypt was despised and spurned, namely, that of a shepherd.

When Israel, utterly disregarding the mission entrusted to them, danced around the golden calf, God said to Moses: "I shall destroy Israel, but make of thee a great nation." A selfish man seeing such an exhibition of base ingratitude on the part of those who thus defeated the work of his life, might have permitted things to take their course or even rejoiced at such a turn. But not so the unselfish "man Moses." Outraged though he was at the horrible sin of his people, the man who could wield an iron hand when circumstances demanded it, prostrated himself and sought forgiveness for the backsliders, saying: "Oh, if thou wilt not forgive their sin, then blot me out of the book that thou hast written." (Ex. xxxii, 32.)

When Eldad and Medad prophesied in the camp and Joshua said, "My master Moses forbid them to do so," did he selfishly interfere with those "outsiders"? On the contrary, "Art thou zealous for my sake"? And "Oh, that one might render all the people of God prophets that he would put His spirit upon them." (Num. xi, 30.) Such was the answer of the "man Moses," who was the very incarnation of unselfishness.

When the spies, by false reports, endeavored to discourage the Israelites from fighting for the promised land, and Jahveh wanted to destroy Israel and make of Moses a great and powerful nation, he again prayed, "Forgive the sin of this people in accord with thy great love, as thou, oh God, hast always done" (Num. xiv, 19); and thus he saved the nation.

When Korah and his followers attempted to create a rebellion against Moses, charging him with hierarchical proclivities, Moses, the true man, could face the excited masses and exclaim "Who can say that I ever took an ass from him or that I ever injured a fellow-man?" (Num. xvi, 15.)

Indeed, Moses did not even ask for a sepulchre. Moses never gave an office to one of his sons. When this "man Moses" was commanded to ascend the mount of Abarim, to see from afar the "promised land" which he would not be permitted to enter, what was his foremost thought? Not self, not mortification at his own sad bitter fate, but the welfare of the nation. He said: "Let the eternal, the God of the spirits of all flesh, set a *man* over the congregation so that the congregation of God may not be as sheep without a shepherd." (Num. xxvii, 12 to 20.)

Here is the same loftiness of spirit rising above every thought of self which marks the whole career of this "man Moses." Wade through folios of biography and history and you will seek in vain such a high degree of manhood and unselfishness. The annals of history preserve names of great statesmen who proved unselfish, so far as material gain was concerned, but they were not free from egotism and jealousy, when their power, glory and influence were to be taken from them. Bismarck, whose greatness cannot be denied, proved petty, and adhered to the despicable "rule or ruin" policy under similar circumstances.

Once only this "man Moses" appears to have been influenced by a spirit of selfishness. He wanted to see the "promised land," the fruit of the hard work, the earnest labor of a life-time. Our sages, however, give a touching psychological explanation of this natural, this truly human desire of the great man. "Did Moses," they ask, "care to eat of the luscious fruits which grew in Palestine"? No; he said to God: "So long have I labored and suffered for Israel, so long have I seen their sorrows and sins, their trials and tribulations, that now, when the dream of my ambition is about to be realized, I am anxious to see the fulfilment of my hopes, my people's happiness."

This "man Moses" was only a *man*, no god, no angel. His faults are not concealed in the Biblical records. He was, like all great men, very impulsive. Every noble deed is the result of impulse, of pressure, of excitement. Enthusiasm and fanaticism grow on the same tree, are children of passion. Cool, cunning, calculating men of policy, tricky, crafty, intriguing diplomats may be successful schemers, but they are small people. They fail to inspire, to lift up, to elevate, and to carry multitudes. Our sages justly say: "If there were no passion, who would build a house, take a wife, or plant a vineyard?"

He who deserves the title of man, must be impulsive. He must be indignant at the sight of sin, must be outraged at the sight of wrong triumphant, must be impatient at the sight of justice down-trodden, truth dethroned, and crime, superstition and hypocrisy enthroned in high places. It might not have been dignified in Moses to strike the Egyptian, but do not his impulsiveness and righteous indignation find full justification in the words of Isaiah:—"And justice was forced to the background, and righteousness stood far off. And *he saw there was no man* and wondered that there was no intercessor, therefore his *own arm brought him aid?* (Isa. lix, 14–16.)

It was impulsiveness, and, perhaps, lack of dignity which prompted Moses to say to God, "Since I came to speak in Thy name to Pharaoh, *the people suffer more,*" or to address the nation of Israel as follows: "Oh hear, *ye rebels!*" But "the greater the man, the greater his temper and passion," so teaches the Talmud. It was most certainly impulsive and undignified in Moses to break the tablets of the law into a thousand pieces. Yet, according to the old sages, God said to Moses, after having seen Israel's wild dance around the golden idol, "Thou hast done well in breaking the tablets."

This conveys the important lesson that the true honest teachers of religion must possess the courage to break, to destroy the idols of the masses, whenever the exigencies of the times demand it. The message of God entrusted to Jeremiah, "I have sent thee to destroy and to build anew," is the principle of every reform movement, which is "destructive in its first stages, in order to be constructive in the end."

And this brings us to another test of manhood, namely—*Decision*. Impulsiveness and decision go hand in hand. Moses was a man, therefore decision, regardless of consequences, was one of the leading features of his character. Neither Moses nor the prophets were men of compromise. When Hezekiah saw that the people worshiped the brazen serpent he destroyed it, although Moses had made it. Elijah exclaimed, "How long will ye halt between two opinions?" If Jehovah is God, follow him; and if Baal, then follow him." (I Kings xviii, 21.)

Modesty and humility is finally another criterion of true manhood and in this also, the "man Moses" may be our ideal.

I do not mean that false humility of the Pecksniff, Tartuffe and Uriah Heep style, which hides its haughtiness and arrogance toward man, under the cloak of humility before God. But the "man Moses" is a type of the noble pride of humility. He recognizes the merits of the Aarons, Joshuas, Calebs and even of the Eldads and Medads who "prophesied in the camp." He leaves his work unfinished, he does not want to be regarded as the atlas who carries the whole world upon his shoulders, who completes the great work, without the co-operation of others. He was indeed עניו מאד "very humble." When the message came to him "Go and redeem my people," he who was not afraid to fight for justice single-handed in the land of the Pharaohs, and in the face of violent, rough, Ethiopian shepherds, hesitated to accept the noble appointment. "Who am I, that I should go to Pharaoh"? "I am not eloquent." "Send some one else." This is the language of true humility and true manhood.

Such was the "man Moses." Humbly as he lived he died; "and no man knoweth the place of his grave." "His grave should not be regarded as a place of pilgrimage, whither men go to do honor to one, and thus raise him above the level of man." So say our ancient teachers, and so say we.

Let us be proud that we can point to such a "man Moses," and doubly proud that he was *only* "a man," who, with his faults, foibles and errors, stands so much nearer to us.

Oh, let us emulate the *unselfishness*, *decision* and *humility* of the "man Moses." To-day, more than ever before, do we need new *whole men*, inspired men, enthusiastic men. Men do we need in the congregations, men do we need in the pulpits, men who do not measure by the yardstick the success of the congregation. Unselfish men do we need in the pulpit, who never ask whether truth, half-truth or falsehood will best advance their interests; who do not cringe before the powerful, who do not cater to every fad of the day and do not change their views with every turn of the tide. Men of decision do we need who, like the old prophets, possess the boldness and courage to teach a living, broad, all-embracing Judaism, based on the principles of service, sacrifice, righteousness, freedom, justice and truth. Men do we need who do not sell their convictions for a mess of pottage, who would rather be right than popular, who lead and are not led and who dare to ignore the applause or the ridicule of ignorant or unprincipled critics. Men do we need who amid the ravages of ambition, the mean aims of egotism and under the burden of great trials and tribulations spurn the fairest gifts of fortune in the pursuit of duty and the vindication of the cause of humanity. Men do we need who in this age of materialism dare to believe that purity of motive is not a dream of fancy, but that it is placed within our reach and is the very end of our being. Such men and *such men only* will make our pulpit an attractive source of centralization and a power of spiritual elevation. They will contribute towards the spread of Jewish ideas and hasten the Messianic time when "righteousness will flow like water and justice like a mighty stream." Amen.

THE DELUGE.

BY REV. DR. F. DE SOLA MENDES.

One of the most striking features of the Mosaic records we have commenced to read anew, is the episode of the Deluge. And I call it thus striking, not so much because it is a plain, unvarnished, unpretentious delineation of a remarkable event which other sources and other authorities tell about, though in far more fanciful and pretentious guise, but because of the fundamental religious doctrine that in it and by it is inculcated, that moral decay and moral corruption are followed by punishment or disaster of a physical order. We shall not stop to-day to examine the historical corroboration of the Deluge received from those sources, no longer than to suggest that, old as the history is, and familiar as we all may claim to be with it, closer study very often will be rewarded by new light and new facts. Thus, for instance: I suppose nine out of every ten of us who know all about the Deluge, or think we do, imagine it as having been simply of the nature of a protracted rain, and picture to ourselves the desolate and persistent down-pour from the hurrying clouds; and so scarcely notice that remarkable expression: "all the fountains of the great deep were split open" ("broken up," the English version lamely says), which fills in the picture with the far more serious suggestion of an inundation from the sea, a bursting forth of the ocean, a tidal wave, or possibly even the settling down of the land and its sinking, while from countless springs the water rushed up and flooded everything. The subsidence of whole continents, we know, has often happened in the geological history of the globe, and this is the account of what happened among men during one of them. Both in its physical aspects and in its historical ones, as illustrated by the clay tablets found in Assyria and deciphered in recent days, this whole subject of the Deluge furnishes a highly interesting topic but one from which the lecture-platform would be the best place and some other opportunity the best time.

Dwelling then to-day only on the topic of physical suffering and physical extinction following upon moral disregard and violence, the question will undoubtedly arise in the mind of every thoughtful Bible reader, "Was all this necessary?" Was such a world-catastrophe, which more modern research is beginning to show us was of far larger extent than we have been accustomed to consider it, requisite to wipe out the wrong-doing of a wicked generation of men? True, Scripture tells us, *hish'hit kol basar darko* "all flesh had corrupted its way upon the earth," but why had they been permitted to do so? Why had corruption been allowed to reach such a pitch of vileness that a terrible cataclysm of nature had to be brought about, earth convulsed, and ocean-floods invoked to wipe it clean? And they who ask thus are not mere curious students of the past, mere archæological inquirers delving amid the rubbish and the ruins of bygone ages. The inquiry has pertinence to-day; it applies to our own times; it echoes among us as well as among the sinful generation of Noah. Why is corruption allowed to-day? why are sin and suffering still permitted to defile and deface the surface of earth? There can be no greater trial or torture for right-thinking men and women than to see, as they too often are called upon to see, the suffering, the sorrows and privation of those who they conceive are meritorious enough to escape such hardship.

A bright and gifted child, a girl of sixteen, known to many among you, possibly a former pupil of our Sunday-school, died a few weeks ago, after a period of protracted and severe pain. *Why* was all that? To say that the poor child inherited her ailment, that she contracted it from one cause or another, does not answer the question: why was such suffering, why was such death, permitted by the Almighty Providence, which most certainly rules us? And when I formulate the question thus for any one particular case or set of cases, you understand of course that it stands not for one, but for a dozen sets of cases or more, more or less similar, which everyone of us meets with in his or her journey through life. Why are these things allowed?

The problem here presented will be best solved perhaps by seeking the analogy of appropriate illustrations. One of the oldest sciences, chemistry—its very name comes to us from the early Arabs—gets revolutionized about every thirty years: that is to say, the chemistry of one generation, by continued research and discovery, comes to be quite different from that of the generation preceding. It is not many months ago since the discovery was made in England that the air we breathe contains in large quantities a gas entirely unknown or unrecognized a year ago, but yet which we have been breathing all our lives; and not only we, but, so far as we know, all the countless generations of man hitherto on earth. See, too, the vast strides made in discovery, in other sciences, in arts of various kinds; in mechanical appliances, in time-saving and labor-saving devices, all educed and built up by the patient, persistent life-work of countless investigators, very many of whom have sacrificed their comfort, some their lives, to the researches they had in hand, for the benefit of mankind's progress. Now would it not have been impossible for Almighty Benevolence to have at once revealed all this vast fund of knowledge in former ages, and so have given all our predecessors the benefit of all the comforts and aids we now enjoy, and at the same time have spared those patient discoverers and inventors the bitter years of their toil, and the numerous disappointments? Yes, you will say: it would have been possible, of course; you are not sure whether it would have been wise. Men of earlier ages were not ready for discoveries and comforts resulting; they would not have appreciated them or utilized them. Besides, and this is the chief point, all the healthful exercises of the thinking faculties, of ingenuity and suggestion, of experiment in a word, would have been lost to the world if mankind had been born knowing all about chemistry, all about mechanics, all about electricity. Without the constant spur of intellectual exercise and practice, men would have been learned babies, knowing everything already, and with their brains and their energies growing soft, and slack, and pithy, and useless.

Now let us go a step further. There is a science—almost entirely a modern one—which deals with the circumstances of men in their organized communities, sociology. It treats of such things as labor and capital, poverty and wealth, crime and its prevention or repression and so forth. Its problems are some of the most perplexing, most heart-rending of any, for human hearts and human lives are its materials of experiment, human sufferings, the things which it must study. Mistakes are made, terrible mistakes, blunders which have heart-rending results with such materials; could not God have given us a revelation on sociology which would have taught us once and forever how we are to handle wealth and labor, how poverty can be remedied or prevented, and crime checked and stifled? He could, of course; but if He had, if we knew exactly how to handle these things, in the first place, such a life of complete happiness and universal comfort as would ensue, would enervate and relax our energy, would dull every ambition, and in reality give us the life of the brute or the vegetable; we should only have to feed and grow large. And in the second place, if all such problems were already solved for us, one of the sources of our keenest delight, of our most lasting and purest satisfaction, would be taken away from us; the delight of being useful to our kind, of ministering to their wants in some degree, assuaging pain and bringing comfort. We should be much the poorer off, did we possess consummate knowledge of true principles of sociology, but at the same time have no practice, whatever, in sympathy, in helpfulness, in brotherhood. Those who practice these things are the noblest of our kind.

In these and other departments, then, of practical knowledge God has given us no relevation: He has left us to find out the laws and results of various circumstances. We very soon ascertain that there is a fixed uniformity about things, that fire always burns, even an innocent child; that alcohol always maddens, no matter how learned the imbiber; that unthriftiness always impoverishes, no matter how much capital you start with. The collection of these multiple facts constitutes education, and they are as accessible to all of us as much as to any favored few. Until we learn that fire burns everyone, that intoxicants brutalize everyone, that extravagance, want of management, impoverish everyone, we are simply ignorant, and it is our ignorance which subjects us every time to the sharp, severe lesson so surely awaiting our transgressing offenses. When, therefore, your sympathizing heart is bruised by the aspect of suffering or affliction, before accusing the kindness of Providence, be sure that none of the laws of nature have been sinned against. It would not be wise to ask God to change these laws when the innocent child grasps the hot coal or the professor yields to the temptation of intoxicants; they must learn, we all must learn, the wisely arranged laws of our nature, and we must help all to learn them.

You will observe that I do not include death among the experiences which properly excite our pity. I have always considered it both folly and impertinence to do so; folly: because we know nothing of what becomes of us after passing that portal; impertinence: for the unwarrantable assumption that this life is the best possible life awaiting us, and therefore departure from it a calamity. To the contrary, I think life is a blessing if properly spent, no matter whether short or long. The next step, I sincerely believe, is a promotion, an advance, not a step to be deplored; all nature is built that way, always higher, upward, never downward, backward, to inferior states.

In conclusion, then, we may say that, just as God

has left chemistry, mechanics, electricity, sociology, for us to find out about, in the very best and most advantageous manner, by experience, or education, so in the field of practical morality, we must ascertain, for ourselves, or by the experience of others, contemporaries or predecessors, that sinfulness brings suffering, that wilful corruption has its undetachable penalty, that anarchy and violence bring ruin and deluge. We were not made—Providence be thanked—mere automata; we can do wrongfully if we wish to, freedom of choice is inseparable from nobility and progress; but we must recognize the unchangeable laws which God has wisely set, governing the results as we are upright or the reverse, as we choose the good or choose the evil.

THE JEWISH HOUSE A SANCTUARY OF THE LORD.

BY REV. DR. B. FELSENTHAL.

"I shall dwell amongst them" (Exod. xxv, 8). These brief words of our Torah shall be the text of my to-day's sermon, and the subject shall be: "The Jewish house must be, or ought to be, a sanctuary, dedicated to divine service, and in which the spirit of God shall dwell."

The very announcement of this theme may call forth some of my hearers' contradiction, or at least some doubting and shaking of the head. What! Our houses shall be sanctuaries? Shall they be temples, or synagogues, in which every-day prayer meetings are to be held? No! Our houses and dwelling places are erected for other purposes. We must have a parlor where we receive our visitors and friends; a dining-room, where we take our meals; a kitchen, where the meals are prepared; the necessary sleeping-rooms for the members of our family, and for our servants, and so forth. If any one feels the desire to enter a sanctuary, a house for divine worship, let him go to the temple, erected and dedicated for such purposes. Thus some may argue.

These arguments, however, rest upon totally false premises, and they therefore lead to false conclusions. They presuppose, first, the thought that religious ideas and sentiments should be fostered only and exclusively, and should be promulgated and advocated only and exclusively, in special buildings dedicated to divine worship—that is, in churches and synagogues. They presuppose, furthermore, the idea that religion should have a right of speech only at special days and seasons set aside for such a purpose—that is, on Sabbaths and on festivals, and at such other times which may be agreed upon by a community. And, thirdly, they presume that this right of speech should be exercised only and exclusively under certain forms and formalities—that is, in accordance with certain rituals and certain ceremonies and usages. Proceeding from these premises, the conclusion is drawn that outside of the appointed buildings and of the days consecrated and divested of traditional forms, religion has no voice whatsoever.

This entire line of reasoning is false and misleading. Religion has a voice, or ought to have a voice, not only in temples and synagogues, but in our dwelling houses too, and in our business houses too, in our private affairs and the affairs of city government and State government too—ay, even in the conduct and shaping of international matters; in short, in everything occupying the human mind and calling forth human activity. Religion has a voice, or ought to have a voice, at all times, and not only on Sabbaths and festive days but on so-called week-days too; in the age of childhood, of youth, of a more mature period of manhood and womanhood, and of the closing years of our earthly life. Religion has a voice, or ought to have a voice, not only in the prescribed rituals and ritualistic usages, but in the common everyday speech of business and in the social intercourse between individuals and individuals.

Religion ought to be a controlling power anywhere and everywhere and at every time.

And therefore I repeat it: The Jewish house ought to be a sanctuary dedicated to whatsoever is godly and divine. To-day I shall restrict myself in my remarks to the dwelling house especially, reserving to myself for other times to speak of business houses, of government offices in cities and States, of halls of legislature, of clubhouses and similar gathering places.

The house is to be a temple. And who are to be the priests in this temple?

You know that in all religious denominations there are certain persons specially designated to conduct the services and what is connected therewith—priests, pastors, rabbis, ministers, or by whatever names they may be called. In ancient times, when our forefathers, the Israelites, dwelt in their own country, in Palestine, and had their own central sanctuary, the temple in Jerusalem, the descendants of Aaron served as priests in this temple and conducted the sacrificial cult then in vogue. It was a hereditary priesthood which in those remote ancient days officiated in the temple. Of course the priests officiating in our houses must be other persons. And who are they? Who are naturally to be the priests there? Ah, you know it, and I need not tell you. It is you, the head of the household; you, the father of the family. And your assistant in the sacred office is to be your wife, the mother of the children, the mistress of the house. You combined, husband and wife, father and mother, you must watch and take good care that a truly religious spirit permeates your house, early and late, on Sabbaths and on week-days, and that all virtues possible be fostered and practised in the house governed by you, and that nothing whatsoever that is unclean—I mean nothing that is irreligious or immoral—may find an entrance in this sanctuary, your house.

Therefore let mutual kindness and love, harmony and peace constantly prevail between husband and wife. Keep your hearts pure and your soul-life unsullied, and out of this good soil of pure thoughts and sentiments will grow up such a good outward conduct of life as true religion demands. Educate the children more by the silent power of your example than by your words. Angry scolding, fitful words, at irregular times, then and now, will rarely, will hardly ever have the effect desired, and will not be of any good educational influence. They will, as a rule, be more harmful than good and useful. But if, by your own exemplary life, you give to your children a model how to lead a life in truthfulness, industry, cleanliness, order, punctuality, modesty, politeness, kindness toward the poor and suffering ones, and so forth, then you have rendered and you do render a sacred service in the sanctuary of your house; you will be priests of the Most High, of the Eternal our God, and your house will be, in as far as you can make it so, a temple, and God's holy spirit will dwell therein.

And the children, too, living in this house, must never forget that under the parental roof they also stand before God—before God, whose all-seeing eyes see everything, whose all-hearing ears perceive every word, who even knows our innermost thoughts and the most hidden of our aspirations. Children, be obedient to your parents; be respectful toward them; be thankful to them for all the deeds of kindness and of goodness which they do for you; love them and honor them as long as they are with you, and honor them and keep them in grateful remembrance even when they are no more with you and after they have departed from this life and when their bodily remains sleep their eternal slumber in the silent grave. Children, if you are mindful of that law which you will find in the center of the Ten Commandments — I mean if you always pay due regard to the fifth commandment: "Honor thy father and thy mother"— and if, besides this, you maintain a truly fraternal and sisterly relationship among yourselves, never forgetting the words of the Psalmist that it is good and pleasant when brothers live together in harmony, then you, on your part, help toward transforming the house into a sanctuary, a temple of the Lord, and a divine spirit will dwell therein and God will be worshiped there constantly.

There are other persons belonging to the family occupying a house, though there are some who maintain that these other persons have no claim toward being counted as members of the family. I speak of the class called *servants*. Where religion—I mean *true* religion—has a voice, and where his voice is heard, and where man and wife, ruling over the house, honestly endeavor to have their house be a temple of the Lord, there the servant *is* considered a member of the family. It is a sign of lack of religion if such is not the case and if the servant is treated with unkindness and without sympathy. The pious Job, among the claims which he made in order to demonstrate that his conduct of life was good and that he did not deserve as punishment all the visitations by robbery, sickness, death, suffered by him— this pious Job also maintained that he never wronged or treated unkindly his man-servant or his maid-servant. Listen to his words: "If I should despise the cause of my man-servant or my maid-servant, when they contend with me, what, then, should I do when God riseth up? And when He visiteth, what should I answer Him? Did not He that made me make him also? And did not one and the same create us?"

You see that already in Biblical times our ancient prophets and sages laid great stress and accent upon the thought that all men are born equal. As it is well known to you, this is almost a self-understood axiom with Americans; it is an idea underlying the whole political and social life of the American people. And we Americans are so very proud of this idea because it was, in modern times, so sharply and distinctly enunciated by the fathers of the Republic in 1776 in the Declaration of Independence. We admit that this idea is not true in the sense that all men are equal in natural talents or abilities, or in bodily strength and powers, or in mental capacities and qualifications. In this sense men are not born equal. But they are equal in their rights as human beings. Concerning such rights and concerning such claims based upon these rights, no one is privileged, neither is one to be assigned to a back seat or pushed down to a lower grade because of poverty or because he has to be a servant or a laborer. The servant, too, has a full claim upon being treated by you kindly, humanely, sympathetically. And Israelites especially should be models in this regard, and their treatment of servants and of employees in general should be a shining example for others. Long before the time of Job the duty was impressed upon the Israelites to be kind, merciful, considerate toward servants.

In the fourth of the Ten Commandments we are

enjoined to grant rest on the Sabbath to our man-servants and our maid-servants, just as well as to our sons and daughters. In other passages of our Torah it is repeatedly said that our servants also shall participate in the joys of the festal days, as well as the other members of the family. Thus it is written in the Torah: "And thou shalt be rejoicing on thy festive day—thou, and thy son, and thy daughter, and thy man-servant, and thy maid-servant, and the Levite, and the stranger, and the orphan, and the widow who are in thy gates." And there is one passage in the Scriptures which particularly appeals to every Israelite: "Remember that thou thyself hast been a slave in Egypt." And in another place: "You should know how a stranger, a friendless one feels in his soul and heart; you should know it, and with sympathy take cognizance of his sad thoughts and depressed mind, for you also have been strangers." O friends, do not set up the plea that such treatment of servants is unfashionable; that it may have been well enough in olden times to maintain such a relationship between master and laborer, between mistress and servant, between employer and employee, but that now such a reconstruction of society is out of date. Out of date! Not fashionable! The laws of morality, the behests of religion are never out of date—never! These laws and these behests are eternally binding. If they are not observed, if, on the contrary, they are disregarded, then the house is not a temple of the Lord, and the spirit of God is not dwelling therein. Instead of true culture, unculture has its habitation there; and instead of true refinement, vulgarity prevails there.

A kind master or mistress has sufficient psychological insight and judgment to know how a servant feels whom circumstances compel to find employment with other people; how grateful he or she is for being treated with kindness; how sad he or she is if treated unkindly; and how happy many of them would feel if they would know that they are considered as members of the family and if they would be able to say that they have found a home! And how would they show their gratitude by faithfulness and by sincere attachment to those who employ them! And should we not also sometimes think that we ought to be thankful to them for doing all the drudgery and all the rough work in and around the house or elsewhere while in our employ? And, besides this, should we not also sometimes think that the servant too has a father and a mother who loved him or her dearly and who educated him or her as well as they could afford, and who, if they still live, would feel sad and sorrowful, and would perhaps have their eyes filled by tears, if they would learn that their son or their daughter is roughly spoken to or unkindly treated in the house of strangers? How would any of us feel if a child of ours should be among strangers and we would learn that the same meets a heartless treatment?

There is a spirit of restlessness widespread in the present age. Unrest and dissatisfaction prevail in large circles and in many countries. The laborer and the employer, the servant and the master, the poor and the rich—they do not live together as harmoniously and as peacefully and as happily as it was the case in former times. We shall not enter to-day into an examination of the various causes which brought forth this state of affairs. One of the causes is, no doubt, the lack of sympathy with the poor ones and the forsaken ones, with those in the lower stratum of society. Our times have become degenerated at least in some regards, and they stand now, in these regards, lower than the times passed. Do not speak so boastfully of progress, of the achievements in natural philosophy, in chemistry and mechanics, in medical science and surgical art, and so forth. There was progress made—a wonderful progress —in these fields. But how in some departments of morals? How in *Humanitat?* Are we as humane, and sympathetic, and considerate, and noble-souled as our parents and grandparents have been? Are we, are all of us so kindly and tenderly disposed toward the poorer classes of our fellow-men as our ancestors have been? Have all of us become more humanized? Have not some of us become more brutalized?

The spirit of unrest in our modern world is, to a certain degree, explainable and perfectly excusable. Not all the demands of the so-called socialists are unreasonable. While a radical reconstruction of society upon a new basis, such as the extreme ones among the socialistic dreamers would like to see, is undoubtedly visionary and of an utopian character, yet some of their claims—among them the claim that all human beings shall be considered equal in the enjoyment of the innate and inalienable rights of man, and that all of them have the right to demand that they be treated with consideration and in true kindness, and that the poor ones shall be considered essentially just as good as the rich ones are and as the so-called higher classes are—these claims will be and must be fulfilled, and in so far the socialistic demands will be realized and will not remain mere dreams. Society is in unrest, is in a state of fermentation, and it may safely be predicted that the harmonious living together of the various classes of which society is composed will not take place until these claims have found a hearing and a

realization. Other times will come, and better times—
not in the nineteenth century, for this will soon close,
but in the twentieth century.

Friends, I know that these ideas advanced by me
this day are not shared by all my hearers. I know
that some will think them to be out of date; that
some up-to-date people will say: "The servants are
servants, and have to be treated as servants; we pay
them so much wages per week or month, and in consideration of these wages they have to do our work
and have to receive our treatment, of whatever nature
it may be; if they do not like it they may go," and
so forth. I know that many entertain such ideas, but
I do not express other people's views. I stand here as
a teacher of religion and of morality, and as such I
teach the laws of religion and the demands of morality.
I would be derelict in my duty would I act otherwise
and would I, in such questions, first shrewdly consider
whether my teachings are popular or not, fashionable
or not, and whether they are shared by the majority or
not. He who, like the prophet Ezekiel, can say that
he has been appointed as a watchman over the house
of Israel, he must fearlessly denounce the moral failings and shortcomings of the people; he must warn
the people and must show them the right ways, without fear and without hesitation. If his words of admonition, and of warning, and of instruction fall upon
barren ground, then he, the watchman, has at least
the consciousness of having done his duty, and, with
the prophet, he can at least say: "I have spoken and
I have saved my soul."

In the beginning of my discourse I stated the subject of the same to be: "The Jewish house must be,
or ought to be, a sanctuary dedicated to what is godly
or divine." I conclude now by appealing to you.

Let your houses be sanctuaries, temples of the Lord, dedicated to what is godly or divine, and be you, fathers and mothers, priests in these temples. Amen.

www.ingramcontent.com/pod-product-compliance
Lightning Source LLC
Chambersburg PA
CBHW032028220426
43664CB00006B/406